Gerry Stahl's assembled texts volume #9

Essays in Computer- Supported Collaborative Learning

Gerry Stahl

Gerry Stahl's Assembled Texts

1. *Marx and Heidegger*

2. *Tacit and Explicit Understanding in Computer Support*

3. *Group Cognition: Computer Support for Building Collaborative Knowledge*

4. *Studying Virtual Math Teams*

5. *Translating Euclid: Designing a Human-Centered Mathematics.*

6. *Constructing Dynamic Triangles Together: The Development of Mathematical Group Cognition*

7. *Essays in Social Philosophy*

8. *Essays in Personalizable Software*

9. *Essays in Computer-Supported Collaborative Learning*

10. *Essays in Group-Cognitive Science*

11. *Essays in Philosophy of Group Cognition*

12. *Essays in Online Mathematics Interaction*

13. *Essays in Collaborative Dynamic Geometry*

14. *Adventures in Dynamic Geometry*

15. *Global Introduction to CSCL*

16. *Editorial Introductions to ijCSCL*

17. *Proposals for Research*

18. *Overview and Autobiographical Essays*

19. *Theoretical Investigations*

20. *Works of 3-D Form*

21. *Dynamic Geometry Game for Pods*

Gerry Stahl's assembled texts volume #9

Essays in Computer-Supported Collaborative Learning

Gerry Stahl

Gerry Stahl

Gerry@GerryStahl.net

www.GerryStahl.net

Published by Gerry Stahl at Lulu.com

Printed in the USA

ISBN: 978-1-329-85956-2 (paperback)
ISBN: 978-1-329-85952-4 (ebook)

Preface

This volume reports on the findings of my research on computer-supported collaborative learning (CSCL) from 2006 to the present (2011). In 2006, I published *Group Cognition: Computer Support for Building Collaborative Knowledge* (Stahl, 2006b), a compilation of my most important CSCL papers from the first decade of my work in the field (1993-2003), as well as some newer chapters devoted to exploring the proposed notion of group cognition. At the 2007 CSCL conference, I organized a workshop of papers related to the Virtual Math Teams (VMT) Project, which I directed from 2003 to the present. That collection of workshop papers grew into *Studying Virtual Math Teams* (Stahl, 2009). Now I have collected all my papers on CSCL, group cognition and VMT that did not appear in either of those collections. This includes both journal articles and other papers from 2006 to the present. These papers are presented in two volumes: the current volume of *Essays in CSCL* (Stahl, 2011a) and a separate volume of *Essays in Online Mathematics Interaction* (Stahl, 2011b).

Essays in Online Mathematics Interaction is organized around a specific VMT event: the four-session online interaction of Team B in the 2006 VMT Spring Fest. Grounded in analysis of the data from this event, a coherent series of chapters discusses the theory of analyzing group cognition in such events.

Essays in CSCL, then, includes the papers that remain. It covers a somewhat broader range, as will be outlined in this Preface. It begins with my general reflections on the importance of CSCL as a research field, situating my work on the VMT Project and my theory of group cognition within the field of CSCL. It describes the VMT research project, including its research approach, technology, pedagogy and analysis methods. Mostly, it discusses in some detail the findings that have emerged from the VMT Project about the nature of online interaction in that type of CSCL setting. The volume concludes with reports of current work in the project and future directions that are underway. In this way, it elaborates, deepens and extends the presentation in *Studying Virtual Math Teams* and prepares the broader background for the companion volume, *Essays in Group Cognition.*

1. Introduction to CSCL 2011

The introduction to the proceedings for the CSCL 2011 conference in Hong Kong provides a kind of introduction to the field of computer-supported collaborative learning (CSCL). I drafted the introduction as co-Conferene

Chair, along with Hans Spada, Naomi Miyake and Nancy Law (Stahl, G., Spada, H., Miyake, N., & Law, N., 2011).

2. Engaging with Engaged Learning

The opening essay touches on themes of engagement with the world, with learning and with technology. It sets the stage for the concerns of CSCL as involving people engaged with others, with collaborative learning and with computer support. This brief chapter served as the Preface to an edited volume of CSCL research (Stahl, 2006a).

3. Toward a New Science of Collaborative Learning

Next is an interview I gave to a journal in Mainland China. It is designed to introduce my research to the growing audience of scholars in Asia who are becoming increasingly interested in CSCL. It describes my particular perspective on CSCL and shows how my work on group cognition and the VMT project fit in. The interview was published in Chinese in *China Education Technology* (Stahl & Chai, 2010).

4. Team Cognition in Socio-Technical Systems

In a commentary to a special issue of the American journal, *Human Factors*, I try to define how my approach to studying group cognition can be distinguished from traditional approaches to human-computer interaction and to systems-theory approaches to team interaction. This introduces themes of post-cognitivism and design-based research that will be detailed later. This essay appeared in a special issue on complex socio-technical systems in (Stahl, 2010).

5. Analyzing Cognition in Online Teams

This essay was originally written for inclusion in a book on different theories and perspectives on analyzing team cognition (Stahl & Rosé, 2011). It was co-authored with Carolyn Rosé, a researcher at Carnegie Mellon University who collaborates on studies using the VMT environment. Most of the essay discusses a hierarchy of structural and temporal levels that can be analyzed to understand the interactions that contribute to group cognition. Taking as an example an excerpt from session 3 of Group B's chats in VMT Spring Fest 2006, the essay distinguishes: the Group B event, a session from that event, a theme that was discussed during the session, a discourse move that contributed to the discussion of the theme, a closely related pair of chat postings that was pivotal for that discourse move, an individual posting that was part of the interactional pair and a detailed reference to what that posting was about. These structural levels are not just creations of the researcher, but are constructed by

Group B in the discourse. Analyzing the collaboration at these multiple levels and seeing how they are interrelated, provides insight into the group-cognitive processes at work in the excerpt. Conducting such an analysis is time consuming and could benefit from computer support. The essay concludes with comments about current work to develop computer support, not only for the analysis of group cognition, but also for facilitating the interaction itself.

6. Sustaining Interaction in a CSCL Environment

The flow of discussion and problem solving in a VMT session is largely carried on through a succession of proposals. Although the proposals may be initiated by individuals, they function as mini interactions. To be effective, a proposal by one person must elicit a certain kind of response from the other members of the group. In this essay, the mechanism whereby a proposal elicits a response is called a "math-proposal adjacency pair." The structure of this mechanism is described. In particular, it is worked out with an analysis of an example of a breach of the mechanism, a "failed proposal." The mutual understanding of a proposal within a group presupposes that members of the group have a shared understanding of the mathematical objects referenced by the proposal. The essay analyzes a case in which such a shared understanding had to be co-constructed by the group members by pointing at a geometric diagram with a tool of the VMT software and with narrative descriptions. This allowed the group to look at the mathematical object together and share the interpretive view assumed by the proposal. The proposals and pointing allowed the group to be together, to work together and to learn together. A version of this essay won the best paper prize at ICCE 2005 (Stahl, 2005) and was published in the journal of the Asia-Pacific Society for Computers in Education (Stahl, 2006c).

7. Synchronous Chat in CSCL

Much research and practice in CSCL takes place in asynchronous environments like Knowledge Forum, Sakai or Blackboard. Alternatively, it takes place in specialized environments that scaffold and guide the students with constrained options, such as an environment for constructing arguments, an algebra tutor with specific areas to fill in or a tightly scripted application that steps the students along. In contrast, the VMT environment offers groups the full power of interacting synchronously through text chat, where they can type whatever they want and get immediate responses. In addition, it provides some math-related resources, such as a generic shared whiteboard, special math notation options and most recently multi-user GeoGebra. Because student interaction is relatively unconstrained, it is complicated to analyze and incredibly creative and divergent from case to case. This essay looks at some of the typical behaviors of student groups interacting through text chat in the VMT environment. Because group interaction is highly situated in its own unique, irreproducible contexts, analysis is case-based. Here, four cases are presented. They come from the four dissertations that were undertaken by research assistants on the VMT Project (Çakir, 2009; Sarmiento-Klapper, 2009; Toledo, 2009; Zhou, 2010). They discuss (1) cognitive conflict at the group level, (2) the role of questions as interactive proposals, (3) how the joint problem space is co-constructed as a basis for shared understanding and (4) how a group can coordinate visual, narrative and symbolic reasoning across the chat and whiteboard. This essay is based on Stahl, G. (2009a).

8. Temporality of the Joint Problem Space

This essay picks up on the third case study in the previous essay. It differentiates a group-cognitive concept of the problem space from the classic information-processing conceptualization. The joint problem space is not a mental model, but a shared set of experiences and references that grows as a group explores a problem. It has strong ties to external inscriptions, such as the shared whiteboard, which provide continuing visual support for cognition and create experiences shared by the group. Due to the unembodied nature of virtual teams and the disruptions of sessions ending and people coming and going, it is necessary for groups to "bridge" across various discontinuities. The joint problem space can provide some continuity for a group, but it often needs to be refreshed in multiple ways. Whereas the classic theory centered on individual mental reasoning procedures, the presentation in this essay argues for three primary dimensions: (1) a social dimension in which participation is managed, (2) a temporal dimension in which sequentialities are co-constructed and temporality itself is constituted and (3) a content dimension dominated by the role of knowledge artifacts. This essay was nominated for the best student paper at ICLS 2008 (Sarmiento & Stahl, 2008).

9. Designing Problems to Support Knowledge Building

The VMT software environment has been mainly used with problems of middle-school and high-school algebra, combinatorics and geometry. For his dissertation in Singapore, Juan Dee Wee used it at the junior college level for courses in calculus (Wee, 2010). In particular, he explored different pedagogical approaches, for instance having groups of students discuss errors made in examples of typical math mistakes. In this essay, presented at ICCE 2007 (Stahl, Wee & Looi, 2007), the use of traditional-closed, open-ended and problem-solving approaches to problem design are discussed. The results of these different cases are analyzed using Wee's Collaboration Interaction Model, which highlights "pivotal moments" (Wee & Looi, 2009).

10. Enhancing Mathematical Communication for Virtual Math Teams

The final three essays bring the description of development of the VMT software up to date (as of early 2011). In particular, work has been focused on porting GeoGebra to VMT, thereby transforming it from a single-user dynamic mathematics application into a multi-user system embedded in the other VMT components (text chat, shared whiteboard, wiki, web browser, social networking portal, etc.). These essays were specifically written to introduce VMT to the international GeoGebra community. This lengthy review of VMT—published in a Romanian mathematics journal (Stahl, Çakir et al., 2010)—shows its major features and illustrates how it has typically been used.

11. Analyzing the Discourse of GeoGebra Collaborations

This essay, presented at the first North American GeoGebra conference (Stahl, Rosé & Goggins, 2010), briefly presents three approaches to analyzing the discourse of groups working in VMT. One approach is that of most of the analyses of group cognition in this volume, based on an adaptation of conversation analysis to virtual math teams engaged in text chat and whiteboard drawing. The second approach is a more quantitative approach to analyzing and comparing structural features of sessions, such as conducting social network analyses at consecutive time slices. The third approach involves automated natural language processing, using toolkits of algorithms that are currently under development for application to VMT data.

12. Software Conversational Agents

The potential of computer analysis of the VMT chats could make possible the programming of software agents within the VMT software, which would monitor the student discourse and periodically intervene. In this report (Stahl, Rosé et al., 2010) on current research, the idea of conversational agents is proposed. Such agents would provide guidance to students. They could suggest discourse moves that might deepen the group knowledge building, help stalled discussions or even provide math hints when needed. They could also give a group feedback on its group process. Alternatively, the agents could alert a teacher when a group needs the teacher's assistance. Without replacing the role of the teacher or limiting student initiative and group agency, carefully designed software agents could provide scaffolding to enhance the online collaborative mathematical experience.

References

Çakir, M. P. (2009). *How online small groups co-construct mathematical artifacts to do collaborative problem solving.* Unpublished Dissertation, Ph.D., College of Information Science and Technology, Drexel University. Philadelphia, PA, USA.

Sarmiento, J., & Stahl, G. (2008). *Extending the joint problem space: Time and sequence as essential features of knowledge building.* Paper presented at the International Conference of the Learning Sciences (ICLS 2008). Utrecht, Netherlands. Web: http://GerryStahl.net/pub/icls2008johann.pdf

Sarmiento-Klapper, J. W. (2009). *Bridging mechanisms in team-based online problem solving: Continuity in building collaborative knowledge.* Unpublished Dissertation, Ph.D., College of Information Science and Technology, Drexel University. Philadelphia, PA, USA.

Stahl, G. (2005). *Sustaining online collaborative problem solving with math proposals [winner of best paper award].* Paper presented at the International Conference on Computers and Education (ICCE 2005). Singapore, Singapore. Proceedings pp. 436-443. Web: http://GerryStahl.net/pub/icce2005.pdf & http://GerryStahl.net/pub/icce2005ppt.pdf

Stahl, G. (2006a). Engaging with engaged learning. In D. Hung & M. S. Khine (Eds.), *Engaged learning with emerging technologies.* (pp. i-v). Boston: Springer. Web: http://GerryStahl.net/pub/engagement.pdf

Stahl, G. (2006b). *Group cognition: Computer support for building collaborative knowledge.* Cambridge, MA: MIT Press. 510 + viii pages. Web: http://GerryStahl.net/mit/

Stahl, G. (2006c). Sustaining group cognition in a math chat environment. *Research and Practice in Technology Enhanced Learning (RPTEL). 1*(2), 85-113. Web: http://GerryStahl.net/pub/rptel.pdf

Stahl, G. (2009a). *Collaborative learning through practices of group cognition.* In the proceedings of the international conference on Computer Support for Collaborative Learning (CSCL 2009). Rhodes, Greece. Web: http://GerryStahl.net/pub/cscl2009stahl.pdf.

Stahl, G. (2009b). *Studying virtual math teams.* New York, NY: Springer. 626 +xxi pages. Web: http://GerryStahl.net/vmt/book Doi: http://dx.doi.org/10.1007/978-1-4419-0228-3

Stahl, G. (2010). Group-cognition factors in sociotechnical systems. *Human Factors. Special issue on Collaboration, Coordination, and Adaptation in Complex Sociotechnical Systems 52*(2), 340-343. Web: http://GerryStahl.net/pub/humanfactors2010.pdf

Stahl, G. (2011a). *Essays in computer-supported collaborative learning.* Philadelphia, PA: Gerry Stahl at Lulu. 215 pages. Web: http://GerryStahl.net/elibrary/cscl

Stahl, G. (2011b). *Essays in Online Mathematics Interaction.* Philadelphia, PA: Gerry Stahl at Lulu. 200 pages. Web: http://GerryStahl.net/elibrary/math .

Stahl, G., Çakir, M. P., Weimar, S., Weusijana, B. K., & Ou, J. X. (2010). Enhancing mathematical communication for virtual math teams. *Acta Didactica Napocensia. 3*(2), 101-114. Web: http://GerryStahl.net/pub/adn2010.pdf

Stahl, G., & Chai, S. (2010). Group cognition as a new science of learning: An interview with Gerry Stahl. *China Education Technology [in Chinese]. 2010* (May). Web: http://GerryStahl.net/pub/chinaed2009.pdf

Stahl, G., & Rosé, C. P. (2011). Group cognition in online teams. In E. Salas & S. M. Fiore (Eds.), *Theories of team cognition: Cross-disciplinary perspectives.* New York, NY: Routledge/Taylor & Francis. Web: http://GerryStahl.net/pub/gcot.pdf

Stahl, G., Rosé, C. P., & Goggins, S. (2010). *Analyzing the discourse of geogebra collaborations.* Paper presented at the First North American GeoGebra Conference. Ithaca, NY. Web: http://GerryStahl.net/pub/geogebrana2010b.pdf

Stahl, G., Rosé, C. P., O'Hara, K., & Powell, A. B. (2010). *Supporting group math cognition in virtual math teams with software conversational agents.* Paper presented at the First North American GeoGebra Conference. Ithaca, NY. Web: http://GerryStahl.net/pub/geogebrana2010a.pdf

Stahl, G., Spada, H., Miyake, N., & Law, N. (2011). Introduction to the proceedings of CSCL 2011. In H. Spada, G. Stahl, N. Miyake & N. Law (Eds.), *Connecting computer-supported collaborative learning to policy and practice: CSCL 2011 conference proceedings. Volume I — long papers.* (Vol. I, pp. viii-xi). Lulu: ISLS. Web: http://GerryStahl.net/pub/cscl2011intro.pdf.

Stahl, G., Wee, J. D., & Looi, C.-K. (2007). *Using chat, whiteboard and wiki to support knowledge building.* Paper presented at the International Conference on Computers in Education (ICCE 07). Hiroshima, Japan. Web: http://GerryStahl.net/pub/icce07.pdf

Toledo, R. P. S. (2009). Resolving differences of perspective in a VMT session. In G. Stahl (Ed.), *Studying virtual math teams.* (ch. 9, pp. 161-178). New York, NY: Springer. Web: http://GerryStahl.net/vmt/book/9.pdf Doi: http://dx.doi.org/10.1007/978-1-4419-0228-3_9

Wee, J. D. (2010). *Reinventing mathematics problem design and analysis of chat interactions in quasi-synchronous chat environments.* Unpublished Dissertation, Ph.D., National Institute of Education, Nanyang Techological University. Singapore.

Wee, J. D., & Looi, C.-K. (2009). A model for analyzing math knowledge building in VMT. In G. Stahl (Ed.), *Studying virtual math teams.* (ch. 25, pp. 475-497). New York, NY: Springer. Web: http://GerryStahl.net/vmt/book/25.pdf Doi: http://dx.doi.org/10.1007/978-1-4419-0228-3_25

Zhou, N. (2010). *Troubles of understanding in virtual math teams.* Unpublished Dissertation, Ph.D., College of Information Science and Technology, Drexel University. Philadelphia, PA, USA.

Contents

1.   Introduction to the Proceedings of CSCL 2011

Gerry Stahl, Hans Spada, Naomi Miyake, Nancy Law

The Scientific Field of CSCL

Computer-Supported Collaborative Learning (CSCL) is a multidisciplinary research field inspired by the power of collaborative learning and by the promise of computer technologies to support collaborative learning. It draws on and explores constructivist and socio-cultural theories, which view learning as a social, interpersonal, meaning-making process that takes place largely through interaction among people and within communities. It also designs, adopts and refines technologies that mediate communication among learners and that help to guide their inquiry or structure their work.

As a research field, CSCL builds on conceptual frameworks and analytic approaches of many academic fields, including education, psychology, communication, computer science and social science. It applies a variety of quantitative and qualitative research methods, often combining them to develop richer understandings of complex phenomena. Likewise, it may involve both laboratory and classroom studies, formal and informal learning settings, different temporal scales and the study of a wide range of influential factors.

Policies and Practices for CSCL

While the CSCL conference series has centered on research studies, the field has always been strongly oriented toward practical concerns of educational practice and associated educational policy. CSCL research frequently involves teachers in school classrooms and seeks to influence or implement governmental education policies.

The CSCL 2011 conference theme, *"Connecting computer-supported collaborative learning to policy and practice,"* builds on previous CSCL conferences to examine whether and how CSCL practices can bring deep changes to formal and informal educational practices at all levels, and contribute to educational improvement at a system level by informing education policy. This theme is addressed by keynote talks, symposia, trips to schools, and other events at the conference and the post-conference. It is hoped that this conference theme will contribute to bringing greater recognition to the fields of CSCL and the Learning Sciences by drawing the attention of a wider public, including policy makers and the professional educational community to their research and development contributions.

One important feature of this year's conference is the inclusion of three parallel tracks of interactive events, demonstrations and CSCL-in-practice showcases, which serve as the foci for attracting practitioners to the conference. Included in these practitioner-oriented events are presentations from several prominent school-university partnership projects that are themselves good exemplars of the conference theme in action. The conference has the support of policy makers in Hong Kong to sponsor teacher participation at the conference; the Education Bureau of the HKSAR Bureau is a supporting organization for this conference. The practitioner tracks are also made possible through the merger of other conferences into this year's CSCL conference. This year, the annual Knowledge Building Summer Institute, which has usually been held in Toronto, Canada, has been integrated into the CSCL conference in Hong Kong and Guangzhou.

To take advantage of CSCL 2011 being held in Hong Kong, CITE collaborated with East China Normal University, South China University and Beijing Normal University to co-organize a series of CSCL 2011 post-conference events in Shanghai, Guangzhou and Beijing respectively on July 11-15. It is the first time that there are such major post-conference events for the CSCL conference and we hope this will provide more opportunities for academic exchange and collaboration between CSCL and learning sciences researchers in Greater China and their global counterparts.

The CSCL Community and Conference

Since 1995, the CSCL conference has provided a stimulating and friendly venue for people interested in the multi-disciplinary issues of computer-supported collaborative learning to meet in a relaxed atmosphere with a variety of formal and informal events. Structured activities and social occasions promote interpersonal relations and knowledge building. The conference's human size and structure facilitate getting to know international colleagues and discussing cutting-edge ideas in educational practice, technology design, CSCL theory and diverse research approaches.

The bi-annual conferences have been instrumental in developing the field of CSCL and in building the research community around it. The conferences took place in Bloomington, USA (1995), Toronto, Canada (1997), Stanford, USA (1999), Maastricht, Netherlands (2001), Boulder, USA (2002), Bergen, Norway (2003), Taipei, Taiwan (2005), New Brunswick, USA (2007) and Rhodes, Greece (2009).

Further efforts to build the CSCL field include the founding of the International Society of the Learning Sciences (ISLS) by the CSCL community and the Learning Sciences research community. ISLS now provides an institutional framework for running the CSCL and ICLS conferences in alternating years and for publishing the *International Journal of Computer-Supported Collaborative Learning (ijCSCL)* and the *Journal of the Learning Sciences (JLS)*. In the early days of CSCL research, there was no publication venue specifically oriented to the field and it was hard to locate publications in the field. Now, in addition to the CSCL journal, there is also a CSCL book series sponsored by ISLS and published by Springer. Furthermore, papers from the CSCL and ICLS conferences are available in the ACM Digital Library and both *ijCSCL* and *JLS* are abstracted in the major indexing services, where they are highly ranked.

Toward a Global CSCL

The first CSCL conference was a relatively simple event, held in the middle of the United States. Over the years, the conference expanded to include a variety of sessions to meet the needs of a growing research community. It now features long papers presented lecture style, posters presented interactively and short papers presented in a hybrid style, to accommodate research findings ranging from early work to more mature reports. There are also tutorials for newcomers and workshops for special hot topics. For doctoral students and new faculty, there is a doctoral consortium and an early career workshop. There are also opportunities for software demos and other interactive events. And of course there are receptions and other social events to give extra times for people to get to know each other.

Although the CSCL community always had a strong base in Western Europe—partially associated with the AI and Education community—the first official CSCL conferences were held in North America. In 2001, a Euro-CSCL conference was organized in the Netherlands, attracting mainly European researchers. In 2002, the conference in the US achieved a good balance of European and American researchers; it initiated a policy of rotating the conferences to Europe (in 2003 and 2009), Asia (in 2005 and 2011) and North America (in 2007 and 2013). The conference in Taipei (2005) succeeded in achieving a good balance of paper authors, program committee members and conference participants from Western Europe, North America and the Asia-Pacific region.

Internationalization has always been a goal of the CSCL community. An analysis of trends during the first decade of the conferences documented strong progress in that direction (Kienle & Wessner, 2006). Analysis of authors included in the CSCL 2011 main conference shows approximately equal participation from Western Europe, North America and Asia-Pacific. Another important trend is an increase in the number of international collaborations in research and in the co-authorship of papers reporting on that research. Such collaboration is necessary for the spread of expertise and deep understanding of innovative ideas, methods and tools. This year's post-conference activities are an additional opportunity to promote exchange with researchers, practitioners and policy makers in Mainland China, an important area in which CSCL approaches seem to be spreading rapidly.

Of course, there are still major regions of the world under-represented in the CSCL community, such as the Middle East, Eastern Europe, Central Asia, South America and Africa. To some extent this may be due to limited traditions of collaborative learning or relatively low levels of computerization in schools in those areas. It may also be due to limitations in resources for traveling to international conferences or in awareness of the field. We have seen that strong involvement in CSCL research generally requires policy initiatives backed up with funding commitments. The European Union Network of Excellence funding programs like Kaleidoscope and Stellar have made a significant difference. NSF support for educational research has helped in the USA as well. Case studies elsewhere underline this factor (Chan, 2011; Looi et al., 2011).

A Delphi survey of researchers and stakeholders in technology-enhanced learning recently ranked CSCL as the second most important core research area for the next decade—just behind "connection between informal and formal learning" and ahead of nine other areas, like "personalized learning" (Kaendler et al., these Proceedings, Vol. II). We hope this recognition will spread around the world. In order to address the challenges facing CSCL in the coming years—not least of which are those related to practice and policy—we need the combined efforts of a global collaborative effort. Such an effort would bring together the unique perspectives of many labs and diverse educational cultures, acknowledging and strengthening their individual perspectives while incorporating them into a global synthesis.

Hong Kong University Centenary

The CSCL 2011 conference coincides with a major local milestone as well as an advance of the CSCL community. A century ago, in 1911, the University of Hong Kong was incorporated by Ordinance. A group of visionaries founded the first university in Hong Kong, from which generations of leaders across the region would come forth. The University of Hong Kong was to be important for China and for the world. In celebrating the first centenary, HKU upholds its commitment to Knowledge, Heritage and Service. The Centre for Information Technology in Education (CITE) of the Faculty of Education is proud to be hosting the CSCL 2011 main conference and co-organizing the CSCL 2011 post-conferences in three Mainland Chinese cities as part of the HKU Centenary celebration events.

References

Chan, C. (2011). CSCL theory-research-practice synergy: The Hong Kong experience of implementing knowledge building in classrooms. *International Journal of Computer-Supported Collaborative Learning. 6*(2). Doi: http://dx.doi.org/10.1007/s11412-011-9121-0.

Kienle, A., & Wessner, M. (2006). The CSCL community in its first decade: Development, continuity, connectivity. *International Journal of Computer-Supported Collaborative Learning. 1*(1), 9-33. Doi: http://dx.doi.org/10.1007/s11412-006-6843-5.

Looi, C.-K., So, H.-j., Toh, Y., & Chen, W. (2011). CSCL in classrooms: The Singapore experience of synergizing policy, practice and research. *International Journal of Computer-Supported Collaborative Learning. 6*(1), 9-38. Doi: http://dx.doi.org/10.1007/s11412-010-9102-8.

2.   Engaging with Engaged Learning

The theme of engaged learning with emerging technology is a timely and important one. The following remarks formed the Preface to *Engaged Learning with Emerging Technologies* (Hung & Khine, 2006). That book proclaims the global relevance of the theme and sharpens its focus. I wanted to open the book by sketching some of the historical context and dimensions of application, before the chapter authors provided the substance.

Engagement with the world

To be human is to be engaged with other people in the world. Yet, there has been a dominant strain of thought, at least in the West, which directs attention primarily to the isolated individual as naked mind. From classical Greece to modern times, engagement in the daily activities of human existence has been denigrated. Plato (340 BC/1941) banished worldly engagement to a realm of shadows, removed from the bright light of ideas, and Descartes (1633/1999) even divorced our minds from our own bodies. It can be suggested that this is a particularly Western tendency, supportive of the emphasis on the individual agent in Christianity and capitalism. But the view of people as originally unengaged has spread around the globe to the point where it is now necessary everywhere to take steps to reinstate engagement through explicit efforts.

Perhaps the most systematic effort to rethink the nature of human being in terms of engagement in the world was Heidegger's (1927/1996). He argued that human existence takes place through our concern with other people and things that are meaningful to us. This analysis reversed many philosophic assumptions, including the priority of explicit knowledge. Our understanding of stated facts requires interpretation based on our previous and primary tacit understanding of our world and our concerns. Our active engagement in the world is a prerequisite for any learning.

Vygotsky's (1930/1978) socio-cultural psychology can be seen as an expansion of Heidegger's critique of Western assumptions. Not only is explicit theoretical knowledge reliant upon tacit practical knowledge, but also individual learning is reliant upon collaborative learning. Vygotsky showed how most learning begins with interpersonal interactions and is only secondarily internalized as individual knowledge. So it is our engagement with other people—whether in our family, tribe, classroom or workplace—that provides the primary context, motivation and source of new knowledge.

In the past several years, a number of theories have elaborated the perspectives of Heidegger and Vygotsky in ways that are particularly relevant to issues of engaged learning. Situated learning (Lave & Wenger, 1991) has stressed that learning is a matter of participating in communities of practice. Distributed cognition (Hutchins, 1996) has shown how engagement with artifacts can be central to learning. Activity theory (Engeström, Miettinen, & Punamäki, 1999) emphasizes engagement in a whole activity structure including tasks, people, artifacts and social structures. Group cognition (Stahl, 2006) argues that knowledge is primarily built in the interactions of small groups.

Dewey (1949/1991) is a major source of the current discussion of engaged learning. Adapting the philosophic critique of individualism in Hegel (1807/1967) and Marx (1867/1976) to his pragmatist viewpoint, Dewey drew out the consequences for education. He opposed behaviorist and didactic training that emphasized drill and practice in favor of engaging students in inquiry into open-ended problem contexts. Fifty years after Dewey, we are still trying to introduce engaged learning into the classroom.

Engagement with learning

There are many dimensions to engagement with learning. As a number of the chapters will stress and illustrate, the nature of the problems that students are given is critical. If we want students to engage with a problem, it must be one that they "care about" in Heidegger's terms; it must involve issues that make sense to them within their interpretive perspectives on the world. In terms of Vygotsky's zone of proximal development, it should be a problem that challenges their current understanding but is within reach of their understanding, given some support by the people who are working on the problem with them. This may mean that they work collaboratively on a problem that they could not master on their own, or that adequate computer support is provided to guide them the way a mentor might.

Of course, not every problem can be in an interest area of every student. One student might have a passion for science, another for reading, drawing, sports or music. By having students work together on stimulating problems that have been designed and supported to optimize chances of successful knowledge building, educational activities can lead to increased interest and engagement with a new learning domain. Engagement with problems, people and domains can have a synergistic effect.

People are engaged in many communities simultaneously: family, neighborhood, religious, school, friendship, online, etc. These are primary contexts and motivators of engagement. People tend to learn the culture of their communities quickly and effortlessly. Communities of various sizes and formats can be formed for purposes of engaged learning. In some cases, students can be introduced to professional communities (e.g., NASA), in other cases mini-communities can be constructed that are based on the professional community but are more accessible to the students (e.g., model rocket clubs). Communities can be built online so that people with a particular interest can interact with others around the world. Groups can also be formed to create new engagements, such as classrooms in different countries corresponding with each other as a way of learning foreign languages. Engagement generally grows through involvement in such communities. Often, small groups form within larger communities so that participants can get to know each other better and establish a shared history. It is in the intense interactions within such small groups that knowledge is likely to be constructed and shared.

One should not think of engagement as an individual attribute. Communities are engaged with specific issues; that may well be why they originally formed and continue to persist. Small groups also engage in activities. The community or group engagement may not so much be motivated by the desires of their individual members as vice versa. Individual engagement is often a consequence of being involved in an engaged group. One is motivated by the group effort. If a researcher looks closely at the behavior of a group, what appears is not a clear causation in either direction between individual and group; they tend to constitute each other's engagement through subtle interactional moves.

Similarly, engagement is neither a purely intellectual, affective nor social phenomenon. Engagement may involve cognitive tasks and the manipulation of conceptual materials. However, it is also a feeling that people have that they are participating in something that is important and interesting. Further, it is a social undertaking, done with, for or because of other people and groups. The impetus to do something, the options available and the methods for accomplishing it are likely to be defined by the culture of some community. What is learned, the motivation to learn it and its socially accepted value are intimately intertwined in ways specific to each case.

So engaged learning can involve engagement with problems, with a domain of knowledge, with communities and with small groups. It can be observed at the individual, small group and community unit of analysis. It appears as a blending of intellectual, affective and social relations.

Engagement with technology

These days, engagement with learning is likely to mean engagement with technology. This is because networked computers seem to offer open-ended possibilities for promoting and supporting engaged learning. They can connect geographically isolated and dispersed individuals into collaborative groups. They can provide scaffolding for learning without requiring the presence of a skilled mentor. They can offer access to worldwide resources. They can incorporate computationally powerful tools.

Unfortunately, this tantalizing potential is not yet at hand. Commercially available media do not support engagement. They are largely designed based on the individual transmission model: they allow individuals to access facts and to transmit opinions. To go beyond this, we need to design technologies that can serve as mediators of person-to-person interaction that goes beyond superficial socializing and exchange of opinions to engagement in deep knowledge building (Scardamalia & Bereiter, 1996). But to do this, we need to understand computer-mediated collaborative learning interaction much better than we do now. It is a complicated process, sensitive to many factors and not predictable from any. It is easy to know what will prevent successful engaged learning, but hard to know how to foster it, particularly given today's technology. While computers are indeed computationally powerful, the technology for programming learning environments is frustratingly rigid. Educational innovators face a wicked problem in trying to realize the potential of emergent technologies.

The far-reaching goal set forth in this book, to design and promote technologies for engaged learning, requires a worldwide effort. Fortunately, the book simultaneously represents a global engagement with this task. Its chapters pursue the educational and technical potential from diverse international perspectives.

References

Descartes, R. (1633/1999). *Discourse on Method and Meditations on First Philosophy*. New York, NY: Hackett.

Dewey, J., & Bentley, A. (1949/1991). Knowing and the known. In J. A. Boydston (Ed.), *John Dewey: The Later Works, 1925-1953* (Vol. 16). Carbondale, IL: SIU Press.

Engeström, Y., Miettinen, R., & Punamäki, R.-L. (Eds.). (1999). *Perspectives on Activity Theory*. New York, NY: Cambridge University Press.

Hegel, G. W. F. (1807/1967). *Phenomenology of Spirit* (J. B. Baillie, Trans.). New York, NY: Harper & Row.

Heidegger, M. (1927/1996). *Being and Time: A Translation of Sein und Zeit* (J. Stambaugh, Trans.). Albany, NY: SUNY Press.

Hutchins, E. (1996). *Cognition in the Wild*. Cambridge, MA: MIT Press.

Hung & Khine (2006).*Engaged Learning with Emerging Technologies*. New York, NY: Springer.

Lave, J., & Wenger, E. (1991). *Situated Learning: Legitimate Peripheral Participation*. Cambridge, UK: Cambridge University Press.

Marx, K. (1867/1976). *Capital* (B. Fowkes, Trans. Vol. I). New York, NY: Vintage.

Plato. (340 BC/1941). *The Republic* (F. Cornford, Trans.). London, UK: Oxford University Press.

Scardamalia, M., & Bereiter, C. (1996). Computer support for knowledge-building communities. In T. Koschmann (Ed.), *CSCL: Theory and Practice of an Emerging Paradigm* (pp. 249-268). Hillsdale, NJ: Lawrence Erlbaum Associates.

Stahl, G. (2006). *Group Cognition: Computer Support for Building Collaborative Knowledge*. Cambridge, MA: MIT Press.

Vygotsky, L. (1930/1978). *Mind in Society*. Cambridge, MA: Harvard University Press.

3.   Toward a New Science of Collaborative Learning

Interview by Shaoming Chai (School of Educational Information Technology, South China Normal University, Guangzhou, Guangdong, China)

1. Professor Stahl, you have been a leading proponent of CSCL during the past decade and an active researcher in the learning sciences. The chapter in the Cambridge Handbook of the Learning Sciences by you with Koschmann and Suthers has introduced CSCL and given a general picture of how CSCL developed and what it is mainly about. In that chapter, you proposed that computer applications in education or instructional technologies have undergone a sequence of approaches, and that CSCL represents the most recent stage in that progression. My question is: What is the striking difference between CSCL and the previous approaches? Does that mean CSCL represents a new paradigm of instructional technology?

First, let me emphasize that CSCL is a diverse field with researchers working in a variety of different ways. Some CSCL researchers come from education, psychology, computer science or social science; some are more interested in computer software design, in research methodology, in psychological models or in classroom practices. I hope that all these approaches fit together and complement each other, although there are some tensions and apparent incompatibilities, as in any active interdisciplinary field. Koschmann, Suthers and I have similar backgrounds, interests and research agendas, so we co-authored an introduction to CSCL that reflected our common orientation. We are particularly interested in detailed analysis of discourse in small groups of learners, and in developing a theory of what Koschmann calls "practices of understanding," Suthers calls "intersubjective meaning making," and I call "group cognition." Our chapter (Stahl, Koschmann, & Suthers, 2006)—which is available in Chinese and other languages—reports on the history of CSCL, important research projects and books in the field, software design issues, alternative research methodologies and theories.

We argue that what is important and new in CSCL is the focus on collaborative groups of learners. Previous instructional software, educational research and pedagogical theory looked almost exclusively at individual learners. CSCL looks at how learning takes place in small groups working together, thanks to networked computers, computer support for learning and computer simulations. Whereas previous instructional software was designed for individual users, CSCL software is multi-user, supporting communication, coordination and collaboration. Whereas previous educational research tried to get at individual knowledge and mental models through individual testing, surveys and interviews, CSCL tries to study the group interactions that build collaborative learning. This makes for a huge paradigm shift. While we believe that learning has always been a fundamentally social, interpersonal process, the availability of networked computers (and mobile devices) creates new opportunities for supporting and for studying collaborative learning.

2. As a branch of the learning sciences, CSCL is concerned with the themes of cognition, social context and design. Can you explain where CSCL locates learning? What is the nature of collaborative learning? What role does social context play in CSCL? And what is the purpose and goal of design in CSCL?

These are large research questions without easy answers. The CSCL research field itself is an attempt at collaborative learning on a global scale to understand these issues better—and to redefine the questions and answers as part of a gradual paradigm shift within education as it is practiced in schools and universities. The term "learning" itself carries traditional connotations of an increase in factual knowledge by an individual. So in CSCL, we often talk about "collaborative knowledge building" rather than learning, in order to avoid the connotations of traditional views so we can re-think the basic concepts of our field. Our goal in a CSCL classroom might be to have groups of students develop knowledge artifacts like documents expressing a theory, where the document gradually becomes more and more developed. The nature of collaborative learning is such that a group working together is likely to develop a document that takes into account more issues, uses more abstract conceptualizations and develops more sophisticated arguments than any individual member would have produced on their own. Through participating in the group process, the individuals may not only learn the theory that the group developed, but also learn to think about the theory from multiple perspectives as well as learning how to work well together with others on this kind of learning task.

The "social context" that you refer to is not just some kind of external factor influencing individual learning, but it is the group process itself, created in the interaction of the group and making the learning at every level possible. When a software designer understands collaborative learning this way, the goal of design is to support productive collaborative knowledge building. This certainly includes providing media for communication within the group across networked computers. But it also involves supporting group processes, like argumentation, seeking information, explaining terms, pointing things out. In addition, it may include making the created knowledge documents easy to modify, persistent for later use and sharable within a larger community.

3. In the past decade you and your research team have been studying collaborative knowledge building at the group level and published many findings. One of the main achievements is that you proposed the theory of group cognition, which looks at a group as engaged in cognitive activities. This seems a very radical shift from the traditional learning view. What is the difference between group learning and individual learning? You argue that group cognition should serve as a foundation of a new science of learning, providing a coherent approach to computer support of collaborative learning in a global society. What is the core idea of your theory of group cognition? What is its implication for CSCL research and the learning sciences?

I developed the notion of "group cognition" while I was assembling selected writings from 1993-2002 into my book, *Group Cognition: Computer Support for Building Collaborative Knowledge* (Stahl, 2006). I realized that this was a hard concept to understand, and I wrote a couple of new chapters for the book to address this, as well as writing several papers on it later. My research from 2002 to the present has been on the Virtual Math Teams (VMT) project, with a wonderful group of collaborators. Highlights of this research are now available in *Studying Virtual Math Teams* (Stahl, 2009). Here, we try to study how small groups of students discuss math issues in an online environment.

By looking closely at their discussions, we can see many interesting group processes taking place: the groups propose strategies for approaching a math problem, they construct diagrams, they divide problems into sub-problems, they point out patterns, they define new terms, they develop algebraic formulae, they engage in argumentation, etc. These are cognitive processes. We often attribute these activities to individual students, but here we can see them being conducted by small groups of students. The activities are not simple expressions of mental representations that were originally in the head of one student; we can see how they emerge from the interactions of the students and build on resources that exist in the context of the on-going discourse. Rather than seeing the origin of the shared ideas in the head of one student, we see it arising from the group—and possibly then being taken up by the individuals in the group within their individual learning.

Most of the theories important in CSCL stress the social nature of learning. Vygotsky (1930/1978) argues that all higher cognitive abilities of people develop first through interpersonal interactions. Lave & Wenger (1991) show how learning is often situated in communities of practice. In the VMT project, we know nothing about the individual students and their cognitive processes, but we can see how a group of three or four students can engage in a variety of group cognitive processes while discussing math in an online environment. We have developed research methods for analyzing the computer logs of their discourse. Our approach is inspired by ethnomethodology and conversation analysis, which focus on interpersonal interaction (Koschmann, Stahl, & Zemel, 2007). This approach contrasts with methods from education and psychology, which focus on individual minds.

So when I write about "group cognition" I am writing about ways in which small groups accomplish cognitive tasks, like solving math problems and the sub-tasks involved in doing that like considering alternative proposals. I would not say that "groups think" or "groups learn" because that conjures up images based on our traditional conceptions of learning and thinking. But I would say that small groups can consider shared problems and can build joint knowledge. In fact, I would say that involving students in group cognition experiences can be a powerful way to teach them. To understand the power of collaborative learning or group cognition and to see how it can provide a foundation for individual intellectual development, the learning sciences must take CSCL seriously.

4. As we know traditional learning theory is mainly based on psychology, and it tries to explore what happen in individual minds in the learning process. It usually employs an experimental paradigm to examine whether one variable in the learning context is more effective or not with the comparison of pre-test and post-test. However, in collaborative learning, you argue that small groups are the most fruitful unit of study and it is in principle easier to study learning in groups than in individuals. Can you explain your view? How should we analyze group learning or group cognition?

Yes. In situations of collaborative learning, the interactions are far too complex and uncontrollable to isolate simple linear causal variables or to test for learning when the participants are no longer involved in the collaborative setting. What a student is likely to do in a collaborative situation is radically different from what they might do in a controlled laboratory, or in an isolated test situation or in an interview with a researcher. Direct access to individual cognition and learning is impossible, and indirect access is difficult and necessarily relies on questionable hypotheses and theories. In contrast, group cognitive processes are observable and can be captured rather rigorously in logs of computer-mediated interaction. The reason these group processes are observable is that the students in a group must make things visible for the other group members in order for the group to make progress together. Things must be visibly shared in the group. In a computer-supported group, making something visible means displaying it in the computer interface, and this can be captured in a computer log and played back by researchers. If the researchers understand the language of the students—including their mathematical moves—the researchers can observe the group processes that take place in the group discussion of the mathematics (although understanding what is going on often requires training, experience and hard work).

5. Just like the learning sciences generally, CSCL is an interdisciplinary field of research, including education, cognitive science, sociology, computer science, anthropology, and so on. This poses a challenge for a CSCL researcher to conduct deep and broad research. From your education background, we know you have studied philosophy, mathematics, cognitive science and computer science. With this rich interdisciplinary background, how do you integrate the various knowledge domains into your CSCL research? Do your have a holistic or coherent theoretical framework in your mind when you conduct your research? What theory and knowledge should researchers have when they conduct interdisciplinary research in CSCL?

It no doubt helps to have an interdisciplinary background, as many CSCL researchers do. The issues in CSCL are intertwined, requiring some perspective on software design, pedagogy, psychology and social theory. One also needs some understanding of the particular learning domain, such as mathematics. In addition, I have had to study ethnomethodology and conversation analysis as well as recent theories relevant to CSCL—activity theory, situated action, actor-network theory, distributed cognition. My students have had to pick some of this up on the side in order to follow our work in the VMT project. This is certainly a challenge. I am sure that it is even more of a challenge for people who—like the four Ph.D. students in the VMT project— are not from the USA or Western Europe and have not been exposed to many of these new theories.

There is no easy answer to how to prepare for conducting CSCL research, other than becoming associated with an existing CSCL lab. In my writings, I have tried to provide pointers to readings and ideas that I consider important and helpful. However, the field is constantly changing and one must gather together resources that one finds helpful to what one is trying to accomplish.

I do not see theory as a pre-defined guide to research. For me, theory has to emerge from the research. It has to be grounded in analysis of real data from collaborative learning sessions. Otherwise, it will not be interesting theory, but will be some version of commonsense conceptualizations and preconceptions. If we have learned anything in the twentieth century, it is that reality is quite different from what we imagine it to be like. When you look carefully at the log of a chat among several young students discussing math in a collaborative way, what you see is very different from the rational propositions that you might imagine. The postings are elliptical fragments, whose meaning depends almost entirely on references to previous text postings or to drawings done in the group. As you become familiar with this kind of data, you realize that it is actually much more sophisticated, complex and interesting than anything you might have imagined based on your previous theories.

Just as the students in a VMT chat rely on the many resources that are available to them at any given moment in their discourse, I do not base my work on some fixed theory but try to take advantage of whatever resources I may be familiar with to respond to my current task. This may be a dialog from Plato that I read in college or a new paper that I heard about and now need to download and read. Working in CSCL involves collaborating with a broad research community through papers, conferences and various joint activities or ways of sharing ideas.

6. CSCL is also a design science and it has both analytic and design components. The goal for design in CSCL is to create artifacts, activities and environments that enhance the practice of group meaning making. To address this issue, explore the group learning practice and establish new theory, researchers began to adopt designed-based research (DBR) in the learning sciences (Barab, 2006). It is used to study learning in real environments, which are designed and systematically changed as part of the research. The goal of DBR is to use the close study of an educational environment as it passes through multiple iterations within a naturalistic context, and to develop new theories, artifacts and practices that can be generalized to other schools and classroom. In one of your journal papers, you mentioned that you adopted this kind of design-based research process. How do you interpret this method? How do you employ this method? How do you bridge practice and theory? In China this method has been introduced, but there is no research practice reported yet. Can you give us some advice on how to use this method to carry out the relevant research?

The VMT project is an example of designing the software, conducting educational sessions, analyzing the data and developing theory as an integrated process. We have now gone through about five years of iterations. We started with a very simple commercial chat system and have expanded it little by little in response to the needs we observed in its usage by groups of students. We now have a very complicated system with a lobby for social networking, text chat, shared whiteboard, wiki, multiple tabs, social awareness, math symbolism, history reviews and explicit referencing. Integration of the different components is important in a complicated interface. In our data analysis, we look at how the student groups themselves coordinate and integrate the different media in which they interact and how they take advantage of the various forms of persistence afforded by the different media. From the analysis, we develop theoretical conceptualizations, such as concepts of deictic referencing, persistence of media, coordination of work across media. These concepts, grounded in actual usage data, improve our theoretical understanding of how group cognition works and feeds back into design changes.

The DBR process can work organically without our having to think about how design, usage, analysis and theory are integrated. The main thing is that we start simply, with a minimum of preconceptions about what the software, pedagogy, analysis and theory should look like. We work as a collaborative team, sharing our observations and insights. And we iterate: re-designing the software, revising the kinds of math problems, digging deeper into the data with increasing understanding and writing theoretical papers—over and over again.

7. The conference on CSCL is an internationally recognized forum for the exchange of ideas related to learning through collaborative activity in technology-based learning environment. It is also one of the major conferences sponsored by the International Society of the Learning Science (ISLS). The CSCL conference has been held every two years since 1995, with the International Conference of the Learning Science (ICLS) in the intervening years. The theme of CSCL 2009 in Greece is "CSCL Practice." What does this mean for CSCL? What do you think will be the main research theme of CSCL and the learning sciences in the next ten years?

The organizers of CSCL 2009, which will take place in June 2009, wanted to highlight the practice of CSCL in the classroom. They are interested in seeing what ideas from the field of CSCL are ready to be used now in school classrooms, in colleges, in informal life-long learning and in workplace training. Some researchers feel this is premature; that the important systems and pedagogies for collaborative learning are yet to be developed and that the conference should concentrate on the needs of researchers, letting teachers go to other conferences to find out about commercial and open source applications. Other people interpreted the theme to mean the study of collaborative learning practices. My papers at the conference analyze the group cognitive practices that groups of students use in VMT.

The CSCL community is a global research community. CSCL 2005 was held in Taipei. The conference will return to Asia in 2011, with CSCL 2011 being held in Hong Kong or Singapore. The special theme then will likely have to do with educational policy at national levels.

The important themes in CSCL have remained quite consistent and are likely to continue into the next decade. CSCL is about how to best educate students for the world of the future. This will be a global world, making heavy use of networked computers and other digital devices, and requiring high levels of collaboration. So we have to understand how people work and learn together. This will guide us in designing new forms of learning and new resources and technologies to support innovative pedagogies. The learning sciences has redefined our understanding of the learning process and we now see that rote learning is of limited value and collaborative learning is extraordinarily promising. Unfortunately, in almost every country, this new orientation has been systematically resisted and the nineteenth-century practices of drill and testing have been retained. If nothing new were learned in the learning sciences for the next ten years, there would still be plenty to do to bring what we already know to students around the world.

8. At CSCL 2002, Koschmann (2002) offered this definition for the CSCL domain in his keynote: "CSCL is a field of study centrally concerned with meaning and the practices of meaning making in the context of joint activity, and the ways in which these practices are mediated through designed artifacts." *Now, after seven years has passed, what do you think of this definition in terms of your research and CSCL community research themes? Is it necessary to redefine CSCL again?*

I loved that definition the first time I read it and I made it a focus of my introduction to the CSCL 2002 proceedings. I would still say that the phrase, *"the practices of meaning making in the context of joint activity"* is a good definition of what I mean when I say, "group cognition." The rest of the sentence, *"the ways in which these practices are mediated through designed artifacts,"* completes the unity of DBR by relating the analysis of student practices to the design of the software that they use. The wording of the sentence uses the theoretical concepts that help us to understand the behavior of students in CSCL settings. It is about practices, meaning making, joint activity and mediation by technology. This is the post-cognitivist language, which has replaced talk of facts being transferred from one form of memory to another. I do not think we need to redefine this as much as we need to understand it more deeply and put its implications into practice.

9. Can you introduce your research team's project? What is your main concern in your research? What is the goal of your research?

I have written a lot about this, most recently in *Studying Virtual Math Teams* (Stahl, 2009), which includes the most important papers by me and others involved in the project. The final chapter looks back over the project and its findings to argue that the VMT project can be taken as a tentative model for a new science of groups. I claim that the project was an example of design-based research that developed a software environment, a data corpus, a set of analyses, an appropriate analytic methodology and a theory of group cognition through an iterative process. This new science avoids using technology, methodology and theory that are oriented to individual minds and instead orients the whole activity toward the group as the unit of analysis. The findings from the project exemplify practices of group cognition.

Until recently, the goal of the project was to generate a rich data corpus for studying group cognition. It has now served that purpose for me, my colleagues, visiting researchers and collaborators at other labs. We are currently trying to prepare it to be a practical online service at the Math Forum (http://mathforum.org) for people around the world to work on stimulating math problems together.

The ultimate goal of my research is to contribute in a small way to changing education in our world by helping researchers to understand the nature and potential of group cognition. Thank you, Shaoming, for asking such challenging and important questions and introducing my ideas in China.

References

Barab, S. (2006). Design-based research: A methodological toolkit for the learning scientist. In R. K. Sawyer (Ed.), *The Cambridge handbook of the learning sciences* (pp. 153-170). Cambridge, UK: Cambridge University Press.

Koschmann, T. (2002). Dewey's contribution to the foundations of CSCL research. In G. Stahl (Ed.), *Computer support for collaborative learning: Foundations for a CSCL community: Proceedings of CSCL 2002* (pp. 17-22). Boulder, CO: Lawrence Erlbaum Associates.

Koschmann, T., Stahl, G., & Zemel, A. (2007). The video analyst's manifesto (or the implications of Garfinkel's policies for the development of a program of video analytic research within the learning sciences). In R. Goldman, R. Pea, B. Barron & S. Derry (Eds.), *Video research in the learning sciences* (pp. 133-144). Mahway, NJ: Lawrence Erlbaum Associates. Available at http://GerryStahl.net/publications/journals/manifesto.pdf.

Lave, J., & Wenger, E. (1991). *Situated learning: Legitimate peripheral participation.* Cambridge, UK: Cambridge University Press.

Stahl, G. (2006). *Group cognition: Computer support for building collaborative knowledge.* Cambridge, MA: MIT Press. Available at http://GerryStahl.net/mit/.

Stahl, G. (Ed.). (2009). *Studying virtual math teams.* New York, NY: Springer. Available at http://GerryStahl.net/vmt/book.

Stahl, G., Koschmann, T., & Suthers, D. (2006). Computer-supported collaborative learning: An historical perspective. In R. K. Sawyer (Ed.), *Cambridge handbook of the learning sciences* (pp. 409-426). Cambridge, UK: Cambridge University Press. Available at http://GerryStahl.net/cscl/CSCL_English.pdf in English, http://GerryStahl.net/cscl/CSCL_Chinese_simplified.pdf in simplified Chinese, http://GerryStahl.net/cscl/CSCL_Chinese_traditional.pdf in traditional Chinese, http://GerryStahl.net/cscl/CSCL_Spanish.pdf in Spanish,

http://GerryStahl.net/cscl/CSCL_Portuguese.pdf in Portuguese,
http://GerryStahl.net/cscl/CSCL_German.pdf in German,
http://GerryStahl.net/cscl/CSCL_Romanian.pdf in Romanian.
Vygotsky, L. (1930/1978). *Mind in society*. Cambridge, MA: Harvard University Press.

4.   Team Cognition in Socio-Technical Systems

Objective: This commentary on the special issue suggests a focus on group-cognition factors in investigations of teamwork involving socio-technical systems. *Background*: The author has conducted research in Computer-Supported Collaborative Learning and has found the need to re-think the theory and methodology of that field to take account of its defining characteristics of small-group interaction and socio-technical mediation. *Method*: A brief literature review is undertaken of major findings in post-cognitive theory and Conversation Analysis. This suggests a methodological priority to group phenomena as sources for the genesis of individual phenomena and for understanding of processes of coordination and communication in small groups. *Results*: It is seen that many recent studies of teams take place within traditional disciplinary frameworks that analyze phenomena primarily at the individual unit of analysis, reducing group phenomena to additive sums of individual phenomena. For instance, processes of coordination and communication are treated as secondary to the expression of individuals' mental models or external expressions of internal representations. *Conclusion*: The commentary calls for development of a new science of groups, with the development of appropriate theory, conceptualizations of core phenomena, experimental methods, analytic analyses and presentational formats. Examples are: focus on discourse analysis, use of design-based research, conceptualization of mediation rather than causation and publication of case studies. *Application*: A focus on the group unit of analysis can shed new light on socio-technical issues.

The articles in this special issue of *Human Factors* illustrate impressively the application of a widely diverse set of theoretical perspectives, experimental approaches, analytic methodologies and disciplinary concerns. In terms of subject matter as well, the variety of coordination strategies, communication media and socio-technical contexts investigated is no less daunting. Many of the papers express the feeling that they are partaking in a grand beginning of investigating this vast new territory; that they have just begun to peek into a realm that is still quite unexplored. At the same time, one repeatedly finds familiar categories, computations and theoretical moves borrowed uncritically from well-established domains. One wonders if the brave new world of socio-technical systems and ubiquitous teamwork might require a more radical re-tooling of the machinery of research than such facile re-application. Sure, one can extend analyses of human factors from the situation of an individual computer user staring at the screen of a desktop computer in a sterile lab to that of teams of people interacting with extensive and messy networks of robots, software, communication systems and other teams. But it may also be true that there is much to be gained from thinking about what is new and essentially different here, and what the implications of that might be for the methods of the science(s) that we pursue.

Coming from the field of computer-supported collaborative learning (CSCL), I have been led to view socio-technical systems primarily from the perspective of the small-group unit of analysis. CSCL explores how networked computers can support collaborative learning not only through the design of socio-technical systems that include communication support for students learning together, but also through innovative teacher/facilitator roles, scaffolded pedagogy and effective peer coordination. Many CSCL researchers come from education, psychology, cognitive science and computer science and still tend to focus on learning as an individual process involving mental processes, internal representations and mental models. Rather than assuming that the categories of traditional approaches still get at the fundamental phenomena in an essentially transformed educational practice, I have tried to identify what is at the root of collaborative learning—such as group processes of coordination and communication.

In CSCL, learning takes place as group discourse. Coordination and communication are not accidental secondary factors, but the primary interaction through which everything else happens. Discourse—which can include speech, text, gesture, intonation, gaze, etc., even in an online environment in which these are indicated in various ways on a computer screen—is the shared world in which participants are engaged as contributors to a joint meaning-making process (Stahl, Koschmann & Suthers, 2006).

Taking the lead from various post-cognitive theories—from mediated cognition (Vygotsky, 1930/1978) to distributed (Hutchins, 1996), situated (Lave, 1991; Suchman, 2007) and embodied cognition (Dourish, 2001)—I try to push the theoretical viewpoint that focuses on the small group as the unit of analysis, as opposed to the many researchers who try to reduce group phenomena to the psychological individual as the ultimate basis of all cognition. I was driven to this approach by my empirical work designing and deploying socio-technical systems for collaborative learning in the 1990s (Stahl, 2006). In the past decade,

I have explored what I call "group cognition" through design-based research developing support for virtual math teams (Stahl, 2009).

In his seminal work on distributed cognition, Hutchins (1996) critiques the foundations of traditional cognitive science (Newell & Simon, 1972) along Vygotskian lines by arguing not only that cognition can extend beyond the individual mind, but that group-cognitive processes have a micro-genetic priority and that there are some group-cognitive processes that cannot be internalized by individuals. For instance, the navigational skills that sailors on large naval ships have, they originally learned from their apprenticeship in navigation teams; furthermore, although they have internalized these skills enough to accomplish some navigational tasks as individuals, there are certain group-cognitive tasks that are too complex to be internalized by any one individual.

In our world of global economics and large socio-technical systems, there must be more such irreducibly group-cognitive tasks than we realize. Just as the Navy trains its navigators to work in teams that accomplish joint cognitive tasks—tasks evidencing a high level of computational complexity that cannot be reduced to the cognitive functions of individuals—so society generally must educate the work force and leadership of the next generation to think collaboratively as effective, innovative, knowledge-producing teams.

To radically re-think group cognition requires more than minimal extensions of traditional information-processing theories. That approach in some ways modeled human cognition on a model of computer computation and adopted an image of science based on the advances of natural sciences as opposed to human sciences. Group cognition involves meaning making and interpretation; it requires a new scientific paradigm, replacing mechanistic causal notions of statistical results under reproducible conditions with a notion of mediation under unique situations (Stahl, 2010). It must be grounded in detailed case studies of group interactions "in the wild." Hutchins, Lave, Suchman and Dourish approach this through ethnography. I approach it through an adaptation of Conversation Analysis (Sacks, 1962/1995; Schegloff, 2007) to the online context. Just as the tape recorder and then video technology once made it possible for the first time to document face-to-face conversation in enough detail to support detailed analysis, so computer logs in carefully designed interventions can now capture everything at the group level of interaction and make it available for rigorous, situated detailed analysis. Group cognition is an emergent phenomenon, but it emerges from the semiotic interactions within the group discourse observed at the group unit of analysis, not directly from some hypothesized comparison or agreement of mental models or computations among internal representations at the individual unit of analysis.

While it may initially seem that naturalistic online interaction mediated by complex socio-technical systems would be much harder to analyze than the cognitive efforts of an individual in a controlled lab setting, the opposite can be true. That is because everything that is shared in the group interaction must by definition be made visible for the multiple participants, whereas individual cognition is posited as not directly accessible. Once it is visible in a computer system, group cognition may be captured and made visible to analysts in a persistent form that can be studied in depth. For instance, a group's trains of thought and references to various concepts, images or experiences are displayed by the participants and these aspects of the group cognition are thereby made available for analysis. Whereas psychological or educational analyses of collaboration generally "black-box" key cognitive processes—e.g., by hypothesizing mental models or internal representations whose details cannot be explored empirically, but only inferred—these processes can be observed at work in the group discourse. For instance, an analyst can follow how a concept develops as it is successively used by different participants building on each other's utterance. One can see precisely what references are made to specific artifacts in the discourse context. Drawings—which often ground mathematical thinking—can be shared in the whiteboard, which then functions as part of the external memory of the group, its common ground or its joint problem space (Çakir, Zemel & Stahl, 2009; Sarmiento & Stahl, 2008). All this interactional data can be captured without interrupting cognition with think-aloud protocols or removing individuals from their interactive group context to administer surveys or interviews.

In particular, fine-grained analysis of discourse can reveal group-cognitive processes of communication and coordination—but also of argumentation, deduction, problem solving, explanation, etc. Conversation Analysis (CA) as a field has built up an impressive analysis of how everyday conversations work: what the rules are by which people take turns talking, how they respond to each other, what kinds of linguistic maneuvers they make to accomplish interpersonal moves, and so on. Specifically, CA looks at "adjacency pairs" as the elementary building blocks of face-to-face informal interaction. Because an adjacency pair includes an interchange between at least two people, it is irreducibly a group phenomenon.

For virtual math teams, we must adapt the CA approach to our context of online quasi-synchronous, text-based chat and whiteboard drawing. Rather than transcribing speaking and listening, we analyze typing and reading. Rather than observing socially enforced sequential turn taking, we reconstruct an implied sequential threading. Rather than studying social conversation, we follow problem solving and mathematical exploration. Rather than tracking adult behavior, we examine novice learning of new math-discourse skills. So, in addition to the normal communication processes of interpersonal interaction, we can analyze effects of technological mediation; progressions attributable to learning; reasoning or explanation processes specific to math discourse; and coordination practices for collaborative problem solving.

Our approach to the study of group cognition in socio-technical systems involves a design-based research (Design-Based Research Collective, 2003) process that drives a co-evolution of technology, theory, intervention and analysis methodology—as can be seen in the diverse themes of the chapters of (Stahl, 2009). Our technology for virtual math teams has grown to support cognition and learning at the individual, small-group and community units, as required by our multi-level theory. Our analysis—focused for practical and theoretical reasons on the small-group unit of analysis—has resulted in many case studies that motivated new technical functionality as well as new pedagogical theories and interventions. We believe we have just begun to understand group cognition mediated by socio-technical systems and that there is much more to be learned by pursuing analysis that takes seriously the priority of the group unit of analysis.

References

Çakır, M. P., Zemel, A., & Stahl, G. (2009). The joint organization of interaction within a multimodal CSCL medium. *International Journal of Computer-Supported Collaborative Learning, 4*(2), 115-149. Web: http://GerryStahl.net/pub/ijCSCL_4_2_1.pdf

Design-Based Research Collective. (2003). Design-based research: An emerging paradigm for educational inquiry. *Educational Researcher, 32*(1), 5-8

Dourish, P. (2001). *Where the action is: The foundations of embodied interaction.* Cambridge, MA: MIT Press.

Hutchins, E. (1996). *Cognition in the wild.* Cambridge, MA: MIT Press.

Lave, J. (1991). Situating learning in communities of practice. In L. Resnick, J. Levine & S. Teasley (Eds.), *Perspectives on socially shared cognition* (pp. 63-83). Washington, DC: APA

Newell, A., & Simon, H. A. (1972). *Human problem solving.* Englewood Cliffs, NJ: Prentice-Hall.

Sacks, H. (1962/1995). *Lectures on conversation.* Oxford, UK: Blackwell.

Sarmiento, J., & Stahl, G. (2008). *Extending the joint problem space: Time and sequence as essential features of knowledge building.* Paper presented at the International Conference of the Learning Sciences (ICLS 2008), Utrecht, Netherlands. Web: http://GerryStahl.net/pub/icls2008johann.pdf

Schegloff, E. A. (2007). *Sequence organization in interaction: A primer in conversation analysis.* Cambridge, UK: Cambridge University Press.

Stahl, G. (2006). *Group cognition: Computer support for building collaborative knowledge*. Cambridge, MA: MIT Press. 510 + viii pages. Web: http://GerryStahl.net/mit/

Stahl, G. (2009). *Studying virtual math teams*. New York, NY: Springer. 626 +xxi pages. Web: http://GerryStahl.net/vmt/book Doi: http://dx.doi.org/10.1007/978-1-4419-0228-3

Stahl, G. (2010). Group cognition as a foundation for the new science of learning. In M. S. Khine & I. M. Saleh (Eds.), *New science of learning: Computers, cognition and collaboration in education*. New York, NY: Springer. Web: http://GerryStahl.net/pub/scienceoflearning.pdf

Stahl, G., Koschmann, T., & Suthers, D. (2006). Computer-supported collaborative learning: An historical perspective. In R. K. Sawyer (Ed.), *Cambridge handbook of the learning sciences* (pp. 409-426). Cambridge, UK: Cambridge University Press. Web: http://GerryStahl.net/cscl/CSCL_English.pdf in English, http://GerryStahl.net/cscl/CSCL_Chinese_simplified.pdf in simplified Chinese, http://GerryStahl.net/cscl/CSCL_Chinese_traditional.pdf in traditional Chinese, http://GerryStahl.net/cscl/CSCL_Spanish.pdf in Spanish, http://GerryStahl.net/cscl/CSCL_Portuguese.pdf in Portuguese, http://GerryStahl.net/cscl/CSCL_German.pdf in German, http://GerryStahl.net/cscl/CSCL_Romanian.pdf in Romanian, http://GerryStahl.net/cscl/CSCL_Japanese.pdf in Japanese

Suchman, L. A. (2007). *Human-machine reconfigurations: Plans and situated actions* (2nd ed.). Cambridge, UK: Cambridge University Press. xii, 314 p. pages.

Vygotsky, L. (1930/1978). *Mind in society*. Cambridge, MA: Harvard University Press.

5.   Analyzing Cognition in Online Teams

Gerry Stahl & Carolyn Penstein Rosé

This chapter represents a disciplinary perspective from Computer-Supported Collaborative Learning (CSCL), an interdisciplinary field concerned with leveraging technology for education and with analyzing cognitive processes like learning and meaning making in small groups of students (Stahl, Koschmann & Suthers, 2006). *Group cognition* is a theory developed to support CSCL research by describing how collaborative groups of students could achieve cognitive accomplishments together and how that could benefit the individual learning of the participants (Stahl, 2006). It is important to note that while it may very well be the case that a group of students working together manage to solve problems faster than any of them may have been able to do alone, the most important benefits to group cognition are the potential for genuinely innovative solutions that go beyond the expertise of any individual in the group, the deeper understanding that is achieved through the interaction as part of that creative process, and the lasting impact of that deep understanding that the students take with them when they move on from that interaction, which they may then carry with them as new resources into subsequent group problem-solving scenarios. Group cognition can then be seen as what transforms groups into factories for the creation of new knowledge.

The types of problems that have been the focus of exploration within the group cognition paradigm have not been routine, well-structured problems where every participant can know exactly what their piece of the puzzle is up front in such a way that the team can function as a well oiled machine. Many critical group tasks do not fit into well-known and practiced protocols—for example, low-resource circumstances that may occur in disaster situations, where standard solutions are not an option. In acknowledgement of this, the focus within the group-cognition research has been on problems that offer groups the opportunity to explore creatively how those problems can be approached from a variety of perspectives, where the groups are encouraged to explore unique perspectives. The processes that are the concern of group-cognition research have not primarily been those that are related to efficiency of problem solving (as in some other chapters of this volume (Salas & Fiore, 2011)). Rather, the focus has been on the pivotal moments where a creative spark or a process of collaborative knowledge building occurs through interaction. Our fascination has been with identifying the conditions under which these moments of inspiration are triggered, with the goal of facilitating this process of group innovation and collaborative knowledge creation.

In this collaboratively written chapter, we consider insights from group cognition in light of synergistic ideas from other subcommunities within CSCL. Within the field of computer-supported collaborative learning, the topic of what makes group discussions productive for learning has been explored—with a similar focus and very similar findings, perhaps with subtle distinctions—under different names, such as *transactivity* (Berkowitz & Gibbs, 1983; Teasley, 1997; Azmitia & Montgomery, 1993; di Lisi & Golbeck, 1999), *uptake* (Suthers, 2006), *social modes of co-construction* (Weinberger & Fischer, 2006), or *productive agency* (Schwartz, 1998). Despite differences in orientation between the subcommunities where these frameworks have originated, the conversational behaviors that have been identified as valuable are quite similar. Specifically, these different frameworks universally value explicit articulation of reasoning and making connections between instances of articulated reasoning. For example, Schwartz and colleagues (1998) and de Lisi and Golbeck (1999) make very similar arguments for the significance of these behaviors from the Vygotskian and Piagetian theoretical frameworks, respectively. The idea of transactivity as a property of a conversational contribution originates from a Piagetian framework and requires that a contribution contain an explicit reasoning display and encode an acknowledgement of a previous explicit reasoning display. However, note that when Schwartz describes from a Vygotskian framework the kind of mental scaffolding that collaborating peers offer one another, he describes it in terms of one student using words that serve as a starting place for the other student's reasoning and construction of knowledge. This implies explicit displays of reasoning, so that the reasoning can be known by the partner and then built upon by that partner. Thus, the process is very similar to what we describe for the production of transactive contributions. In both cases, a transactive analysis would say that mental models are articulated, shared, mutually examined and potentially integrated.

The theory of group cognition has been explored primarily using data from the Virtual Math Teams (VMT) Project, documented in (Stahl, 2009a). While much of the analysis of VMT data takes the form of detailed case studies conducted manually (often in group data sessions), the VMT Project and CSCL generally are also interested in the use of software algorithms to aid in the analysis of online discourse (Rosé et al., 2007; Rosé et al., 2008; Kang et al., 2008) or collaborative recorded speech (Gweon et al., 2009), especially with the promise that effective facilitation of collaborating groups can eventually be automated (Kumar et al., 2007; Cui et al., 2009; Chaudhuri et al., 2009; Kumar et al., in press). Some of this automatic analysis work has focused explicitly on properties like transactivity (Joshi & Rosé, 2007; Rosé et al., 2008), while other work focuses on lower-level conversational processes that can be seen as building blocks that enable the recognition of transactivity (Wang & Rosé, 2007; Wang & Rosé, in press; Ai et al., submitted) or more general-purpose text-mining techniques related to making fine-grained stylistic distinctions (Joshi & Rosé, 2009; Arora, Joshi, & Rosé, 2009; Mayfield et al., submitted). As part of this effort, we have worked to transcend the theoretical underpinnings of frameworks like transactivity to think more about a linguistic-level lens through which to view the data that might serve as a form of *interlingua*, or intermediate representation, that would make it more natural to bridge between different theoretical frameworks (Howley, Mayfield, & Rosé, in press). This objective of working towards a linguistic-level lens that is close to being theory neutral with respect to learning-science theories is particularly key for our collaboration because of the way that the group-cognition framework does not make the same assumptions about mental models and cognitive processes as do many of the above-mentioned other frameworks.

Group cognition is a post-cognitive theory, like some of the theories presented in other chapters of this book. Post-cognitivism is a tradition characterized by situated, non-dualistic, practice-based approaches, as described by Musaeus (this volume). Cognitivism—which tends to retain theoretical remnants of the Cartesian dualism of the mental and physical worlds—originally arose through the critique of behaviorism, with the argument that human responses to stimulae in the world are mediated by cognitive activity in the mind of the human agent. This argument was particularly strong in considerations of linguistic behavior (Chomsky, 1959). More recently, post-cognitivist theories have argued that cognitive activity can span multiple people (as well as artifacts), such as when knowledge develops through a sequence of utterances by different people and the emergent knowledge cannot be attributed to any one person or assumed to be an expression of any individual's prior mental representations (e.g., Bereiter, 2002, p. 283).

In his seminal statement of post-cognitivist theory, Hutchins (1996) pointed to group-cognitive phenomena: "The group performing the cognitive task may have cognitive properties that differ from the cognitive properties of any individual" (p. 176). "The cognitive properties of groups are produced by interaction between structures internal to individuals and structures external to individuals" (p. 262). However, rather than focusing on these group phenomena themselves, Hutchins usually analyzes socio-technical systems and the cognitive role of highly developed artifacts (airplane cockpits, ship navigation tools). In focusing on the cultural level—characteristically for a cultural anthropologist—he does not often analyze the cognitive meaning making of the group itself.

Group-cognition theory explicitly focuses on these inter-personal phenomena and investigates data in which one can observe the development of cognitive achievements in the interactions of small groups of people, often in online collaborative settings, where interactions can be automatically logged. By interaction, we mean the discourse that takes place in the group. Thus, what Beck & Keyton (this volume) say for macrocognition or team cognition applies to group cognition, namely that it is communicatively based and can be tracked in team members' interdependent messages. Group cognition is fundamentally a linguistic (speech or text) process, rather than a psychological (mental) one, as mentioned above. Thus, unlike the theory of transactivity described above, this post-cognitive approach does not assume cognitive constructs such as mental models, internal representations or retrievable stores of personal knowledge. In the online setting of VMT, cognition is analyzed by looking closely at the ways in which meaning is built up through the interplay of text postings, graphical constructions and algebraic formulations (Çakır, Zemel & Stahl, 2009). Methodologically, our case studies of group cognition use a form of interaction analysis (Jordan & Henderson, 1995) adapted from conversation analysis (Sacks, 1962/1995) to the CSCL context (Stahl, 2009a, p. 47). In our ongoing collaboration, we are exploring ways of extending these approaches in light of linguistic frameworks such as systemic functional linguistics (Christie, 1999; Martin & Rose, 2003; Martin & White, 2005).

The title of this chapter already reflects a tension that permeates this book as a whole (see Koschmann, this volume): that between the human sciences and the natural sciences, between *understanding* team cognition (e.g., with micro-analysis of situated case studies) and *explaining* it (e.g., modeling, confirming general hypotheses, formulating laws and specifying predictive causal relations). Group cognition in online teams involves both humans and computers, both highly situated collaborative interactions and programmed computer support. Our methodology therefore includes both micro-analysis of group discourse in unique case studies and the automated coding of the discourse log for statistical hypothesis testing.

The field of CSCL is particularly interested in the ways small groups can build knowledge together thanks to communication and support from networking technology. We hope that CSCL environments can be designed that make possible and encourage groups to think and learn collaboratively. In our research, our colleagues and we look at logs of student groups chatting and drawing about mathematics in order to see if they build on each other's ideas to achieve more than they would individually. How do they understand each other and build shared language and a joint problem focus? What kinds of problems of understanding do they run into and how do they overcome those? How do they accomplish intersubjective meaning making, interpersonal trains of thought, shared understandings of diagrams, joint problem conceptualizations, common references, coordination of problem-solving efforts; planning, deducing, designing, describing; problem solving, explaining, defining, generalizing, representing, remembering and reflecting as a group? What can we say about the general methods that small groups use to learn and think as groups? How can we support and encourage this better with software support for social awareness, social networking, simulations, visualizations, communication; with intelligent software agents; with pedagogical scaffolds and guidance; with training and mentoring; with access to digital resources; with new theories of learning and thinking? To answer these complex questions, we must look carefully at the details of discourse in CSCL groups and develop innovative tools (both analytic and automated) and theories (of cognition by individuals, small groups and discourse communities).

Views of learning and thinking

The learning sciences view learning as involving meaning making by the learners (Stahl, Koschmann & Suthers, 2006). Students who just passively accept instruction without thinking about it and coming to understand it in their own way of making sense of things will be wasting everyone's time. Why? Because they will not be able to *use* the new knowledge or to *explain* it. Of course, this construction of meaning takes place over time: someone can learn something one day and make sense of it later, when they try to use it in different circumstances and to explain their use to other people and to themselves. But if they never integrate what they have learned into their own thinking and acting—by applying it where appropriate and talking about it clearly—then they will not have really learned. What sociologists like Bernstein, as presented in Hasan's overview (1999), know about social interactions and contribute to our understanding of the significance of group cognition is the way participants internalize the resources that evolve within one interactional context and then recontextualize them in new and radically different contexts they find themselves in later. In this way, the new knowledge that is created, or the new or enhanced knowledge-building skills that are appropriated, can replicate and spread contagiously. It is the magic that, for instance, makes seemingly inconsequential interactions between mothers and children while cleaning the oven play a key role in a child's preparation for schooling (Cloran, 1999). It is precisely because of the tremendous impact the results of these interactions can have going forward that the local sacrifice that may occur in terms of efficiency of the interaction can be viewed as a small price to pay when one considers the long-term cost-benefit ratio, the profound impact of one transformational experience of group cognition.

Vygotsky *(1930/1978)* made an even stronger argument. He showed for the major forms of human psychological functioning that the individual capabilities were derived from interpersonal experiences:

> *An interpersonal process is transformed into an intrapersonal one.* Every function in the child's cultural development appears twice: first, on the social level and later, on the individual level; first *between* people (*interpsychological*), and then *inside* the child. This applies equally to voluntary attention, to logical memory, and to the formation of concepts. All the higher functions originate as actual relations between human individuals. (p. 57)

Although all functions of individual cognition are derived from group cognition, the reverse is not true. As Hutchins (1996) demonstrated with his example of the bridge of a large Navy ship, not all group cognition can be internalized by an individual: "The distribution of knowledge described [in the book] is a property of the navigation team, and there are processes that are enabled by that distribution that can never be internalized by a single individual" (p. 284). Whether or not specific skills and knowledge can be mastered by individuals or only by teams, the learning of those skills or knowledge seems to rely heavily and essentially on group cognition. That is why we try to promote and to study group cognition.

What we, as learning scientists, have learned about learning and thinking in recent decades in the West is influenced by what philosophers before us said. For instance, most Western philosophers until the middle of the 1900s thought that knowledge could be expressed by propositions, sentences or explicit statements. If that were true, then the learning of knowledge could, indeed, consist simply of students individually hearing or reading the right sentences and remembering them.

But Ludwig Wittgenstein's book, *Philosophical Investigations*, published in 1953, questioned this view of learning and thinking. It looked at math as a prime example. Mathematical knowledge can be seen as a set of procedures, algorithms or rules. Wittgenstein asked how one can learn to follow a mathematical rule (Wittgenstein, 1944/1956, Part VI; 1953, §185-243, esp.

§201). For instance, if someone shows you how to count by fours by saying, "4, 8, 12, 16," how do you know how to go on? Is there a rule for applying the rule of counting by fours? (Such as, "Take the last number and add 4 to it.") And if so, how do you learn to apply that rule? By another rule? Eventually, you need to know how to do something that is not based on following a propositional rule—like counting and naming numbers and recognizing which numbers are larger. The use of explicit rules must be somehow grounded in other kinds of knowledge. These other kinds include the tacit knowledge of how to behave as a human being in our culture: how to speak, count, ask questions, generalize, put different ideas together, apply knowledge from one situation in another context and so on. *And these are the kinds of things that one initially learns socially, in small groups or in child-parent dyads.* Wittgenstein's question brought the logical view of knowledge as explicit propositions into a paradox: if knowledge involves knowing rules, then it must involve knowing how to use rules, which is itself *not* a rule.

Wittgenstein was an unusual philosopher because he said that problems like this one could not be solved by contemplation, but rather by looking at how people actually do things. He said, "Don't think, look!" (1953, §66). In studying group cognition, we try to follow Wittgenstein's advice. We try to view how small groups of people actually *do* things. Our focus is on understanding how the group magic occurs concretely in interaction.

A perspective on cognition is a particular way of viewing it. Rather than telling you what our *views* or ideas are about learning and thinking in CSCL groups, we will show you how we *view* or observe learning and thinking in CSCL groups. The term "view" has this double meaning: it means both viewing by looking at something with ones eyes and also viewing in the metaphorical sense of thinking about something from a conceptual perspective. Although Wittgenstein himself did not actually look at empirical examples of how people follow rules in math, we can. By carefully setting up a CSCL session, we can produce data that allows us to view groups of students learning how to follow math rules and thinking about the math rules. This is what we do to view learning and thinking in CSCL groups. It is the basic approach of the science of group cognition (see Stahl, 2009b for a discussion of the scientific methodology).

The work of our research teams and other colleagues involves looking closely at some rich examples of student groups learning and thinking about math. We would like to share a brief excerpt from one of these examples with you and talk about how we go about viewing the learning and thinking of this group of students. In particular, how do they construct their group cognition through collaborative meaning-making activities?

In this chapter, we will look at the meaning-making work of a group of students, analyzing their language-based interaction at multiple levels: the overall *event*, a specific hour-long *session* of the two-week event, a discussion *theme* that arose, a discourse *move* that triggered that theme, a pivotal *interchange*, a single *utterance* and a particular *reference* in the utterance. By looking at the linguistic connections, we can see how the syntax, semantics and pragmatics weave a network of meaningful references that accomplishes a set of cognitive achievements.

On the one hand, we can see the linguistic elements of the log and their structure of temporal and hierarchical relationships as accomplishing group cognition by, at each moment, constraining the next utterance as situated in the context of event, session, theme, discourse moves, eliciting adjacency pairs, preceding utterances and network of references. On the other hand, human actors creatively design accountable responses (see Koschmann, this volume) within the constraining situation defined by these contextual elements. That is, among the constraints on the actors is the requirement that their linguistic actions make sense in the on-going discourse and that they reveal their meaning and relevance in their linguistic design. Although people often design their utterances to convey the impression that they are the result of psychological processes (change of mental state, expression of internal reflections), we can analyze the group cognition in terms of the linguistic effects of the observable words and drawing actions, without making any assumptions about individual mental representations. The individual students are active as linguistic processors—interpreting and designing the utterances—but the larger mathematical and cognitive accomplishments are achieved through the group discourse, which exists in the computer displays, observable by the students and—even years later—by analysts. As Koschmann suggests, we can see and make explicit how teams become teams in the ways that they manifest the contingencies and accountabilities of their unique situation, using conventional linguistic structures as resources.

The event: VMT Spring Fest 2006 Team B

Here, we will be talking about an online event that occurred three-and-a-half years ago. The interaction is preserved in a computer log, which can be replayed by researchers. Three students, probably about 16 years old, were assigned to be Team B and they met with a facilitator in an online chat environment on May 9, 10, 16 and 18, in 2006, for about an hour in the late afternoon each day. The participants were distributed across three time zones in the US. The event was part of the VMT research project. Neither the students nor we know anything more about each other's personal characteristics or background.

Figure 1. Topic for VMT Spring Fest 2006.

The topic for this event was to explore a pattern of sticks forming a stair-step arrangement of squares (see Figure 1) and then to explore similar patterns chosen by the students themselves. The VMT online environment consisted primarily of a synchronous chat window and a shared whiteboard. At the end of each session, the students were supposed to post their findings on a wiki, shared with other teams participating in the Spring Fest. Between sessions, the facilitator posted feedback to the students in a textbox on the whiteboard.

The session: Session 3, May 16, 7 pm

Let's look at an excerpt from the end of the third session. The three students had already solved the original problem of the stair-step pattern of squares. They had also made up their own problem involving three-dimensional pyramids. Now they turned to look at the problem that Team C had described on the wiki after session 2. Team B is looking at an algebraic expression that the other team of students had derived for a diamond pattern of squares. They start to draw the pattern in their whiteboard (see Figure 2) and they chat as a team about the problem of this new pattern.

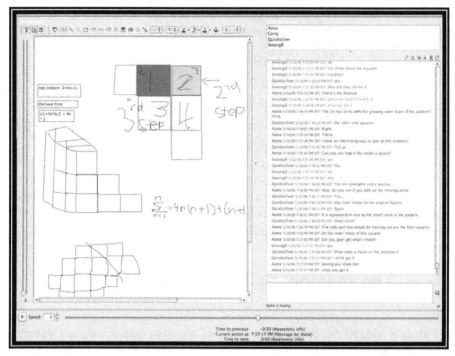

Figure 2. The VMT Replayer showing the VMT online environment.

The theme: "I have an interesting way to look at this problem"

One of the students, Aznx, begins to make a proposal on how to "look" at their problem. First, he announces, "`I have an interesting way to look at this problem.`" Note that he uses the word "`look`" in the same double meaning of "`view`" that was mentioned above. As we will see, he means he has a new way to think about the problem mathematically—and that involves a way of observing a visual image of the problem. The group does its thinking both by typing text and algebraic expressions in the chat window and by simultaneously drawing and viewing diagrams or geometric constructions of the problem in the shared whiteboard (see Çakır, Zemel & Stahl, 2009 for an analysis of the coordination by the group of their text, symbols and drawings).

Aznx' announcement opens an opportunity for the group to discuss a way of looking at the problem. In fact, the group takes up the offer that is implicit in Aznx' statement and the students spend the next eight minutes trying to each understand it. As it turns out, they will work on this view of the problem for the rest of this session and most of their final session.

A VMT chat session can generally be analyzed as a series of themes or discussion topics. Often, themes come and go, and different themes overlap, with one wrapping up while another gets started. Researchers can identify the boundaries of a theme: when a new theme opens and an old one closes (Zemel, Xhafa & Çakir, 2009).

In this case, the group has been talking about how the diamond pattern grows as a geometric figure for a couple of minutes and then they discuss Team C's algebraic expression for a couple of minutes. As those themes get played out and there is a pause in the chat, Aznx makes a move to open a new theme for the group.

A move: Showing how to view the problem

Aznx' announcement that he has a perspective to share with the group is a way of introducing a new theme, a "pre-announcement" (Schegloff, 2007, pp. 37-44; Terasaki, 2004). Conversations often flow by new contributions picking up on something that was already being discussed. Online text chat tends to be more open than face-to-face talking; chat does not follow the strict turn-taking rules of conversation. However, it is still common to do some extra work to change themes even in chat. In a sense, Aznx is asking permission from the group to start a new theme. Quicksilver responds encouragingly right away by saying, "Tell us" (see Figure 3).

line	date	start	post	delay		
919	5/16/06	19:35:26	19:35:36	0:00:06	Aznx	I have an interesting way to look at this problem.
920	5/16/06	19:35:41	19:35:42	0:00:03	Quicksilver	Tell us
921	5/16/06	19:35:38	19:35:45	0:00:00	Aznx	Can you see how it fits inside a quare?
922	5/16/06	19:35:45	19:35:45	0:00:00	Bwang	yes
	5/16/06	19:35:49	19:35:52	0:00:00	Bwang	[user erased message]
923	5/16/06	19:35:51	19:35:52	0:00:01	Quicksilver	Yes
924	5/16/06	19:35:52	19:35:53	0:00:02	Bwang	oh
925	5/16/06	19:35:55	19:35:55	0:00:06	Bwang	yes
926	5/16/06	19:35:53	19:36:01	0:00:04	Quicksilver	You are sayingthe extra spaces...
927	5/16/06	19:35:58	19:36:05	0:00:06	Aznx	Also, do you see if you add up the missing areas

Figure 3. The move to introduce Aznx' new way of looking at the group's problem.

Actually, Aznx already starts typing his proposal before he gets Quicksilver's response, but it is not posted until afterward. The next step in his proposal is: "Can you see how it fits inside a square?" Here, he structures his contribution as a question, which elicits a response from the other members of the team. Note that he uses the term "see" in his proposal with the same double meaning as the term "look" in his prior announcement. As we shall see (in both senses), the group tries to work out and comprehend Aznx' proposal both conceptually and visually.

Both Bwang and Quicksilver respond to Aznx's proposal with "Yes". However, both modify this response. Bwang starts to type something else, but erases it; then he posts two messages: "oh" and "yes". This suggests some hesitation in responding to the proposal immediately. Quicksilver follows his initial positive response with, "You are saying the extra spaces …" He is asking for more clarification of the proposal. While Quicksilver is typing his request for clarification, Aznx is typing an expansion of his initial proposal: "Also, do you see if you add up the missing areas …"

The analysis of interaction moves is central to the science of group cognition. This is the level of granularity of many typical group-cognitive actions. Discourse moves are ways in which small online groups get their work done. They often follow conventional patterns—speech genres (Bakhtin, 1986) or member methods (Garfinkel, 1967)—which makes them much easier for participants to understand. Researchers can also look for these patterns to help them understand what the group is doing.

In this case, a new theme is being opened, one that will provide direction for the rest of this group's event together. This move is an example of one way in which a group can establish a shared understanding of a diagram or select a joint problem conceptualization (depending on how we take the terms "look" and "see"). Other moves that we often see in VMT logs are, for instance, defining shared references, coordinating problem-solving efforts, planning, deducing, designing, describing, solving, explaining, defining, generalizing, representing, remembering and reflecting as a group.

A pair: Question/response: "Can you see how it fits inside a square?" / "Yes"

In conversation analysis, one typically looks for "adjacency pairs" (Duranti, 1998; Sacks, 1962/1995; Schegloff, 2007). A prototypical adjacency pair is question/answer. Aznx' offering of a question—"Can you see how it fits inside a square?"—followed by Bwang and Quicksilver's responses—"yes", "Yes"—illustrate this structure for the simplest ("preferred") case: one person poses a yes/no question and the others respond with an affirmative answer.

Response structures are often more complicated than this. Text chat differs from talk in that people can be typing comments at the same time; they do not have to take turns and wait until one person stops talking and relinquishes the floor. They will not miss what the other person is saying, because unlike with talk, the message remains observable for a while. The disadvantage is that one does not observe how people put together their messages, with pauses, restarts, corrections, visual cues, intonations and personal characteristics. While it is possible to wait when you see a message that someone else is typing, people often type simultaneously, so that the two normal parts of an adjacency pair may be separated by other postings. For example, Quicksilver's question (line 926 in Figure 3) separated Aznx's continuation of his line 921 posting in line 927, because 926 appeared before 927 although 927 was typed without seeing 926. So in chat we might call these "response pairs" rather than "adjacency pairs." While they may be less sequentially *adjacent* than in talk, they are still direct *responses* of one posting to another.

Because the sequencing in online chat texting is less tightly controlled than in face-to-face talk, response pairs are likely to become entangled in the longer sequences of group moves. This may result in the common problem of "chat confusion" (Fuks, Pimentel & Pereira de Lucena, 2006; Herring, 1999). It can also complicate the job of the researcher. In particular, it makes the task of automated analysis more complicated. In convoluted chat logs, it is essential to work out the response structure (threading) before trying to determine the meaning making. The meaning making still involves participants interacting through the construction of response pairs, but in chat people have to recreate the ties among these pairs. Realizing this, the group members design their postings to be read in ways that make the response pair or threading structure apparent, as we will see (Zemel & Çakir, 2009).

An utterance: Question: "Can you see how it fits inside a square?"

In his posting—"Can you see how it fits inside a square?"— Aznx is comparing the relatively complicated diamond shape to a simple square. This is a nice strategy for solving the group's problem. The group can easily compute the number of stick squares that fill a large square area. For instance if there are five little squares across the width of a square area (and therefore five along the height), then there will be five-squared, or 25 little squares in the area. In general, if there are N little squares across the width, there will be N-squared to fill the area. This is a strategy of simplifying the problem to a simple or already known situation—and then perhaps having to account for some differences. So Aznx' posting seems to be relevant to thinking about the math problem conceptually.

At the same time, Aznx poses his proposal in visual or graphical terms as one of "seeing" how one shape "fits inside" of the other. The group has been looking at diagrams of squares in different patterns, both a drawing by Team C in their wiki posting and Team B's own drawings in their whiteboard. So Aznx's proposal suggests visualizing a possible modification to one of the diamond drawings, enclosing it in a square figure (see the white diamond pattern enclosed in the red square in Figure 4).

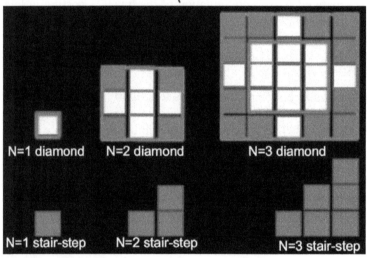

Figure 4. White diamond patterns and red stair-step patterns.

Aznx is asking the others if they can visualize this also, so that the group can use this to simplify and solve their problem with the diamond. He presents his proposal about re-thinking the problem as a question about visualizing the diagram. The group has been working in the VMT environment, going back and forth between text in the chat and drawings in the whiteboard. They have started with problems presented graphically and have discussed these graphical problems in their text chat. They have shared different ways of viewing the relationships within the drawings and they have gradually developed symbolic algebraic ways of expressing general relationships about patterns in these drawings, working out these symbolic expressions in the chat and then storing them more persistently in the whiteboard.

We have been calling Aznx' chat posting a "problem-solving math proposal" (Stahl, 2006, chapter 21). However, it is presented in the grammatical form of a *question*. Aznx did not simply state a proposal like, "`I think we should enclose the diamond in a square, calculate the size of the square and then subtract the missing areas.`" Rather, he first announced that he had "`an interesting way to look at this problem`" and then explained his way of looking by asking if the others could "`see how it fits inside a square.`" Presenting a proposal calls on the others to accept the proposal and to start to work on it. Of course, the others can reject the proposal, ask for clarifications about it, make a counter-proposal or ignore the proposal.

But Aznx' utterance is not a full proposal that the others must accept or reject. It is another preliminary step. It asks the others if they can visualize something. It puts this to them as a question. If they say yes, then Aznx can proceed to make his proposal—or perhaps the others will see the implications of his interesting way to look at the problem and propose the strategy without Aznx having to advocate it, explain it and defend it. If they say no—that they cannot see how it fits inside a square—then he can explain his view further so they will be better prepared to accept his proposal.

Aznx' chat posting avoids articulating a complete proposal; by starting the conversation about the visualization, it involves the others in articulating the proposal *collaboratively*. In fact, in the subsequent discussion, the others do "`see`" the strategy that is implicit in Aznx' interesting view of the problem and they do help to articulate the strategy and then pursue it. By designing his proposal as this preliminary question about viewing the problem, Aznx succeeds in directing the group problem solving in a certain direction without his having to fully work out a detailed, explicit proposal. Aznx does not seem to be presenting a solution that he has worked out in his head. Rather, he is presenting his "`interesting idea`" for an approach to solving the problem so that the group will proceed to use the idea and work as a group to try to solve the problem with this approach.

A reference: "It"

Aznx' question is ambiguous at a purely syntactic level. It asks the others, "`Can you see how it fits inside a square?`" To what does the term "`it`" refer? People use pronouns like "`it`" rather than lengthy explicit noun phrases when the reference is clear from the context. This situates the utterance in its context—it's meaning cannot be gathered from the utterance considered in isolation. Often, "it" will reference something that was recently referred to in a previous contribution that the new utterance is building on. For instance, "it" could refer to something mentioned in Aznx' previous utterance, "I have an interesting way to look at this problem." But to say that it refers to "this problem" does not make complete sense. The *problem* does not fit inside a square.

However, a minute earlier, when the group was discussing Team C's equations, Aznx said about part of an equation, "The 3n has to do with the growing outer layer of the pattern I think." He was referencing different aspects of the growth of the diamond pattern, particularly its "outer layer." So when he announces that he has an interesting way to view the problem, it is reasonable to assume that his new way of looking may be closely related to the observation that he had just reported about the outer layer of the diamond pattern. Because everyone in the group was following the flow of the discussion, Aznx could refer to the topic of the outer layer of the diamond pattern in the shorthand of the pronoun "it". When he typed, "Can you see how it fits inside a square?" he could assume that the readers of this posting would understand that he was referring to how some aspect of the diamond pattern can be seen as fitting inside of some square shape.

Although the reference to some aspect of the diamond pattern is relatively clear, the details are not clear about just what aspect of the diamond is to be visualized or focused on visually, where a square is to be constructed, and how the diamond fits inside the square. At this point, only a rather confusing image of a diamond pattern is visible on the whiteboard (see Figure 2). To *make sense* of "it", everyone has to follow the flow of discussion and the way in which the math topic is being developed as a "joint problem space", understood and visualized by the whole group.

Bwang and Quicksilver both respond initially to Aznx' question with "Yes." However, as we saw, Bwang indicates some hesitancy in his response and Quicksilver asks for further clarification. Aznx and Quicksilver discuss what they see when they fit a diamond pattern inside a square. Quicksilver notes that the "extra spaces" (colored red in Figure 4) look similar to the stair-step pattern that the team worked on previously. But Aznx goes on to talk about the four squares on the outer areas of the square, confusing Quicksilver. That is, as they each try to work out the details of Aznx' view, they display that they are not *seeing* things quite the same way. They have not yet achieved an adequate shared understanding or shared view.

Quicksilver suggests that Aznx show what he means on the whiteboard, so the ambiguity of his proposal can be resolved. Rather than drawing it himself, Aznx asks Bwang to do a drawing, since Bwang said he could see what Aznx was talking about. Bwang has in the past shown himself to be skilled at making drawings on the whiteboard, while Aznx has not tried to draw much.

Bwang draws a very clear diagram on the whiteboard for the diamond pattern when N=2 (see Figure 5). As soon as Bwang completes his drawing, he makes explicit the problem-solving proposal that is implicit in Aznx' way of viewing the problem or the pattern: "`We just have to find the whole square and minus the four corners.`" His drawing has made this process very visible. He drew the diamond pattern with white squares and then filled in a large square that the diamond fits into by adding red squares. The red squares fill in symmetrical spaces in the four corners of the diamond pattern. The group can now look at this together in the shared whiteboard, providing a shared view of the matter to the group.

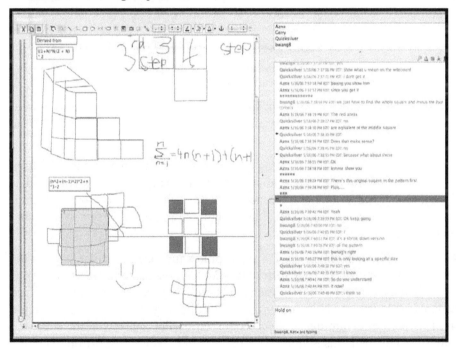

Figure 5. Bwang has drawn the white diamond for N=2 with red squares filling in the corners of an enclosing square. Quicksilver is pointing to a diamond pattern for N=3, also re-drawn lower on the whiteboard.

The group then discusses the view of the diamond pattern fitting into an enclosing square. They eventually realize that some of their observations are only true for the diamond pattern at a certain stage, like N=2.

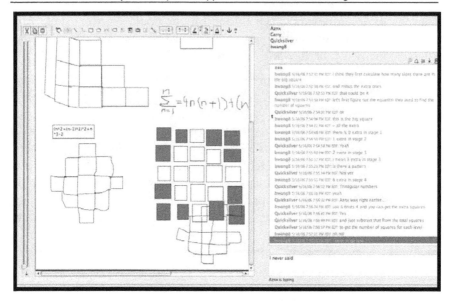

Figure 6. Bwang expanded his drawing to make the diamond for N=3. Note the red corners are now stair-step patterns.

So Bwang then draws the pattern for N=3. Here it starts to become visible to the group that the red squares in each corner follow the stair-step pattern (see Figure 6).

The group has realized that viewing a graphical image of a mathematical pattern can be very helpful in thinking about the pattern. They treat the whiteboard as a shared, viewable image of aspects of the joint problem space of their collaborative work. Viewing this image and pointing out elements of it ground their chat discourse.

However, the image drawn by Bwang captures just one particular stage in the pattern, one value of N. They then start to look at images for different values of N or different stages in the growing pattern. They count the number of red squares in a corner as N increases and notice that it goes: 0, 1, 3, 6 (see Figure 4). This pattern is familiar to them from their earlier analysis of the stair-step pattern. They call this sequence "triangular numbers," from Pascal's triangle, which is often useful in combinatorics math problems. They know that this sequence can be generated by Gauss' formula for the sum of the consecutive integers from 1 to N: (N+1)N/2. Unfortunately, at that point Bwang has to leave the group. But when they return in session 4, they will quickly put together the simple formula for the enclosing square minus this formula for the number of squares in each of the four corners, to solve their problem.

Viewing the learning and thinking

Let us pause now from all these details about the case study of three students in a virtual math team session and talk about how we view learning and thinking in CSCL groups. We have tried to demonstrate how we view learning and thinking in CSCL groups by *viewing* with you how a group of three students engaged in collaborative thinking and learning processes within an online environment for drawing and chatting.

We went through several levels of analysis of the group discourse (see Figure 7). We started by mentioning the overall context of the *event*. This was an online event in which Team B, consisting of three students, met in the Virtual Math Teams environment to discuss patterns of squares formed by sticks. We then focused on the smaller *session* unit, looking at Team B's third session, in which they considered a pattern that another group, Group C, had analyzed. Within this session, we identified one of several *themes* of discussion in that session, namely the one involving Aznx' "interesting way to look at this problem."

Event:	VMT Spring Fest 2006, Team B
Session:	session 3, May 16, 7:00 pm
Theme:	"I have an interesting way to look at this problem"
Move:	Show how to view
Pair:	"Can you see how it fits inside a square?" "Yes"
Utterance:	"Can you see how it fits inside a square?"
Reference:	"it", diamond pattern

Figure 7. Levels of analysis of online group discourse.

Aznx introduced the theme by initiating a group problem-solving *move*. Namely, he got the group to view the problem in a certain way, as a diamond enclosed in a square. We saw how the group ended up drawing images in their shared whiteboard of diamond patterns enclosed in squares. Aznx introduced this group move in a subtle way; he did not simply come out and say, "We should analyze this pattern as partially filling an enclosing square." Rather, he first announced that he had an interesting view, involving the others in his approach to make it a group problem-solving process. Then he asked if the others could view the problem in a certain way. He did this through a question/answer response *pair*: he asked a question, which elicited a yes-or-no response from the others. By eliciting the response, he oriented the others to looking at the diagram in the whiteboard in a certain way—namely in the way that his question implicitly proposed. A set of lines on the whiteboard are not immediately meaningful—they must be seen (interpreted) *as* something (Heidegger, 1927/1996, §32; Wittgenstein, 1953, §II xi).

Aznx' formulation of his question looks like a simple *utterance* in question format, but it entails selection from a number of different ways of picturing the relationships among the diamond pattern, the enclosing square and the empty corners. To begin with, one must decide what the *reference* to "it" is doing.

Indexical references like the pronoun "it" are ubiquitous in online text chat—and unavoidable according to Garfinkel (1967). They require the reader to understand or reconstruct the implicit threading or response structure of the chat. The difficulty of doing this often leads to confusions, which require the participants to spend time clarifying the content and structure of their discussion. For instance, in our example of the move of seeing the diamond in the square, the group had to engage in a couple minutes of chatting and drawing to co-construct a shared understanding of the problem.

Issues of shared understanding can be analyzed as linguistic problems of reference. In other words, in order to view learning and thinking in CSCL groups, we do not try to figure out what is going on in the heads of the students; rather, we try to figure out what is going on in their chat postings and their drawing actions. This is what we call the group's *interaction*. In VMT, the interaction of the virtual math team consists of sequences of chat postings and drawing actions.

Our first step in figuring out what is going on in the chat postings and drawing actions is generally to try to analyze the sequencing of these by reconstructing their response structure—what previous action each new action is responding to and what kinds of action it is eliciting, what it is opening up an interaction space for, or what kinds of responses it is making relevant as next postings. Often, this leads to some kind of threading diagram (Çakir, Xhafa & Zhou, 2009), uptake graph (Suthers et al., 2010), or interaction model (Wee & Looi, 2009). This represents graphically a basic structure of the meaning-making sequencing. Then we try to understand what problem-solving work is being accomplished at each point in the sequence. This involves looking at different levels of granularity, such as the event, session, theme, move, pair, utterance and reference. Understanding the meaning that the group is co-constructing in their interaction generally involves going back and forth through these different levels and integrating partial interpretations from the different levels (Gadamer, 1960/1988).

Through this process, we can gradually view the learning and thinking that takes place in the CSCL group. This learning and thinking is not something that takes place primarily in the minds of the individual participants (although the individuals in the group are each continuously using their linguistic skills to understand what is going on and to respond to it with their postings and drawings). Rather, when there is an intense collaborative process taking place in the online environment, the thinking and learning takes place in the visible text and graphical interactions.

According to the theory of group cognition, thinking in a CSCL collaborative interaction does not take place so much the way we usually think of thinking. Thoughts, or cognitive processes, do not take place by neurons connecting and firing in a brain; they take place by text postings and drawings referring to each other and building on each other, in the spirit of the idea of transactivity introduced earlier. We will look more at how this takes place in a minute. Similarly, learning does not take place the way we learned about learning. It is not a change in the amount of knowledge stored in a brain. Rather it is a matter of knowledge artifacts being gradually refined through sequences of text postings and graphical drawings that are interrelated and that explicate each other. The knowledge artifacts may be statements about a problem the group is working on, as viewed from a new perspective that the group has developed. The knowledge artifact might be a drawing like Bwang's in Figure 6 or an algebraic formula that sums up the group's analysis of pattern growth.

Constructing the joint problem space

When one studies logs of virtual math teams, one sees that the teams spend a lot of time and effort constructing shared understanding about references in their postings. The reason that teams and other small groups devote so much time and energy to resolving confusing references is that the network of references that they build up together plays an essential role in their group learning and thinking. In the theory of CSCL, there is considerable emphasis on the idea of "common ground" (Clark & Brennan, 1991) and "joint problem space" (Teasley & Roschelle, 1993). A group establishes common ground largely by reaching a shared understanding of how references work in their discourse. As it interacts over time, a group co-constructs a network of references that can become quite complex.

The "shared understanding" that is built up is akin to the notion of *co-orientation*, which "refers to the mutual orientation of individuals in a group toward an object (knowledge, belief, attitude), and can be traced back to the interactionist social psychology of John Dewey and George Herbert Mead" (Poole, this volume). Psycho-linguistic metaphors of comparing stored mental representations are unnecessary and can be misleading, reducing all knowledge to individual mental possessions. Team members share a world centered on their task; they orient as a group to the objects that populate that world, such as Aznx' proposals, Bwang's drawings and Quicksilver's queries. *Because they share a common world*—which they co-constitute largely through their discourse, mediated by the larger common social, cultural and historical horizons of their world—*they co-construct a shared understanding.*

The shared network of references defines the context or *situation* in which the group discourse continues to take place (Heidegger, 1927/1996, §18). Aznx' reference to "it" that we looked at contributed to a network of meaning that the group built up continuously through their interaction. This network included images of sticks in various patterns (like diamonds at stage N=2 and N=3), the relationships of the patterns (like a diamond enclosed in a square with stair-step empty corners), concepts referred to by technical terms (like "triangular numbers" or "summation") and symbols representing mathematical operations (like equations for number of squares in a pattern).

As a group builds up its network of shared references, it can use more shortcut references (symbols, names, pronouns) to point to things without creating confusion. People can use deictic references to point to things in the network, like "this formula", "the second equation" or "it". In linguistic terms, the shared network of references provides a background for referring to things, a so-called "indexical ground of deictic reference" (Hanks, 1992).

In problem-solving terms, the network of references forms a joint problem space, a shared view of the topic that the group is addressing (Sarmiento & Stahl, 2008). For Team B, the joint problem space starts in their first session with the stair-step pattern and the chart of the number of sticks and squares for each stage of this pattern as presented in the topic description for the event (Figure 1). By the middle of session 3, it includes the diamond pattern and the view of "it" enclosed in a square, forming empty corners. It also includes triangular numbers and their associated formula, as well as several other equations from Team C and from Team B's own work. The team's interaction (the text postings and drawings) gradually creates this joint problem space and is (reflexively) situated within it. The work and utterances of the team can only be understood (by the participants and by us as researchers) through an on-going understanding of the joint problem space as a network of meaningful reference.

Achievements of group cognition are not automatic and they can be quite fragile. They require work not only to construct shared understandings, but also to maintain the understanding of knowledge artifacts and to transfer their meaning to changing situations. After Bwang left the third session, Aznx and Quicksilver tried to review the group's accomplishments. They become confused about various equations and unsure of their ability to explain what the group has figured out. They ended the session with Quicksilver saying, "then let's pick it up next time when Bwang can explain it." This ends one session and projects what will happen in a future session. When the group meets for its fourth session, Aznx and Quicksilver do eventually get together with Bwang to review the derivation of the equation based on the view of the problem that Aznx introduced in the theme we just considered. The discussion in session four refers back to the group's work in session three and also to Team C's work in session two. But it does this in ways that are situated in Team B's session-four context (Sarmiento-Klapper, 2009). The team members and the memories they bring with them from the past are re-constituted in the new group situation, made relevant to the current themes, problem space and available resources.

Forming groups and co-constructing knowledge artifacts

At the beginning of session one, the students were not part of a particularly effective group or team. They did not build much on each other's contributions and were hesitant to make proposals, ask each other to undertake tasks, produce permanent drawings or manipulate mathematical symbols. That all changed dramatically in the course of their four-session event. By the end, they had many graphical, narrative and symbolic representations or expressions related to their mathematical topic. They worked effectively together and solved their problems well. Problem-solving methods that one person introduced were later proposed and used by the other group members.

You may be wondering if each of the students learned mathematics. An interesting thing about looking closely at what really went on in this event is that what we traditionally consider to be the math content actually plays a relatively minor role in the group's problem solving. Yes, content is brought in: the students talk about triangular numbers and they apply the formula for summing consecutive integers, for instance. Often, this math content is brought in quickly through proposals by individuals. It is then discussed through responses to the proposal that check that everyone understands the math content and agrees on its applicability. However, the bulk of the hard work is not accessing the traditional math content, but selecting, adapting, integrating, visualizing, sharing, explaining, testing, refining, building on and summarizing sequences of group response pairs. These proposals and discussions reference not only math content, but also various related resources that the group has co-constructed or made relevant.

The learning and thinking of the group takes place through the group's discourse, as a temporally unfolding multi-level structure of response/adjacency pairs interwoven into larger sequences of group moves, problem-solving themes and sessions of events. The group learns about the mathematics of its topic by building and exploring an increasingly rich joint problem space. It thinks about the mathematical relationships and patterns by following sequences of proposals, raising and responding to various kinds of questions and engaging in other sorts of interactional moves. Some of this gets summarized in persistent knowledge artifacts like drawings, concepts, equations, solution statements and textual arguments. The building of the joint problem space generally requires a lot of work to resolve references and to co-construct a shared network of meaning.

The math skills—like following certain procedures to do long division or to transform symbols—are not where the deep learning takes place and real knowledge is involved. Rather, the ability to sustain progressive inquiry through methods of group interaction is the real goal. This ability makes use of the math content and skills as resources for answering questions and coming up with new proposals. Learning math is primarily a process of becoming a participant in the discourse community of people conversant in mathematics. Learning math collaboratively involves engaging in linguistic methods of shared meaning making—and other semiotic practices like geometric construction and algebraic symbolization. These are the tacit foundations of mathematics, the abilities needed in order to follow the rules of explicit math procedures.

If you wonder how to view learning and thinking in CSCL groups as an example of team cognition, follow Wittgenstein's advice: "Don't think, look!" Our colleagues and we have tried to do this by looking at the work of virtual math teams in the way we have just described. We have been amazed to discover that collaborative learning and group cognition are a lot different than people traditionally thought.

Looking forward: Towards enhancing transactive interactions with automatic facilitation

In this chapter, we have described the group-cognition framework in relation to work in other subcommunities within the broader CSCL community, where similar conversational processes have been examined from different perspectives, with different styles. While group cognition has not typically been investigated through categorical coding aided by automatic text processing technology as has been done frequently within the transactivity tradition (Joshi & Rosé, 2007; Rosé et al., 2008; Ai et al., in press), the advantage of approaching the analysis that way is that it enables the possibility of automatic monitoring as well as automatic triggering of support.

There have already been quite a few successful studies of student groups benefitting from the support of automatically triggered conversational agents that enrich the interaction between students (Wang et al., 2007; Kumar et al., 2007; Cui et al., 2009; Chaudhuri et al., 2009; Kumar et al., in press), many of which employed a version of the Virtual Math Teams environment augmented with this form of dynamic collaborative learning support (Cui et al., 2009; Kumar et al., 2009). For example, early evaluations measured the extent to which students learned more in conditions when automatic support was offered in the environment in comparison to conditions where it was not (Wang et al., 2007; Kumar et al., 2007). These early studies showed that insertion of a support agent into the environment increased pre to post-test learning gains by about one standard deviation, which is a full letter grade. Subsequent studies compared alternative versions of this form of automatic support. These evaluations showed additional increases in effectiveness as we successively refined the design of the support. For example, Chaudhuri et al. (2009) showed that students learned more when the support agents allowed the students to put off discussion with the support agents until they were ready to give it their full attention. Kumar et al., (submitted) showed that students learned more when the support agents engaged in social behavior in addition to just offering cognitive support.

Encouraged by these early successes, which we celebrate, we are continuing to push forward with this intellectual and technical integration of group-cognition analysis using manual and automated methods. For example, we acknowledge that much of the richness of the type of thick description presented in this chapter is lost when the analysis is reduced to a sequence of a small number of labels, tags or codes. Furthermore, we acknowledge that even with perfect knowledge of where pivotal moments in collaboration are occurring or not occurring, this analysis is not the same thing as having the wisdom to know when to intervene or not, and how to guide the conversation effectively. These recognitions do not leave us discouraged, however. Rather they convince us of the great potential that our collaboration holds. With this in mind, then, in our current work, we are striving for a deeper intellectual integration between these different analytical traditions in order to create a yet more powerful form of dynamic collaboration support that will eventually make the power of group cognition as ubiquitous as the World Wide Web.

References

Ai, H., Kumar, R., Nagasunder, A., Rosé, C. P. (submitted). Exploring the Effectiveness of Social Capabilities and Goal Alignment in Computer Supported Collaborative Learning, submitted to the *Intelligent Tutoring Systems conference (ITS 2010)*.

Ai, H., Sionti, M., Wang, Y. C., Rosé, C. P. (in press). Finding Transactive Contributions in Whole Group Classroom Discussions, in *Proceedings of the International Conference of the Learning Sciences*.

Arora, S., Joshi, M., Rosé, C. P. (2009). Identifying Types of Claims in Online Customer Reviews, *Proceedings of the North American Chapter of the Association for Computational Linguistics*

Azmitia M, Montgomery R. (1993). Friendship, transactive dialogues, and the development of scientific reasoning. *Social Development* 2(3): 202-221

Bakhtin, M. (1986). *Speech genres and other late essays* (V. McGee, Trans.). Austin, TX: University of Texas Press.

Bereiter, C. (2002). *Education and mind in the knowledge age*. Hillsdale, NJ: Lawrence Erlbaum Associates.

Berkowitz M, Gibbs J. (1983). Measuring the developmental features of moral discussion. Merrill-*Palmer Quarterly* 29: 399-410

Çakir, M. P., Xhafa, F., & Zhou, N. (2009). Thread-based analysis of patterns in vmt. In G. Stahl (Ed.), *Studying virtual math teams* (ch. 20, pp. 359-371). New York, NY: Springer. Web: http://GerryStahl.net/vmt/book/20.pdf Doi: http://dx.doi.org/10.1007/978-1-4419-0228-3_20

Çakır, M. P., Zemel, A., & Stahl, G. (2009). The joint organization of interaction within a multimodal CSCL medium. *International Journal of Computer-Supported Collaborative Learning, 4*(2), 115-149. Web: http://GerryStahl.net/pub/ijCSCL_4_2_1.pdf Doi: http://dx.doi.org/10.1007/s11412-009-9061-0

Chaudhuri, S., Kumar, R., Howley, I., Rosé, C. P. (2009). Engaging Collaborative Learners with Helping Agents, *Proceedings of Artificial Intelligence in Education*

Chomsky, N. (1959). Review of verbal behavior, by b. F. Skinner. *Language, 35*(1), 26-57

Christie, F. (ed.) (1999). *Pedagogy and the Shaping of Consciousness: Linguistic and Social Processes,* London: Cassell.

Clark, H., & Brennan, S. (1991). Grounding in communication. In L. Resnick, J. Levine & S. Teasley (Eds.), *Perspectives on socially-shared cognition* (pp. 127-149). Washington, DC: APA

Cloran, C. (1999). Contexts for Learning, in Francis Christie (1999). *Pedagogy and the shaping of consciousness: Linguistics and Social Processes,* New York: Continuum.

Cui, Y., Chaudhuri, S., Kumar, R., Gweon, G., Rosé, C. P. (2009). Helping Agents in VMT, in G. Stahl (Ed.) *Studying Virtual Math Teams,* Springer CSCL Series, Springer.

de Lisi R, Golbeck SL. (1999). Implications of the Piagetian Theory for peer learning. In: O'Donnell A. M, King A. *Cognitive perspectives on peer learning.* New Jersey, Lawrence Erlbaum Associates Inc. pp. 3-37

Duranti, A. (1998). *Linguistic anthropology.* Cambridge, UK: Cambridge University Press.

Fuks, H., Pimentel, M., & Pereira de Lucena, C. (2006). R-u-typing-2-me? Evolving a chat tool to increase understanding in learning activities. *International Journal of Computer-Supported Collaborative Learning, 1*(1), 117-142 Doi: http://dx.doi.org/10.1007/s11412-006-6845-3

Gadamer, H.-G. (1960/1988). *Truth and method.* New York, NY: Crossroads.

Garfinkel, H. (1967). *Studies in ethnomethodology.* Englewood Cliffs, NJ: Prentice-Hall.

Gweon, G, Kumar, R. & Rosé, C. P. (2009). Towards Automatic Assessment for Project Based Learning Groups, *Proceedings of Artificial Intelligence in Education*

Hanks, W. (1992). The indexical ground of deictic reference. In A. Duranti & C. Goodwin (Eds.), *Rethinking context: Language as an interactive phenomenon* (pp. 43-76). Cambridge, UK: Cambridge University Press

Hasan, R. (1999). Society, language and the mind: the meta-dialogism of Basil Bernstein's theory, in Francis Christie (1999). *Pedagogy and the shaping of consciousness: Linguistics and Social Processes,* New York: Continuum.

Heidegger, M. (1927/1996). *Being and time: A translation of sein und zeit* (J. Stambaugh, Trans.). Albany, NY: SUNY Press.

Herring, S. (1999). Interactional coherence in cmc. *Journal of Computer Mediated Communication, 4*(4). Web: http://jcmc.indiana.edu/vol4/issue4/herring.html

Howley, I., Mayfield, E. & Rosé, C. P. (invited). Linguistic Analysis Methods for Studying Small Groups, in Cindy Hmelo-Silver, Angela O'Donnell, Carol Chan, & Clark Chin (Eds.) *International Handbook of Collaborative Learning,* Taylor and Francis, Inc.

Hutchins, E. (1996). *Cognition in the wild.* Cambridge, MA: MIT Press.

Jordan, B., & Henderson, A. (1995). Interaction analysis: Foundations and practice. *Journal of the Learning Sciences, 4*(1), 39-103. Web: http://lrs.ed.uiuc.edu/students/c-merkel/document4.HTM

Joshi, M. & Rosé, C. P. (2009). Generalizing Dependency Features for Opinion Mining, *Proceedings of the Association for Computational Linguistics*

Joshi, M. & Rosé , C. P. (2007). Using transactivity in conversation summarization in educational dialog. *Proceedings of the SLaTE Workshop on Speech and Language Technology in Education.*

Kang, M., Chaudhuri, S., Kumar, R., Wang, Y., Rosé, E., Cui, Y., Rosé, C. P. (2008). Supporting the Guide on the SIDE, in *Proceedings of Intelligent Tutoring Systems (ITS '08)*

Kumar, R., Ai, H., & Rosé, C. P. (submitted). Choosing Optimal Levels of Social Interaction – Towards creating Human-like Conversational Tutors, submitted to the *Intelligent Tutoring Systems conference (ITS 2010)*.

Kumar, R. & Rosé, C. P. (in press). Engaging learning groups using Social Interaction Strategies, In *Proceedings of the North American Chapter of the Association for Computational Linguistics*.

Kumar, R. & Rosé, C. P. (2009). Building Conversational Agents with Basilica, *Proceedings of the North American Chapter of the Association for Computational Linguistics*

Kumar, R., Rosé, C. P., Wang, Y. C., Joshi, M., Robinson, A. (2007). Tutorial Dialogue as Adaptive Collaborative Learning Support, *Proceedings of Artificial Intelligence in Education*

Martin, J. R. & Rose, D. (2003). *Working with Discourse: Meaning Beyond the Clause*, Continuum

Martin, J. R. & White, P. R. (2005). *The Language of Evaluation: Appraisal in English*, Palgrave

Mayfiled, E. & Rosé, C. P. (submitted) Using Feature Construction to Avoid Large Feature Spaces in Text Classification, submitted to *GECCO 2010*

Rosé, C. P., Wang, Y.C., Cui, Y., Arguello, J., Stegmann, K., Weinberger, A., Fischer, F., (2008). Analyzing Collaborative Learning Processes Automatically: Exploiting the Advances of Computational Linguistics in Computer-Supported Collaborative Learning, *International Journal of Computer Supported Collaborative Learning* 3(3), pp237-271.

Rosé, C. P., Gweon, G., Arguello, J., Finger, S., Smailagic, A., Siewiorek, D. (2007). Towards an Interactive Assessment Framework for Engineering Design Learning, *Proceedings of ASME 2007 International Design Engineering Technical Conferences & Computers and Information in Engineering Conference*

Sacks, H. (1962/1995). *Lectures on conversation*. Oxford, UK: Blackwell.

Salas, E. & Fiore, S. M. (Eds.) (2011) *Theories of team cognition: Cross-disciplinary perspectives*. New York, NY: Routledge/Taylor & Francis

Sarmiento, J., & Stahl, G. (2008). *Extending the joint problem space: Time and sequence as essential features of knowledge building*. Paper presented at the International Conference of the Learning Sciences (ICLS 2008), Utrecht, Netherlands. Web: http://GerryStahl.net/pub/icls2008johann.pdf

Sarmiento-Klapper, J. W. (2009). *Bridging mechanisms in team-based online problem solving: Continuity in building collaborative knowledge*. Unpublished Dissertation, Ph.D., College of Information Science and Technology, Drexel University, Philadelphia, PA, USA

Schegloff, E. A. (2007). *Sequence organization in interaction: A primer in conversation analysis*. Cambridge, UK: Cambridge University Press.

Schwartz, D. (1998). The productive agency that drives collaborative learning. In Dillenbourg, P. (Ed.) *Collaborative learning: Cognitive and computational approaches.* NY: Elsevier Science/Permagon

Stahl, G. (2006). *Group cognition: Computer support for building collaborative knowledge.* Cambridge, MA: MIT Press. 510 + viii pages. Web: http://GerryStahl.net/mit/

Stahl, G. (2009a). *Studying virtual math teams.* New York, NY: Springer. 626 +xxi pages. Web: http://GerryStahl.net/vmt/book Doi: http://dx.doi.org/10.1007/978-1-4419-0228-3

Stahl, G. (2009b). Toward a science of group cognition. In G. Stahl (Ed.), *Studying virtual math teams* (ch. 28, pp. 555-579). New York, NY: Springer. Web: http://GerryStahl.net/vmt/book/28.pdf Doi: http://dx.doi.org/10.1007/978-1-4419-0228-3_28

Stahl, G., Koschmann, T., & Suthers, D. (2006). Computer-supported collaborative learning: An historical perspective. In R. K. Sawyer (Ed.), *Cambridge handbook of the learning sciences* (pp. 409-426). Cambridge, UK: Cambridge University Press. Web: http://GerryStahl.net/cscl/CSCL_English.pdf in English, http://GerryStahl.net/cscl/CSCL_Chinese_simplified.pdf in simplified Chinese, http://GerryStahl.net/cscl/CSCL_Chinese_traditional.pdf in traditional Chinese, http://GerryStahl.net/cscl/CSCL_Spanish.pdf in Spanish, http://GerryStahl.net/cscl/CSCL_Portuguese.pdf in Portuguese, http://GerryStahl.net/cscl/CSCL_German.pdf in German, http://GerryStahl.net/cscl/CSCL_Romanian.pdf in Romanian, http://GerryStahl.net/cscl/CSCL_Japanese.pdf in Japanese

Suthers, D. (2006). Technology affordances for inter-subjective meaning making: A research agenda for CSCL. *International Journal of Computer Supported Collaborative Learning*, 1: 315-337.

Suthers, D. D., Dwyer, N., Medina, R., & Vatrapu, R. (2010). A framework for conceptualizing, representing and analyzing distributed interaction *International Journal of Computer-Supported Collaborative Learning, 5*(1), 5-44

Teasley, S. D. (1997). Talking about reasoning: How important is the peer in peer collaboration? In: Resnick L. B, Säljö R, Pontecorvo C, Burge B. (Eds). *Discourse, tools and reasoning: Essays on situated cognition.* New York, Springer , pp. 364-384

Teasley, S. D., & Roschelle, J. (1993). Constructing a joint problem space: The computer as a tool for sharing knowledge. In S. P. Lajoie & S. J. Derry (Eds.), *Computers as cognitive tools* (pp. 229-258). Mahwah, NJ: Lawrence Erlbaum Associates, Inc.

Terasaki, A. K. (2004). Pre-announcement sequences in conversation. In G. Lerner (Ed.), *Conversation analysis: Studies from the first generation* (pp. 171-224). Philadelphia, PA: John Benjamins

Vygotsky, L. (1930/1978). *Mind in society.* Cambridge, MA: Harvard University Press.

Wang, H. C. & Rosé, C. P. (in press). Making Conversation Structure Explicit: Identification of Initiation-response Pairs in Online Discussion, In *Proceedings of the North American Chapter of the Association for Computational Linguistics.*

Wang, H. C. & Rosé, C. P. (2007). Supporting Collaborative Idea Generation: A Closer Look Using Statistical Process Analysis Techniques, *Proceedings of Artificial Intelligence in Education*

Wang, H. C., Rosé, C.P., Cui, Y., Chang, C. Y, Huang, C. C., Li, T. Y. (2007). Thinking Hard Together: The Long and Short of Collaborative Idea Generation for Scientific Inquiry, *Proceedings of Computer Supported Collaborative Learning*

Weinberger A., Fischer F. (2006). A framework to analyze argumentative knowledge construction in computer supported collaborative learning. *Computers & Education* 46: 71 - 95

Wee, J. D., & Looi, C.-K. (2009). A model for analyzing math knowledge building in vmt. In G. Stahl (Ed.), *Studying virtual math teams* (ch. 25, pp. 475-497). New York, NY: Springer. Web: http://GerryStahl.net/vmt/book/25.pdf Doi: http://dx.doi.org/10.1007/978-1-4419-0228-3_25

Wittgenstein, L. (1944/1956). *Remarks on the foundations of mathematics.* Cambridge, MA: MIT Press.

Wittgenstein, L. (1953). *Philosophical investigations.* New York, NY: Macmillan.

Zemel, A., Xhafa, F., & Çakir, M. P. (2009). Combining coding and conversation analysis of vmt chats. In G. Stahl (Ed.), *Studying virtual math teams* (ch. 23, pp. 421-450). New York, NY: Springer. Web: http://GerryStahl.net/vmt/book/23.pdf Doi: http://dx.doi.org/10.1007/978-1-4419-0228-3_23

6.   Sustaining Interaction in a CSCL Environment

Learning takes place over long periods of time that are hard to study directly. Even the learning experience involved in solving a challenging math problem in a collaborative online setting can be spread across hundreds of brief postings during an hour or more. Such long-term interactions are constructed out of posting-level interactions, such as the strategic proposing of a next step. This paper identifies a pattern of exchange of postings that it terms *math-proposal adjacency pair*, and describes its characteristics. Drawing on the methodology of conversation analysis, the paper adapts this approach to investigating mathematical problem-solving communication and to the computer-mediated circumstances of online chat. Math proposals and other interaction methods constitute the collaborative group as a working group, give direction to its problem solving and help to sustain its shared meaning making or group cognition. Groups sustain their online social and intellectual work by building up longer sequences of math proposals, other adjacency pairs and a variety of interaction methods. Experiences of collaboration and products of group cognition emerge over time.

Research in learning has traditionally focused on psychological processes at the individual unit of analysis. With the shift to socio-cultural approaches in recent years, the community unit of analysis has come to the fore. In a new book on group cognition, we have identified small groups as defining a middle ground between individual people and communities of practice:

> Small groups are the engines of knowledge building. The knowing that groups build up in manifold forms is what becomes internalized by their members as individual learning and externalized in their communities as certifiable knowledge. At least, that is a central premise of this book. (Stahl, 2006b, p. 16)

The concept of group cognition, however, retains a certain ambiguity of scale. On the micro level, it is based on the discovery by conversation analysis that a smallest element of meaning in discourse is the adjacency pair, a product of interaction within a dyad or small group, and not an expression of individual cognition (Duranti, 1998; Schegloff, 1991). On the macro level, it is a vision of collaborative knowledge building, where knowledge arises through community, interpersonal or social interaction (Lave & Wenger, 1991; Scardamalia & Bereiter, 1996; Vygotsky, 1930/1978). Taking one approach or the other, we can analyze how a small group of students establishes a detailed point of shared understanding or we can, for instance, analyze how they apprentice participation in the community of math discourse. The question remains: how can we understand what happens in a group at the interesting meso level during a one-hour math chat consisting of many detailed interactions but perhaps not measurably increasing the group's community participation?

This paper tries to address the gap in the methodology of the learning sciences in a preliminary way. It begins with a detailed analysis of a particular interaction that actually occurred in a student chat. It then gradually broadens the discussion of online math chat sessions, discussing various aspects of how the elemental adjacency pairs in such a momentary interaction contribute to a sustained group experience over a somewhat longer period of time. The presentation proceeds through these steps:

The context of online math chats which provide the empirical basis for our observations is first motivated and described.

The concept of adjacency pairs from conversation analysis is adapted to the situation of online math chats and is particularized as "math-proposal adjacency pairs."

A specific adjacency pair is analyzed as a "failed proposal," which by contrast sheds light on the nature of successful proposals.

We then describe our design-based research approach in which we revise our software and pedagogy in response to issues observed during a sequence of evolving trials.

Next, we look at a more extended interaction that occurred in our revised chat environment, involving methods of computer-supported deictic referencing that build from adjacency pairs to longer sequences of cognitive work.

To extrapolate beyond one or two detailed interactions and analyze more extended sessions with some generality would require volumes of exposition. We therefore rely on our other studies, our general impressions from observing and participating in many online math chats, and from related work by others to discuss a number of relevant aspects of sustained group cognition.

We conclude with reflections on how groups construct and sustain their on-going sense of shared experience. This points to future work.

Doing mathematics together online

Technology-enhanced learning offers many opportunities for innovation in education. One of the major avenues is by supporting the building of collaborative meaning and knowledge (Stahl, 2006b). For instance, it is now possible for students around the world to work together on challenging math problems. Through online discussion, they can share problem-solving experiences and gain fluency in communicating mathematically. Research on mathematics education stresses the importance of student discourse about math (NCTM, 2000; Sfard, 2002), something that many students do not have opportunities to practice face-to-face.

While much research on computer-supported collaborative learning (CSCL) has analyzed the use of asynchronous threaded discussion forums, there has been relatively little research on the use of synchronous chat environments in education. The research reported here suggests that chat has great promise as a medium for collaborative learning if the medium and its use are carefully configured. This paper investigates how math discourse takes place within the chat medium and how we use our analyses to inform the design of effective math chat environments.

In the Virtual Math Teams (VMT) research project at the Math Forum (http://mathforum.org/vmt), we invite middle-school students to participate in online chats about interesting problems in beginning algebra and geometry. The following math problem, discussed in the chat excerpt analyzed below, is typical:

> If two equilateral triangles have edge-lengths of 9 cubits and 12
> cubits, what is the edge-length of the equilateral triangle whose area
> is equal to the sum of the areas of the other two?

We rely on a variety of approaches from the learning sciences to guide our research and to analyze the results of our trials, including coding along multiple dimensions (Strijbos & Stahl, 2005), analysis of threading (Cakir *et al.*, 2005) and ethnography (Shumar, 2006). In particular, we have developed an ethnomethodologically-informed (Garfinkel, 1967; Heritage, 1984) chat analysis approach based on conversation analysis (Pomerantz & Fehr, 1991; Psathas, 1995; Sacks, 1992; Sacks, Schegloff, & Jefferson, 1974; ten Have, 1999) to understand the structure of interactions that take place in student chats. In this paper, we adapt a finding of conversation analysis to math chats and analyze a specific form of adjacency pairs that seem to be important for this context. Before presenting these findings, it may be useful to describe briefly how the notion of adjacency pairs differs from naïve conceptions of conversation.

There is a widespread common-sense or folk-theory (Bereiter, 2002; Dennett, 1991) view of conversation as the exchange or transmission of propositions (Shannon & Weaver, 1949). This view was refined and formalized by logicians and cognitive scientists as involving verbal "expression" in meaningful statements by individuals, based on their internal mental representations. Speech served to transfer meanings from the mind of a speaker to the mind of a listener, who then interpreted the expressed message. Following Wittgenstein (1953) in critiquing this view, speech act theory (Austin, 1952; Searle, 1969) argued that the utterances spoken by individuals were ways of acting in the world, and were meaningful in terms of what they accomplished through their use and effects. Of course, the expression, transmission and interpretation of meaning by individuals can be problematic, and people frequently have to do some interactional work in order to re-establish a shared understanding. The construction of common ground has been seen as the attempt to coordinate agreement between individual understandings (Clark & Brennan, 1991).

Conversation analysis takes a different view of conversation. It looks at how interactional mechanisms, like the use of adjacency pairs, co-construct inter-subjectivity.

> *Adjacency pairs* are common sequences of utterances by different people—such as mutual greetings or question/answer interchanges— that form a meaningful speech act spanning multiple utterances, which cannot be attributed to an individual or to the expression of already formed mental states. They achieve meaning in their very interaction.

We are interested in what kinds of adjacency pairs are typical for math chats. The topic of adjacency pairs is taken up extensively in two sections below. Stahl (2006b) further discusses the implications that viewing adjacency pairs as the smallest elements of meaning making has for the intersubjective foundation of group cognition, a process of jointly constructing meaning in discourse.

The medium of online chat has its own peculiarities (Lonchamp, 2006; Mühlpfordt & Wessner, 2005; O'Neill & Martin, 2003). Most importantly, it is a text-based medium, where interaction takes place by the sequential response of brief texts to each other (Livingston, 1995; Zemel, 2005). As a quasi-synchronous medium (Garcia & Jacobs, 1999), chat causes confusion because several people can be typing at once and their texts can appear in an order that obscures to whom or to what they are responding. Furthermore, under time pressure to submit their texts so that they will appear near the post to which they are responding, some chat participants break their messages into several short texts. Because of these peculiarities of chat, it is necessary for researchers to carefully reconstruct the intended threading of texts that respond to each other before attempting to interpret the flow of interaction (Cakir *et al.*, 2005; Strijbos & Stahl, 2005).

Math chats differ from ordinary informal conversation in a number of additional ways. They are focused on the task of solving a specific problem, and they take place within a somewhat formal institutional setting. They involve the *doing* of mathematics (Livingston, 1986). And, of course, they are computer-mediated rather than face-to-face. The approach of conversation analysis is based on ethnomethodology (Garfinkel, 1967), which involves the study of the *methods* that people use to accomplish what they are doing. So, we are interested in working out the methods that are used by students in online math chats. In this paper, we discuss a particular method of collaboration in math chats that we have elsewhere called *exploratory participation*: participants engage each other in the conjoint discovery and production of both the problem and possible solutions (Wegerif, 2006; Zemel, Xhafa, & Stahl, 2005).

Math-proposal adjacency pairs

In order to begin to analyze the methods that students use in math chats, we take a close look at an excerpt from an actual chat. Figure 1 shows an excerpt from near the beginning of the log of one of our first online collaborative math problem-solving sessions. Three students—named Avr, Sup and Pin—have just entered the chat room, said hello to each other and read the problem involving three triangles.

The first thing to notice here is a pattern of proposals, discussions and acceptances similar to what takes place in face-to-face discourse. Bids for proposals about steps in solving the math problem are made by Avr in lines 1, 3, 8, 17 and by Pin in lines 20, 27. These proposals are each affirmed by someone else in lines 2, 6, 10, 19, 22, 28, respectively.

To avoid chat confusion, note that line 21 responds to line 19, while line 22 responds to line 20. The timestamps show that lines 20 and 21 effectively overlapped each other chronologically: Avr was typing line 21 before she saw line 20. Similarly, lines 24 and the following were responses to line 20, not line 23. We will correct for these confusions later, in Figure 2, which reproduces a key passage in this excerpt.

```
1. Avr (8:21:46 PM): Okay, I think we should start with
the formula for the area of a triangle
2. Sup (8:22:17 PM): ok
3. Avr (8:22:28 PM): A = 1/2bh
4. Avr (8:22:31 PM): I believe
5. pin (8:22:35 PM): yes
6. pin (8:22:37 PM): i concue
7. pin (8:22:39 PM): concur*
8. Avr (8:22:42 PM): then find the area of each triangle
9. Avr (8:22:54 PM): oh, wait
10. Sup (8:23:03 PM): the base and heigth are 9 and 12
right?
11. Avr (8:23:11 PM): no
12. Sup (8:23:16 PM): o
13. Avr (8:23:16 PM): that's two separate triangles
14. Sup (8:23:19 PM): ooo
15. Sup (8:23:20 PM): ok
16. Avr (8:23:21 PM): right
17. Avr (8:23:27 PM): i think we have to figure out the
height by ourselves
18. Avr (8:23:29 PM): if possible
19. pin (8:24:05 PM): i know how
20. pin (8:24:09 PM): draw the altitude'
21. Avr (8:24:09 PM): how?
22. Avr (8:24:15 PM): right
23. Sup (8:24:19 PM): proportions?
24. Avr (8:24:19 PM): this is frustrating
25. Avr (8:24:22 PM): I don't have enough paper
26. pin (8:24:43 PM): i think i got it
27. pin (8:24:54 PM): its a 30/60/90 triangle
28. Avr (8:25:06 PM): I see
29. pin (8:25:12 PM): so whats the formula
```

Figure 1. Excerpt of 3½ minutes from a one-hour chat log. Three students chat about a geometry problem. Line numbers have been added and screen-names anonymized; otherwise the transcript is identical to what the participants saw on their screens.

In Figure 1, we see several examples of a three-step pattern:

A proposal bid is made by an individual for the group to work on: "I think we should ...."

A proposal acceptance is made on behalf of the group: "Ok," "right"

There is an elaboration of the proposal by members of the group. The proposed work is begun, often with a secondary proposal for the first sub-step.

The three-step pattern consists of a pair of postings—a bid and an acceptance—that form a proposal about math, and some follow-up effort. This suggests that collaborative problem-solving of mathematics may often involve a particular form of adjacency pair. We will call this a *math-proposal adjacency pair*.

Here are six successful math-proposal adjacency pairs from Figure 1:

1. Avr: Okay, I think we should start with the formula for the area of a triangle

2. Sup: ok

3. Avr: A = 1/2bh

6. pin: i concue

8. Avr: then find the area of each triangle

10. Sup: the base and heigth are 9 and 12 right?

17. Avr: i think we have to figure out the height by ourselves

19. pin: i know how

20. pin: draw the altitude'

22. Avr: right

27. pin: its a 30/60/90 triangle

28. Avr: I see

Note that the response is not always literally immediately adjacent to the bid in the chat log due to the complexities of chat posting. But the response is logically adjacent as an up-take of the bid.

Many varieties of adjacency pairs allow for the insertion of other pairs between the two parts of the original pair, delaying completion of the original pair. For instance, a question/answer pair may be delayed by utterances seeking clarification of the question. As we will see below, the clarification interaction may itself consist of question/answer pairs, possibly with their own clarifications—this may continue recursively. With math-proposal adjacency pairs, the subsidiary pairs seem to come after the completion of the original pair, in the form of secondary proposals, questions or explanations that start to do the work that was proposed in the original pair. This characteristic leads to their role in sustaining group inquiry.

Math proposals tend to lead to some kind of further mathematical work as a response to carrying out what was proposed. Often—as seen in the current example—that work consists of making further proposals. In this way, the three-step structure of the math-proposal adjacency pair starts to sustain the group interaction. The proposal bid by one person calls forth a proposal response by someone else. If the response is one of acceptance, it in turn calls forth some further work to be done or a bid for another proposal. If the response is a rejection, it may lead to justification, discussion and negotiation.

It is striking that the proposed work is not begun until there is agreement with the proposal bid. This may represent consent by the group as a whole to pursue the proposed line of work. Of course, this idea is not so clear in the current example, where there are only three participants and the interaction often seems to take place primarily between pairs of participants. As confirmed by other chat examples, however, the proposal generally seems to be addressed to the whole group and opens the floor for other participants to respond. The use of "we" in "we should" or "we have to" (stated or implied) constitutes the multiple participants as a plural subject—an effective unified group (Lerner, 1993). Any one other than the proposer may respond on behalf of the group. The fact that the multiple participants are posited as a group for certain purposes, like responding to a proposal bid, by no means rules out their individual participation in the group interaction from their personal perspectives, or even their independent follow-up work on the math. It simply means that the individual who responds to the bid may be doing so on behalf of the group.

Moreover, there seems to be what in conversation analysis is called an interactional *preference* (Schegloff, Jefferson, & Sacks, 1977) for acceptance of the proposal. That is, if one accepts a proposal, it suffices to briefly indicate agreement: "ok." If one wants to reject a proposal, however, then one has to account for this response by giving reasons. If the group accepts the bid, one person's response may serve on behalf of the group; if the group rejects the bid, several people may have to get involved.

We would like to characterize in more detail the method of making math-proposal adjacency pairs. Often, the nature of an interactional method is seen most clearly when it is breached (Garfinkel, 1967). Methods are generally taken for granted by people; they are not made visible or conducted consciously. It is only when there is a *breakdown* (Heidegger, 1927/1996; Winograd & Flores, 1986) in the smooth, tacit performance of a method that people focus on its characteristics in order to overcome the breakdown. The normally transparent method becomes visible in its breach. In common-sense terms we say, "The exception proves the rule," meaning that when we see why something is an exceptional case it makes clear the rule to which it is an exception. Heidegger made this into an ontological principle, whereby things first become experience-able during a breakdown of understanding. Garfinkel uses this, in turn, as a methodological fulcrum to make visible that which is commonly assumed and is effective but unseen.

We can interpret Sup's posting in line 23 as a *failed proposal*. Given the mathematics of the triangle problem, a proposal bid related to proportionality, like Sup's, might have been fruitful. However, in this chat, line 23 was effectively ignored by the group. While its character as a failed proposal did not become visible to the participants, it can become clear to us by comparing it to successful proposal bids in the same chat and by reflecting on its sequential position in the chat in order to ask why it was not a successful bid. This will show us by contrast what the characteristics are that make other proposal bids successful.

A failed proposal

Let us look at line 23 in its immediate interactional context in Figure 2. We can distinguish a number of ways in which it differed from successful math proposal bids that solicited responses and formed math-proposal adjacency pairs:

```
17, 18. Avr (8:23:29 PM): i think we have to figure out
the height by ourselves … if possible

19.    pin (8:24:05 PM): i know how

21.    Avr (8:24:09 PM): how?

20.    pin (8:24:09 PM): draw the altitude'

22.    Avr (8:24:15 PM): right

24.    Avr (8:24:19 PM): this is frustrating

23.    Sup (8:24:19 PM): proportions?
```

Figure 2. Part of the chat log excerpt in Figure 1, with order revised for threading.

(a) All the other proposal bids (1, 3, 8, 17, 20, 27) were stated in relatively complete sentences. Additionally, some of them were introduced with a phrase to indicate that they were the speaker's proposal bid (1. "I think we should …," 17. "I think we have to …," 20. "i know how …" and 27. "i think i got it …"). The exceptions to these were simply continuations of previous proposals: line 3 provided the formula proposed in line 1 and line 8 proposed to "then" use that formula. Line 23, by contrast, provided a single word with a question mark. There was no syntactic context (other than the question mark) within the line for interpreting that word and there was no reference to semantic context outside of the line. Line 23 did not respond in any clear way to a previous line and did not provide any alternative reference to a context in the original problem statement or elsewhere. For instance, Sup could have said, "I think we should compute the proportion of the height to the base of those equilateral triangles."

(b) The timing of line 23 was particularly unfortunate. It exactly overlapped a line from Avr. Because Avr had been setting the pace for group problem solving during this part of the chat, the fact that she was involved in following a different line of inquiry spelled doom for any alternative proposal around the time of line 23. Pin either seemed to be continuing on his own thread without acknowledging anyone else at this point, or else he was responding too late to previous postings. So a part of the problem for Sup was that there was little sense of a coherent group process—and what sense there was did not include him. If he was acting as part of the group process, for instance posing a question in reaction to Pin and in parallel to Avr, he was not doing a good job of it and so his contribution was ignored in the group process. It is true that a possible advantage of text-based interaction like chat over face-to-face interaction is that there may be a broader time window for responding to previous contributions. In face-to-face conversation, turn-taking rules may define appropriate turns for response that expire in a fraction of a second as the conversation moves on. In computer-based chat, the turn-taking sequence is more open. However, even here if one is responding to a posting that is several lines away, it is important to make explicit somehow the post to which one is responding. Sup could have said, "I know another way to find the height – using proportions." His posting does not do anything like that; it relies purely upon sequential timing to establish its context, and that fails in this case.

(c) Sup's posting 23 came right after Pin's proposal bid 20: "draw the altitude." Avr had responded to this with 22 ("right"), but Sup seems to have ignored that. Pin's proposal had opened up work to be done and both Avr and Pin responded after line 23 with contributions to this work. So Sup's proposal bid came in the middle of an ongoing line of work without relating to it. In sequential terms, he made a bid for a proposal when it was not time to make a proposal. Sup's proposal bid was not positioned within the group effort to sustain a promising line of inquiry. It is like trying to take a conversational turn when there is not a pause that creates a turn-taking opportunity. Now, it is possible—especially in chat—to introduce a new proposal at any time. However, to do so effectively, one must make a special effort to bring the on-going work to a temporary halt and to present one's new proposal as an alternative. Simply saying "proportions?" will not do it. Sup could have said, "Instead of drawing the altitude, let's use proportions to find it."

(d) To get a proposal response to a proposal bid, one can elicit at least an affirmation or recognition. Again, this is a matter of pre-structuring a sustained interaction. Line 23 does not really solicit a response. For instance, Avr's question, 21: "how?" called for an answer—that was given by Pin in line 20, which actually appeared in the chat window just prior to the question and with the same time stamp. But Sup's posting does not call for a specific kind of answer. Even Sup's own previous proposal bid in line 10 ended with "right?"—requiring agreement or disagreement. Line 10 elicited a clear response from Avr, line 11 ("no") followed by an exchange explaining why Sup's proposal was not right.

(e) Other proposal bids in the excerpt are successful in contributing to sustaining the collaborative knowledge building or group problem solving in that they open up a realm of work to be done. One can look at Avr's successive proposal bids on lines 1, 3, 8 and 17 as laying out a work strategy. This elicits a proposal response from Sup trying to find values to substitute into the formula and from Pin trying to draw a graphical construction that will provide the values for the formula. Sup's proposal bid in line 23, however, neither calls for a response nor opens up a line of work. There is no request for a reaction from the rest of the group, and the proposal bid is simply ignored. Since no one responded to Sup, he could have continued by doing some work on the proposal himself. He could have come back and made the proposal more explicit, reformulated it more strongly, taken a first step in working on it, or posed a specific question related to it. But he did not—at least not until much later— and the matter was lost.

(f) Another serious hurdle for Sup was his status in the group at this time. In lines 10 through 16, Sup had made a contribution that was taken as an indication that he did not have a strong grasp of the math problem. He offered the lengths of the two given triangles as the base and height of a single triangle (line 10). Avr immediately and flatly stated that he was wrong (line 11) and then proceeded to explain why he was wrong (line 13). When he agreed (line 15), Avr summarily dismissed him (line 16) and went on to make a new proposal that implied his approach was all wrong (lines 17 and 18). Then Pin, who had stayed out of the interchange, re-entered, claiming to know how to implement Avr's alternative proposal (lines19 and 20) and Avr confirmed that (line 22). Sup's legitimacy as a source of useful proposals had been totally destroyed at precisely the point just before he made his ineffective proposal bid. Less than two minutes later, Sup tries again to make a contribution, but realizes himself that what he says is wrong. His faulty contributions confirm repeatedly that he is a drag on the group effort. He makes several more unhelpful comments later and then drops out of the discourse for most of the remaining chat. Sustaining a math chat discourse involves work to maintain an ongoing social interaction as well as work to continue the math inquiry. Proposal bids and other postings are constrained along multiple dimensions of efforts to sustain the activity.

The weaknesses of line 23 as a proposal bid suggest (by contrast, exception, breach or breakdown) some characteristics for successful proposals:

A clear semantic and syntactic structure,

Careful timing within the sequence of postings,

A firm interruption of any other flow of discussion,

The elicitation of a response,

The specification of work to be done and

A history of helpful contributions.

In addition, there are other interaction characteristics and mathematical requirements. For instance, the level of mathematical background knowledge assumed in a proposal must be compatible with the expertise of the participants, and the computational methods must correspond with their training. Additional characteristics become visible in other examples of chats. Successful proposals contribute in multiple ways to sustaining the group cognitive process.

As we have just seen, the formulation of effective bids for math proposals involves carefully situating one's posting within the larger flow of the chat. This is highly analogous to taking a turn in face-to-face conversation (Sacks *et al.*, 1974). Where conversation analysis developed a systematics of turn taking, we are trying to discover the systematics of chat interaction. This would describe how math proposals and other chat methods must be designed to fit into—and thereby contribute to—the sustained flow of group interaction.

So far in this paper, the notion of math-proposal adjacency pairs has been illustrated in just a single chat log excerpt. But in our research we have seen both successful and failed math proposals many times. Other researchers have also noted the role of successful and failed proposals in collaborative problem solving (Barron, 2003; Cobb, 1995; Dillenbourg & Traum, 2006; Sfard & McClain, 2003).

Each proposal bid and uptake is unique—in its wording and its context. The interactional work that it does and the structuring that it employs are situated in the local details of its sequential timing and its subtle referencing of unique and irreproducible elements of the on-going chat. Each group of students develops somewhat different methods of engaging with math problems and making math proposals. Even within a given chat, each posting pair that might be a proposal must be analyzed as a unique, meaning-making interaction in order to determine if it is in fact a math-proposal adjacency pair. That is why case studies provide the necessary evidence—the essential details of interaction methods are lost in aggregation, in the attempt to overcome what Garfinkel (1967) terms the "irreducible indexicality" of the event. To the extent that identifying proposal pairs is a useful analytic approach, it is important to determine what interactional methods of producing such proposals are effective (or not) in fostering successful knowledge building and group cognition, as we have begun to do here.

An understanding of methods like proposal making can guide the design of activity structures for collaborative math. As we are collecting and analyzing a corpus of chat logs under different technological conditions, we are evolving the design of computer support through iterative trials and analyses.

Designing computer support

If the failure of Sup's proposal about proportions is considered deleterious to the collaborative knowledge building around the triangles problem, then what are the implications of this for the design of educational computer-based environments? One response would be to help students like Sup formulate stronger proposals. Presumably, giving him positive experiences of interacting with students like Avr and Pin, who are more skilled in chat proposal making, would provide Sup with models and examples from which he can learn—assuming that he perseveres and does not drop out of the chat.

Another approach to the problem would be to build functionality into the software and structures into the activity that scaffold the ability of weak proposal bids to survive. As students like Sup experience success with their proposals, they may become more aware of what it takes to make a strong proposal bid.

Professional mathematicians rely heavily upon inscription—the use of specialized notation, the inclusion of explicit statements of all deductive steps and the format of the formal proof to support the discussion of math proposals—whether posted on an informal whiteboard, scrawled across a university blackboard or published in an academic journal. Everything that is to be referenced in the discussion is labeled unambiguously. To avoid ellipsis, theorems are stated explicitly, with all conditions and dependencies named. The projection of what is to be proven is encapsulated in the form of the proof, which starts with the givens and concludes with what is proven. Perhaps most importantly, proposals for how to proceed are listed in the proof itself as theorems, lemmas, etc. and are organized sequentially. (This view of proof is an idealization that abstracts from unstated tacit background knowledge of the mathematical community, as Livingston (1999) and Wittgenstein (1944/1956) before him have demonstrated.)

One could imagine a chat system supplemented with a window containing an informal list of proposals analogous to the steps of a proof. After Sup's proposal, the list might look like Figure 3. When Sup made a proposal in the chat, he would enter a statement of it in the proof window in logical sequence. He could cross out his own proposal when he felt it had been convincingly argued against by the group (see dashed lines in Figure 3 crossing out the proposal that base and height = 9 and 12).

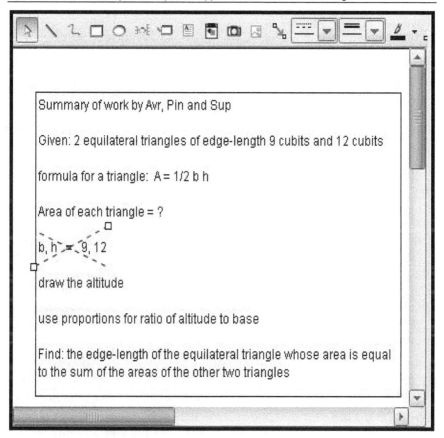

Figure 3. A list of proposals.

The idea is that important proposals that were made would be retained in a visible way and be shared by the group. Of course, there are many design questions and options for doing something like this. Above all, would students understand this functionality and would they use it? The design sketch indicated in Figure 3 is only meant to be suggestive.

Another useful tool for group mathematics would be a shared drawing area. In the chat environment used by Sup, Pin and Avr, there was no shared drawing, but a student could create a drawing and send it to the others. Pin did this twelve minutes after the part of the interaction shown in the excerpt. Before the drawing was shared, much time was lost due to confusion about references to triangles and vertices. For math problems involving geometric figures, it is clearly important to be able to share drawings easily and quickly. Again, there are many design issues, such as how to keep track of who drew what, who is allowed to erase, how to point to items in the drawing and how to capture a record of the graphical interactions in coordination with the text chatting.

Because we are designing a computer-supported experience that has never before existed and because we want our design to be based on detailed study of how students actually create their collaborative experience in the environment we are designing, we follow a highly iterative try-analyze-redesign cycle of design-based research (Design-Based Research Collective, 2003), in order to asymptotically approach an effective computer-supported environment and math discourse community.

We started with a simple online service. We used AOL's IM commercial chat system that was already familiar to many students. We invited students into chat rooms and presented a problem from the Math Forum's well-established Problem of the Month service. An adult facilitator was present in the room to help with any technical problems. When we saw how necessary a shared whiteboard was we tried an open source solution and also WebCT's and Blackboard's interactive classrooms. Eventually we collaborated with researchers in Germany to use and further develop ConcertChat. Together, we have gradually evolved ConcertChat into a sophisticated environment for both students and researchers.

Since the early AOL-based chat analyzed above, we have gone through many cycles of design, trial and analysis. In addition to designing support for persistent summaries of work (such as that in Figure 3) and a shared whiteboard for constructing geometric drawings (discussed in the following section and shown in Figure 4), we have incorporated the following: a referencing tool; a way for users to explicitly thread their chat postings; several forms of social awareness; tutorials on how to use the new features; a help system on using the tools, collaborating and problem-solving; and a lobby to support group formation. We have also experimented extensively with how best to formulate math problems or topics and how to provide feedback to students on their work.

References and threading

The more we study chat logs, the more we see how interwoven the postings are with each other and with the holistic Gestalt of the interactional context that they form. There are many ways in which a posting can reference elements of its context. The importance of indexicality to creating shared meaning was stressed by Garfinkel (1967). Vygotsky also noted the central role of pointing for mediating intersubjectivity in his analysis of the genesis of the infant-and-mother's pointing gesture (1930/1978, p. 56). Our analysis of face-to-face collaboration emphasized that spoken utterances in collaborative settings tend to be elliptical, indexical and projective ways of referencing previous utterances, the conversational context and anticipated responses (Stahl, 2006b, chapter 12).

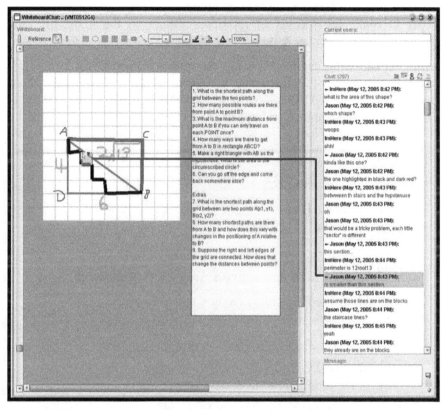

Figure 4. Screen view of VMT-Chat with referencing. Line 12 of the chat is selected.

Based on these practical and theoretical considerations—and working with the ConcertChat developers—we evolved the VMT-Chat environment. As shown in Figure 4, it not only includes a shared whiteboard, but has functionality for referencing areas of the whiteboard from chat postings and for referencing previous postings. The shared whiteboard is necessary for supporting most geometry problems. (This will save Avr the frustration of running out of paper, and also let Pin and Sup see what she is drawing and add to it or reference it.) Sharing drawings is not enough; students must be able to reference specific objects or areas in the drawing. (For example, Sup could have pointed to elements of the triangles that he felt to be significantly proportional.) The whiteboard also provides opportunities to post text where it will not scroll away. (Sup could have put his failed proposal in a text box in the whiteboard, where he or the others could come back to it later.) The graphical references (see the bold line from a selected posting to an area of the drawing in Figure 4) can also be used to reference one or more previous postings from a new posting in order to make the threads of responses clearer in the midst of "chat confusion" (Fuks, Pimentel, & de Lucena, 2006).

In one of our first chats using VMT-Chat, the students engaged in a particularly complex interaction of referencing a figure in the whiteboard whose mathematics they wanted to explore (Stahl, Zemel *et al.*, 2006). Here is the chat log from Figure 4 (graphical references to the whiteboard are indicated by "[REF TO WB]" in the log):

```
1      ImH:  what is the area of this shape? [REF TO WB]

2      Jas:  which shape?

3      ImH:  woops

4      ImH:  ahh!

5      Jas:  kinda like this one? [REF TO WB]

6      Jas:  the one highlighted in black and dark red?

7       ImH: between th stairs and the hypotenuse

8      Jas:  oh

9      Jas:  that would be a tricky problem, each little
"sector" is different

10     Jas:  this section [REF TO WB]

11     ImH:  perimeter is 12root3

12     Jas:  is smaller than this section [REF TO WB]

13     ImH:  assume those lines are on the blocks

14     Jas:  the staircase lines?

15     ImH:  yeah

16     Jas:  they already are on the blocks
```

Line 1 of the chat textually references an abstract characteristic of a complex graphical form in the whiteboard: "the area of this shape." The software function to support this reference failed, presumably because the student, ImH, was not experienced in using it and did not cause the graphical reference line to point to anything in the drawing. Line 5 provides a demo of how to use the referencing tool. Using the tool's line, a definite textual reference ("`the one`") and the use of line color and thickness in the drawing, lines 5 and 6 propose an area to act as the topic of the chat. Line 7 makes explicit in text the definition of a sub-area of the proposed area. Line 8 accepts the new definition and line 9 starts to work on the problem concerning this area. Line 9 references the problem as "`that`" and notes that it is tricky because the area defined does not consist of standard forms whose area would be easy to compute and add up. It refers to the non-uniform sub-areas as little "`sectors`." Line 10 then uses the referencing tool to highlight (roughly) one of these little sectors or "`sections`." Line 12 continues line 10, but is interrupted in the chat log by line 11, a failed proposal bid by ImH. The chat excerpt continues to reference particular line segments using deictic pronouns and articles as well as a growing vocabulary of mathematical objects of concern: sectors, sections, lines, blocks.

Progress is made slowly in the collaborative exploration of mathematical relationships, but having a shared drawing helps considerably. The students use multiple textual and graphical means to reach a shared understanding of mathematical objects that they find interesting but hard to define. In this excerpt, we start to get a sense of the complex ways in which brief textual postings weave dense webs of relationships among each other and with other elements of the collaborative context.

This example shows how creating shared meaning can require more than a simple adjacency pair. In order to establish a reference to "this shape" that could allow the two participants to discuss that math object, the dyad had to construct a complex involving nested question/answer pairs, math proposal pairs, a failed proposal bid, drawing, coloring, labeling, pointing, multiple repairs, computations. Here we see a more sustained group cognitive process. Across 16 postings and considerable coordinated whiteboard activity during two minutes, the student dyad defines a math object for investigation. The definition is articulated by this whole sequence of combined and intricately coordinated textual and graphical work.

Sustaining the group interaction

The goal of our research is to provide a service to students that will allow them to have a rewarding experience collaborating with their peers in online discussions of mathematics. We can never know exactly what kind of subjective experience they had, let alone predict how they will experience life under conditions that we design for them. For instance, it is methodologically illegitimate to ask if ImH already "intended" or "had in mind" in line 1 the shape that the group subsequently arrived at. We know from the log that ImH articulated much of the explicit description, but he only did this in response to Jas. If we interviewed ImH afterwards he might quite innocently and naturally project this explicit understanding back on his earlier state of mind as a retrospective account or rationalization (Suchman, 1987).

Our primary access to information related to the group experiences comes from chat logs (including the whiteboard history). The logs capture most of what student members see of their group on their computer screens. They therefore constitute a fairly complete record of everything that the participants themselves had available to understand their group interaction. We can even replay the logs so that we see how the session unfolded sequentially in time. Of course, we are not engaged in the interaction the way the participants were, and recorded experiences never quite live up to the live version because the engagement is missing. To gain some first-hand experience, we do test out the environments ourselves and enjoy the experience, but we experience math and collaboration differently than do middle-school students. We also interview students and their teachers, but teenagers rarely reveal much of their life to adults.

So we try to understand how collaborative experiences are structured as interpersonal interactions that are sustained over time. The focus is not on the individuals as subjective minds, but on the human, social group as constituted by the interactions that take place within the group. Although we generally try to ground our understanding of interaction through close, detailed analysis of excerpts from chat recordings, we do not have room to document our analysis of longer scale structures at that level of detail in this paper. We have collected over 50 hours of small-group chat about math. We engage in weekly collaborative data sessions (Jordan & Henderson, 1995) to develop case studies of unique chat excerpts. A number of published papers arising from these sessions are available. The discussion in the remainder of this paper is a high-level summary based on what we have observed.

Replies, up-take, pairs and triplets

Figure 5 provides a diagram of the responses of postings in the chat discussed above involving Avr, Pin and Sup. The numbers of the posts by each participant are placed in chronological order in a column for that participant. Math-proposal adjacency pairs are connected with solid arrows and other kinds of responses are indicated with dashed arrows. Note that Sup's failed proposal bid (line 23) is isolated. Most of the chat, however, has coherence, flow or motion because most postings are responses to previous messages. This high level of responses is due to the fact that many postings elicit responses or up-take, the way that a greeting invariably calls forth another greeting in response, or a question typically produces an answer. In a healthy conversation, most contributions by one participant are taken up by others. Conversationalists work hard to fit their offerings into the timing and evolving focus of the on-going interaction. In chat, the timing, rules and practices are different, but the importance of up-take remains.

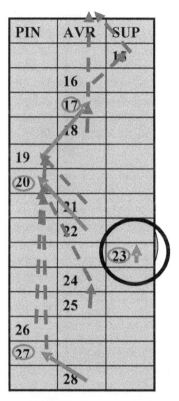

Figure 5. Threading of adjacency pairs and other uptake.

The fact that the group process and the cross ties between people are central to collaborative experiences does not contradict the continuing importance of the individuals. The representation of Figure 5 uses columns to indicate the connections and implicit continuity within the sequence of contributions made by an individual (compare the representation in Sfard & McClain, 2003). We may project psychological characteristics onto the unity of an individual's postings, attributing this unity to personal interests, personality, style, role, etc. Such attributions may change as the chat unfolds. The point is that the individual coherence and unfolding of each participant's contributions adds an important dimension of implicit sustaining connections among the postings.

Adjacency pairs like math proposals, greetings and questionings provide important ties that cut across the connections of individual continuities. They form the smallest elements of shared meaning precisely by binding together postings from different people. A proposal bid that is not taken up is not a meaningful proposal, but at best a failed attempt at a proposal. A one-sided greeting that is not recognized by the other is not an effective greeting. An interrogative expression that does not call for a response is no real questioning of another. These adjacency pairs are all interactional moves whose meaning consists in a give-and-take between two or more people. When we hear something that we recognize as a proposal bid, a greeting or a question, we feel required to attempt an appropriate response. We may ignore the proposal bid, snub the greeter or refuse to answer the question, but then our silence is taken as a response of ignoring, snubbing or refusing—and not simply a lack of response.

In fact, the way that a response is taken is also part of the interaction itself. In discussing the building of "common ground," Clark argues that shared understanding by A and B of A's utterance involves not only B believing that he understands A, but also A agreeing that B understands (Clark & Brennan, 1991). This requires an interaction spanning multiple utterances. For instance, the most prevalent interaction in classroom discourse is when a teacher poses a question, a student provides an answer demonstrating understanding and then the teacher acknowledges the student response as such an understanding (Lemke, 1990). Here, the elemental cell of interactional meaning making is a sequence of contributions by different people.

It is clear in this analysis that the meaning is constructed through the interaction of multiple people, and is not a simple expression of pre-existing mental representations in any one individual's head. This is the philosophical importance of the concept of adjacency pair: that meaning in groups is made through the interaction of multiple people, not completely by an individual's mental activity. In calling this "group cognition," we extend the term "cognition" from individual psychology to apply to processes in which small groups through their discourse construct meaning structures like logical arguments or mathematical proofs—that is, they engage in processes which are considered thinking when conducted by individual people. This approach is consistent with dialogical theories that actually view higher-level thinking by individuals as derivative of such intersubjective meaning making (Bakhtin, 1986; Linell, 2001; Stahl, Koschmann, & Suthers, 2006; Vygotsky, 1930/1978; Wegerif, 2006).

Longer sequences

Although much attention has been given to adjacency pairs in conversation analysis and although such pairs can be thought of as the elements of meaning making in collaborative interaction, they form only one of many levels of analysis. For instance, there are *longer sequences* (Sacks, 1992, vol. II, p. 354), *episodes* (Linell, 2001) and *topics* in dialogs and chats (Zemel, Xhafa, & Cakir, 2005) that provide layers of structure and sense. An hour-long chat is not a homogeneous interchange. A typical math chat might start with a period of introductions, greetings, socializing. Then there could be some problem-solving work. This might be periodically interrupted by joking, playing around, or silliness. People may come and go, requiring catching up and group reorganization. Each of these episodes has boundaries during which the group members must negotiate whether or not to stop what they were doing and start something else. These transitions may themselves be longer sequences of interaction, especially in large groups. We have barely begun to explore these different layers.

In social conversation, people work hard to strike up conversations, to propose new topics of mutual interest and to keep the conversation going. Online math chats face similar challenges. Students hesitantly greet each other and get things started. Math proposals are often used to introduce new topics and to carry forward a train of thought together. Finally, participants engage in considerable interaction work to sustain their sessions, intertwining humor, socializing and math inquiry—often using one of these modes to sustain others. Eventually every group decides to disband, at least until a future session.

The above referencing excerpt from a VMT-Chat was from the second hour-long session in a series of four chats by the same group. The sessions referred back to previous sessions and prepared for future ones. We hope to foster a community of Math Forum users who come back repeatedly to math chats, potentially with their friends. Their chats will reference other chats and different online experiences, building connections at the community level. This adds more layers of interconnections. It may sustain group interaction, inquiry and reflection over more significant periods of time.

Constructing proofs

Learning math involves becoming skillful in the social practices of the math community (Livingston, 1999). The math community is an aspect of the world-historical global community. The most central participants are the great mathematicians, who have invented new mathematical objects and developed new forms of mathematical practice (Sfard & Linchevski, 1994). Most of the population has low math literacy and participates on the periphery of the math discourse community. They are unable to manipulate math concepts fluidly in words or mathematical symbolism (Sfard, 2002). Nevertheless, they can use basic arithmetic methods for practical purposes (Lave, 1988). One of the most fundamental methods of math is counting, which children are drilled at extensively. Formal math assumes that the practitioner is skilled at following rules, such as the non-formalized rules of numeric sequencing (Wittgenstein, 1944/1956).

In our chats, students work on math problems and themes. In solving problems and exploring math worlds or phenomena, the groups construct sequences of mathematical reasoning that are related to proving. Proofs in mathematics have an interesting and subtle structure. To understand this structure, one must distinguish:

The problem statement-and-situation;

The exploratory search for a solution;

The effort to reduce a haphazard solution path to an elegant, formalized proof;

The statement of the proof; and

The lived experience of following the proof (Livingston, 1986, 1987).

Each of these has its own structures and practices. Each implicitly references the others. To engage in mathematics is to become ensnarled in the intricate connections among them. To the extent that these aspects of doing math have been distinguished and theorized, it has been done as though there is simply an individual mathematician at work. There has been virtually no research into how these could be accomplished and experienced collaboratively—despite the fact that talking about math has for some time been seen as a priority in math education (NCTM, 1989; Sfard, 2002).

The stream of group consciousness

Psychologists like William James and novelists like Jack Kerouac have described narratives that we tell ourselves silently about what we are doing or observing as our stream of consciousness. This "inner voice" rattles on even as we sleep, making connections that Sigmund Freud found significant (if somewhat shocking in his day). In what sense might online chats—with their meanderings, flaming, associative referencing, unpredictable meaning making and unexpected images—deserve equal status as streams of (group) consciousness? Group cognition can be self-conscious: The group discourse can talk about the existence of the group discourse itself and comment on its own characteristics.

Our sense of sustained time and the rhythms of life are largely reliant upon the narratives we tell ourselves (Bruner, 1990; Sarmiento, Trausan-Matu, & Stahl, 2005). We know that we have already lived through a certain part of the day or of our life because our present is located within a nexus of ties to the past or hopes for the future. In similar ways, a chat's web of references that connects current postings to prior ones to which they respond and to future postings that they elicit defines a temporality of the chat. This is experienced as a lived sense of time that is shared by the group in the chat. Like our individual internal clocks, the group temporality is attuned to the larger world outside—the world of family life that calls the students away from the chat for dinner or the world of school that interrupts a chat with class changes or homework pressures. The temporality that defines a dimension of the collaborative experience is constrained by the nature of the social situation and by the functionality of the technological environment.

Constructing the group experience

Groups constitute themselves (Garfinkel, 2006, pp. 189ff; Sacks, 1992, vol. I, pp. 144-149). We can see how they do this in the chat logs. At one level, the VMT service brings several students together and locates them in a chat room together. It may supply a math problem for them to work on and it may provide a facilitator who introduces them to the environment. At this point, they are a potential group with a provisionally defined membership. The facilitator might say something like, "Welcome to our first session of Virtual Math Teams! I am the facilitator for your session. . . . As a group, decide which question you would like to work on." (This is, in fact, part of the facilitator script from the session involving ImH and Jas excerpted above.) Here we can see that the facilitator has defined the group ("as a **group** … **you**") and distinguished her own role as outside the group ("**I** am the facilitator … **your** session"). The potential group projected by the facilitator need not necessarily materialize. Individual students may come to the setting, look around, decide it is lame and leave as individuals. However, this rarely happens. Sometimes an individual will leave without ever interacting, but as long as enough students come there, a group emerges.

Students enter the chat environment with certain motivations, expectations and experiences. These are generally sufficient to get the group started. One can see the group form itself. This is often reflected in the shift from singular to plural pronouns: "**Let's** get started. Let **us** do some math." We saw this in Avr's proposal: "**I** think **we** have to figure out the height by `our`selves." The proposal bid comes from an individual, but the projected work is for the group. Through her use of "`we`," Avr constitutes the group. Through her proposal bid, she constitutes the group as a recipient of the bid and elicits a response from them. Someone other than Avr must respond to the bid on behalf of the group. When Pin says, "`I know how: draw the altitude`," he is accepting Avr's proposal as a task for the group to work on and in so doing he makes a proposal about how the group should go about approaching this task (by making a geometric construction). In this interchange, the group (a) is projected as an agent ("`we`") in the math work (Lerner, 1993), and (b) is actually the agent of meaning making because the meaning of Avr's proposal is defined by the interaction within the group (e.g., by a math-proposal adjacency pair).

If the group experience is a positive one for the participants, they may want to return. Some chats end with people making plans to get together again. In some experiments, the same groups attended multiple sessions. We would like to see a community of users form, with teams re-forming repeatedly and with old-timers helping new groups to form and learn how to collaborate effectively.

The recognition that collaborative groups constitute themselves interactionally and that their sense making takes place at the group unit of analysis has implications for the design of cognitive tools for collaborative communities. The field of computer-supported collaborative learning (CSCL) was founded a decade ago to pursue the analysis of group meaning making and the design of media to support it (Stahl, Koschmann *et al.*, 2006). We view the research described here as a contribution to this CSCL tradition.

We are designers of tools for collaborative groups. We want to design an online collaborative service, with strong pedagogical direction and effective computer support. Our goal is to design an environment that fosters exciting mathematical group experiences for students and inspires them to return repeatedly. Our ultimate vision is to foster a sustainable community of math discourse among students. We approach this by trying to understand how groups of students construct their experience in such settings.

When students enter our website now, they are confronted by a densely designed environment. The lobby to our chat rooms is configured to help students find their way to a room that will meet their needs. In the room, there is a daunting array of software functionality for posting and displaying chat notes, drawing geometric forms and annotating them, keeping track of who is doing what and configuring the space to suit oneself. There may be a statement of a math problem to solve or an imaginary world to explore mathematically. The service, problems and software are all designed to enhance the user's experience. But how can a student who is new to all this understand the meanings of the many features and affordances that have been built into the environment?

Groups of students spontaneously develop methods for exploring and responding to their environments. They try things out and discuss what happens. A new group may doodle on the whiteboard and then joke about the results. They bring with them knowledge of paint and draw programs and skills from video games, SMS and IM. The individuals may have considerable experience with single-user apps, but react when someone else erases their drawing; they must learn to integrate coordination and communication into their actions. The math problems they find in the chat rooms may be quite different from the drill-and-practice problems they are used to in traditional math textbooks. It may take the group a while to get started in productive problem solving, so the group has to find ways to keep itself together and interacting in the meantime. There may be various forms of socializing, interspersed with attempts to approach the math. As unaccustomed as the math may be, the students always have some knowledge and experience that they can bring to bear. They may apply numerical computations to given values; try to define unknowns and set up equations; graph relationships; put successive cases in a table; use trigonometric relationships or geometric figures; draw graphical representations or add lines to an existing drawing. Mainly, they put proposals out in the chat stream and respond to the proposals of others. Sometimes the flow of ideas wanders without strong mathematical reflection. Other times, one individual can contribute substantial progress and engage in expository narrative to share her contribution with the group (Stahl, 2006a).

Groupware is never used the way its designers anticipated. The designers of VMT-Chat thought that its referencing tools would immediately clarify references to elements of drawings and transform chat confusion into logical threaded chat. But our studies of the actual use of these designed functions tell a quite different and more interesting story. The shared whiteboard with graphical references from the chat may allow more complex issues to be discussed, but they do not make pointing problem free. We saw in a previous section how much work ImH and Jas engaged in to clarify for each other what they wanted to focus on. In the excerpt and in the longer chat, they used a variety of textual, drawing and referencing methods. Through this process, they learned how to use these methods and they taught each other their use. Within a matter of a fraction of a minute, they were able to reach a shared understanding of a topic to work on mathematically. During that brief time, they used dozens of deictic methods, some that would prove more useful than others for the future.

Chat is a highly constrained medium. Participants feel various pressures to get their individual points of view out there. In a system like VMT-Chat, there is a lot to keep track of: new postings, changes to the whiteboard, signs that people are joining, leaving, typing, drawing. Small details in how something is written, drawn or referenced may have manifold implications through references to present, past or future circumstances. Students learn to track these details; apply them creatively; acknowledge to the group that they have been recognized; check, critique and repair them. Each group responds to the environment in its own way, giving group meaning to the features of the collaborative world and thereby putting their unique stamp on their group experience.

In the process, they create a group experience that they share. This experience is held together with myriad sorts of references and ties among the chat postings and drawings. Often, what is not said is as significant as what is. Individual postings are fragmentary, wildly ambiguous, and frequently confusing. In lively chats, much of what happens remains confusing for most participants. Clarity comes only through explicit reflections, up-takes, appreciations or probing. The interactions among postings, at many levels, cohere into a stream of group consciousness, a flow of collaboration, a shared lived temporality and, with luck, an experience of mathematical group cognition.

The small groups who meet in the VMT-Chat rooms participate in the larger collaborative communities of: the VMT project, the Math Forum user community and the math discourse community at large. In general, interacting small groups mediate between their individual members and the larger communities to which they belong. The discourse within the small group evokes and collects texts, drawings and actions by different participants, who bring multiple interpretive perspectives to the shared meaning making. Enduring ambiguity, mutual inconsistency and down-right contradiction pervade the resultant group cognition, with its "inter-animation of perspectives" (Bakhtin, 1986; Wegerif, 2006). Whether or not we assume that an individual's thoughts are logically consistent and interpretively determinant, it seems that much of a group chat generally remains a mystery to both participants and researchers. Yet, from out of the shrouds of collective fog insights are co-constructed that could not otherwise shine forth. The tension arising from conflicting or ungraspable interpretations in place of harmonious shared meaning fuels the creative work of constructing innovative group understanding.

The chat environment as incorporated in the VMT project is essentially different from familiar conversational situations, as we have seen in this paper. In general, there is little known by the participants about each other, except for what appears in the chat text or whiteboard drawings. No one's age, gender, appearance, accent, ethnicity is known. Even people's real names are replaced in the chat with anonymous login handles. Participants do not observe each other typing and correcting text until it is posted. Nor do they see what people are doing or saying in their lives outside the chat—if they have gone for a snack, are talking on the phone or are engaged in other, simultaneous online interactions. Normally, a person's history, culture and personality are conveyed through their vocal intonation and physical appearance (Bourdieu, 1972/1995); these are absent in chat. The one-hour duration of most VMT chats limits the history that can be established among participants through the available outlets of text and drawing, interaction style, word choice and use of punctuation. Yet, these drastically restricted means somehow allow incredibly rich, unique, creative and sophisticated interactions to take place. Insights take place and are shared; meaning is constructed and made sense of by groups. Perspectives and personal voices are established and acknowledged. Like characters in a Beckett play, chat participants learn to survive using radically impoverished discourse within a sensuously desolate landscape, and they sustain surprising forms of interaction for about an hour.

Conclusion

As we have seen in this paper, when students enter into one of our chats they enter into a complex social world. They typically quickly constitute a working group and begin to engage in activities that configure a group experience. This experience is conditioned by a social, cultural, technological and pedagogical environment that has been designed for them. Within this environment, they adopt, adapt and create methods of social practice for interacting together with the other students who they find in the chat environment. Over time, they explore their situation together, create shared meaning, decide what they will do and how they will behave, engage in some form of mathematical discourse, socialize, and eventually decide to end their session.

Then our job as researchers begins: to analyze what has happened and how the software tools we are designing condition the collaborative experiences that groups construct and sustain. We face the same poverty of knowledge about our subjects that the participants themselves face about each other. But, here too, less can be more. This record is conducive to careful, detailed analysis, without the interpretive complexities of video recording and transcription. We can analyze what happens at the group unit of analysis, with the methods of interaction adopted by the participants, because everything that could have gone into the shared understanding of the participants is available in the persistent record of the chat room history.

We can study this record at our leisure and make explicit the influences that the group experienced tacitly in the flow of its life. We can observe how several students constitute and sustain their group cognition in the math chat environment we are designing with them.

We can identify successful and failed math proposals, questions, greetings and other low-level interactions. We can observe how groups construct, identify, make sense of and explore math objects. But we can also see how these elementary interactions build up longer sequences of group cognition (Stahl, 2006b), intersubjective meaning making (Suthers, 2006) and sustained collaborative group experiences.

Acknowledgments

An earlier version of the first part of this paper won a Best Paper Award at ICCE 2005 in Singapore (Stahl, 2005). The Virtual Math Teams Project is a collaborative effort at Drexel University. The Principal Investigators are Gerry Stahl, Stephen Weimar and Wesley Shumar. A number of Math Forum staff work on the project, especially Stephen Weimar, Annie Fetter and Ian Underwood. The graduate research assistants are Murat Cakir, Johann Sarmiento, Ramon Toledo and Nan Zhou. Alan Zemel is the post-doc; he facilitates weekly conversation analysis data sessions. The following visiting researchers have spent 3 to 6 months on the project: Jan-Willem Strijbos (Netherlands), Fatos Xhafa (Spain), Stefan Trausan-Matu (Romania), Martin Wessner (Germany), Elizabeth Charles (Canada). The VMT-Chat software was developed in collaboration with Martin Wessner, Martin Mühlpfordt and colleagues at the Fraunhofer Institute IPSI in Darmstadt, Germany. The VMT project is supported by grants from the NSDL, IERI and SoL programs of the US National Science Foundation.

References

Austin, J. (1952). *How to do things with words*. Boston, MA: Harvard University Press.
Bakhtin, M. (1986). *Speech genres and other late essays* (V. McGee, Trans.). Austin, TX: University of Texas Press.
Barron, B. (2003). When smart groups fail. *Journal of the Learning Sciences, 12* (3), 307-359.
Bereiter, C. (2002). *Education and mind in the knowledge age*. Hillsdale, NJ: Lawrence Erlbaum Associates.

Bourdieu, P. (1972/1995). Structures and the habitus (R. Nice, Trans.). In *Outline of a theory of practice* (pp. 72-95). Cambridge, UK: Cambridge University Press.

Bruner, J. (1990). *Acts of meaning.* Cambridge, MA: Harvard University Press.

Cakir, M., Xhafa, F., Zhou, N., & Stahl, G. (2005). *Thread-based analysis of patterns of collaborative interaction in chat.* Paper presented at the international conference on AI in Education (AI-Ed 2005), Amsterdam, Netherlands. Retrieved from http://www.cis.drexel.edu/faculty/gerry/pub/aied2005.pdf.

Clark, H., & Brennan, S. (1991). Grounding in communication. In L. Resnick, J. Levine & S. Teasley (Eds.), *Perspectives on socially-shared cognition* (pp. 127-149). Washington, DC: APA.

Cobb, P. (1995). Mathematical learning and small-group interaction: Four case studies. In P. C. H. Bauersfeld (Ed.), *The emergence of mathematical meaning: Interaction in classroom cultures* (pp. 25-129). Mahwah, NJ: Lawrence Erlbaum Associates.

Dennett, D. C. (1991). *Consciousness explained.* Boston, MA: Little Brown and Company.

Design-Based Research Collective. (2003). Design-based research: An emerging paradigm for educational inquiry. *Educational Researcher, 32* (1), 5-8.

Dillenbourg, P., & Traum, D. (2006). Sharing solutions: Persistence and grounding in multimodal collaborative problem solving. *Journal of the Learning Sciences, 15* (1), 121-151.

Duranti, A. (1998). *Linguistic anthropology.* Cambridge, UK: Cambridge University Press.

Fuks, H., Pimentel, M., & de Lucena, C. J. P. (2006). R-u-typing-2-me? Evolving a chat tool to increase understanding in learning activities. *International Journal of Computer-Supported Collaborative Learning, 1* (1). Retrieved from http://ijcscl.org/_preprints/volume1_issue1/fuks_pimentel_lucena.pdf

Garcia, A., & Jacobs, J. B. (1999). The eyes of the beholder: Understanding the turn-taking system in quasi-synchronous computer-mediated communication. *Research on Language and Social Interaction, 34* (4), 337-367.

Garfinkel, H. (1967). *Studies in ethnomethodology.* Englewood Cliffs, NJ: Prentice-Hall.

Garfinkel, H. (2006). *Seeing sociologically: The routine grounds of social action.* Boulder, CO: Paradigm Publishers.

Heidegger, M. (1927/1996). *Being and time: A translation of Sein und Zeit* (J. Stambaugh, Trans.). Albany, NY: SUNY Press.

Heritage, J. (1984). *Garfinkel and ethnomethodology.* Cambridge, UK: Polity Press.

Jordan, B., & Henderson, A. (1995). Interaction analysis: Foundations and practice. *Journal of the Learning Sciences, 4* (1), 39-103. Retrieved from http://lrs.ed.uiuc.edu/students/c-merkel/document4.HTM.

Lave, J. (1988). *Cognition in practice: Mind, mathematics and culture in everyday life.* Cambridge, UK: Cambridge University Press.

Lave, J., & Wenger, E. (1991). *Situated learning: Legitimate peripheral participation.* Cambridge, UK: Cambridge University Press.

Lemke, J. (1990). *Talking science.* Norwood, NJ: Ablex.

Lerner, G. (1993). Collectivities in action: Establishing the relevance of conjoined participation in conversation. *Text, 13* (2), 213-245.

Linell, P. (2001). *Approaching dialogue: Talk, interaction and contexts in dialogical perspectives.* New York, NY: Benjamins.

Livingston, E. (1986). *The ethnomethodological foundations of mathematics.* London, UK: Routledge & Kegan Paul.

Livingston, E. (1987). *Making sense of ethnomethodology.* London, UK: Routledge & Kegan Paul.

Livingston, E. (1995). *An anthropology of reading.* Bloomington: IN: Indiana University Press.

Livingston, E. (1999). Cultures of proving. *Social Studies of Science, 29* (6), 867-888.

Lonchamp, J. (2006). Supporting synchronous collaborative learning: A generic software framework. *International Journal of Computer-Supported Collaborative Learning, 1* (2).

Mühlpfordt, M., & Wessner, M. (2005). *Explicit referencing in chat supports collaborative learning.* Paper presented at the international conference on Computer Support for Collaborative Learning (CSCL 2005), Taipei, Taiwan.

NCTM. (1989). *Curriculum and evaluation standards for school mathematics.* Alexandria, VA: National Council of Teachers of Mathematics.

NCTM. (2000). *Principles and standards for school mathematics.* Alexandria, VA: National Council of Teachers of Mathematics.

O'Neill, J., & Martin, D. (2003). *Text chat in action.* Paper presented at the ACM Conference on Groupware (GROUP 2003), Sanibel Island, FL.

Pomerantz, A., & Fehr, B. J. (1991). Conversation analysis: An approach to the study of social action as sense making practices. In T. A. van Dijk (Ed.), *Discourse as social interaction: Discourse studies, A multidisciplinary introduction, volume 2* (pp. 64-91). London, UK: Sage.

Psathas, G. (1995). *Conversation analysis: The study of talk-in-interaction.* Thousand Oaks, CA: Sage.

Sacks, H. (1992). *Lectures on conversation.* Oxford, UK: Blackwell.

Sacks, H., Schegloff, E. A., & Jefferson, G. (1974). A simplest systematics for the organization of turn-taking for conversation. *Language, 50* (4), 696-735. Retrieved from www.jstor.org.

Sarmiento, J., Trausan-Matu, S., & Stahl, G. (2005). *Co-constructed narratives in online, collaborative mathematics problem solving.* Paper presented at the international conference on AI in Education (AI-Ed 2005), Amsterdam, Netherlands. Retrieved from http://www.cis.drexel.edu/faculty/gerry/pub/aiedwkshp.pdf.

Scardamalia, M., & Bereiter, C. (1996). Computer support for knowledge-building communities. In T. Koschmann (Ed.), *CSCL: Theory and practice of an emerging paradigm* (pp. 249-268). Hillsdale, NJ: Lawrence Erlbaum Associates. D.O.I.: [1996].

Schegloff, E. (1991). Conversation analysis and socially shared cognition. In L. Resnick, J. Levine & S. Teasley (Eds.), *Perspectives on socially shared cognition* (pp. 150-171). Washington, DC: APA.

Schegloff, E. A., Jefferson, G., & Sacks, H. (1977). The preference for self-correction in the organization of repair in conversation. *Language, 53* (2), 361-382. Retrieved from www.jstor.org.

Searle, J. (1969). *Speech acts: An essay in the philosophy of language.* Cambridge, UK: Cambridge University Press.

Sfard, A. (2002). There is more to discourse than meets the ears: Looking at thinking as communicating to learn more about mathematical learning. In C. Kieran, E. Forman & A. Sfard (Eds.), *Learning discourse: Discursive approaches to research in mathematics education* (pp. 13-57). Dordrecht, Netherlands: Kluwer.

Sfard, A., & Linchevski, L. (1994). The gains and the pitfalls of reification -- the case of algebra. *Educational Studies in Mathematics, 26,* 191-228.

Sfard, A., & McClain, K. (2003). Analyzing tools: Perspectives on the role of designed artifacts in mathematics learning: Special issue. *Journal of the Learning Sciences, 11* (2 & 3).

Shannon, C., & Weaver, W. (1949). *The mathematical theory of communication.* Chicago, Il: University of Illinois Press.

Shumar, W. (2006). *The production of self, other and group through f2f and online chat interactions at the Math Forum.* Paper presented at the 27th Urban Ethnography in Education Research Forum, Philadelphia, PA.

Stahl, G. (2005). *Sustaining online collaborative problem solving with math proposals [winner of best paper award].* Paper presented at the International Conference on Computers and Education (ICCE 2005), Singapore, Singapore. Proceedings pp. 436-443. Retrieved from http://www.cis.drexel.edu/faculty/gerry/pub/icce2005.pdf.

Stahl, G. (2006a). Analyzing and designing the group cognitive experience. *International Journal of Cooperative Information Systems.* Retrieved from http://www.cis.drexel.edu/faculty/gerry/pub/ijcis.pdf.

Stahl, G. (2006b). *Group cognition: Computer support for building collaborative knowledge.* Cambridge, MA: MIT Press. Retrieved from http://www.cis.drexel.edu/faculty/gerry/mit/.

Stahl, G., Koschmann, T., & Suthers, D. (2006). Computer-supported collaborative learning: An historical perspective. In R. K. Sawyer (Ed.), *Cambridge handbook of the learning sciences.* Cambridge, UK: Cambridge University Press. Stahl, G., Zemel, A., Sarmiento, J., Cakir, M., Weimar, S., Wessner, M., et al. (2006). *Shared referencing of mathematical objects in chat.* Paper presented at the International Conference of the Learning Sciences (ICLS 2006), Bloomington, IL. Retrieved from http://www.cis.drexel.edu/faculty/gerry/pub/icls2006.pdf.

Strijbos, J. W., & Stahl, G. (2005). *Chat-based problem solving in small groups: Developing a multi-dimensional coding scheme.* Paper presented at the Eleventh Biannual Conference of the European Association for Research in Learning and Instruction (EARLI 2005), Nicosia, Cyprus. Retrieved from http://www.cis.drexel.edu/faculty/gerry/pub/earli2005jw.pdf.

Suchman, L. (1987). *Plans and situated actions: The problem of human-machine communication.* Cambridge, UK: Cambridge University Press.

Suthers, D. D. (2006). Technology affordances for intersubjective meaning making: A research agenda for CSCL. *International Journal of Computer-Supported Collaborative Learning, 1* (3).

ten Have, P. (1999). *Doing conversation analysis: A practical guide.* Thousand Oaks, CA: Sage.

Vygotsky, L. (1930/1978). *Mind in society.* Cambridge, MA: Harvard University Press.

Wegerif, R. (2006). A dialogical understanding of the relationship between CSCL and teaching thinking skills. *International Journal of Computer-Supported Collaborative Learning, 1* (1). Retrieved from http://ijcscl.org/_preprints/volume1_issue1/wegerif.pdf.

Winograd, T., & Flores, F. (1986). *Understanding computers and cognition: A new foundation of design.* Reading, MA: Addison-Wesley.

Wittgenstein, L. (1944/1956). *Remarks on the foundations of mathematics.* Cambridge, MA: MIT Press.

Wittgenstein, L. (1953). *Philosophical investigations.* New York, NY: Macmillan.

Zemel, A. (2005). *Texts-in-interaction: Collaborative problem-solving in quasi-synchronous computer-mediated communication.* Paper presented at the International Conference of Computer-Supported Collaborative Learning (CSCL 05), Taipei, Taiwan.

Zemel, A., Xhafa, F., & Cakir, M. (2005). *What's in the mix? Combining coding and conversation analysis to investigate chat-based problem-solving.* Paper presented at the 11th Biennial Conference of the European Association for Research on Learning and Instruction (EARLI 2005), Nicosia, Cyprus.

Zemel, A., Xhafa, F., & Stahl, G. (2005). *Analyzing the organization of collaborative math problem-solving in online chats using statistics and conversation analysis.* Paper presented at the CRIWG International Workshop on Groupware, Racife, Brazil. Retrieved from http://www.cis.drexel.edu/faculty/gerry/pub/criwg2005zemel.pdf.

7.   Synchronous Chat in CSCL

Underlying deeply successful collaborative learning are processes of group cognition. Where collaborative learning is more than a group of individuals supporting each other's individual learning, there are group processes in which contributions from participants build on each other. The group achieves cognitive tasks such as problem solving in ways that no individual could have on their own. Researchers have often looked for signs of such group cognition in asynchronous online settings like discussion forums. However, the Virtual Math Teams (VMT) Project has produced considerable data of small groups of students using synchronous chat to achieve group cognitive results.

While there have been claims that collaborative learning is a "social" phenomenon—i.e., consists largely of group-level practices—there has been little analysis and description of these processes as such; learning has generally been studied at the individual unit of analysis. The VMT research, in contrast, focuses on describing the interactional small-group practices that take place in synchronous chat learning contexts. This paper considers these practices and how they work together to form the foundation for effective collaborative learning activities. It analyzes collaborative learning activities in VMT's synchronous chat setting to discuss such small-group practices as: resolving cognitive conflict, pursuing inquiry, maintaining a group problem space and coordinating multiple modes of reasoning. These have broad implications for foundational issues of temporality, indexicality and group cognition.

Collaborative learning using synchronous chat

Collaborative learning can be defined as the achievement of progressive knowledge building and other cognitive accomplishments by a small group of people working together. The study of group cognition involves the systematic description of the processes at the group level of analysis whereby a group organizes its joint interaction to achieve such collective cognitive accomplishments as planning, deducing, designing, describing, problem solving, explaining, defining, generalizing, representing, remembering and reflecting as a group (Stahl, 2006a). It is concerned with how small groups establish their intersubjectivity in understanding the meaning of utterances and artifacts so that they can proceed with such joint work. In particular, we are interested in how group cognition can take place in online environments and how technological media can best be designed to support the foundational processes of group cognition. In this chapter, we focus on the use of synchronous text chat and we review studies of how small group interaction and knowledge building are mediated in a chat environment.

Synchronous text chat has a number of advantages over other media that currently exist for supporting small group collaborative learning or knowledge building. For instance, compared to speech, chat can involve multiple people proposing ideas at the same time. It can also involve multiple threads of discussion continuing simultaneously. Text has a persistence, so that participants can study utterances at their leisure and come back to review discussions reflectively. In addition, latecomers can catch up and people can refer back to previous statements. So synchronous chat has many of the advantages that are often attributed to asynchronous text systems as promoting reflective interaction (Hakkarainen, 2009; Scardamalia & Bereiter, 1996). However, in contrast to asynchronous media, chat can be livelier and more engaging because people do not have to wait long periods for responses, not knowing if their messages are being read. However, chat also has well-known drawbacks. If many people are interacting simultaneously, the response structure and coherence of the discourse can become confusing (Fuks, Pimentel & Pereira de Lucena, 2006; Herring, 1999).

Much research about chat has focused on its significant differences from spoken conversation. Chat is not simply an impoverished form of talk; it has its own structure and characteristics (Zemel & Çakir, 2009). It is important to understand chat as a genre. The nature of chat interaction is significantly influenced by the design of the supporting technology (Garcia & Jacobs, 1998; 1999; Lonchamp, 2006; 2009; Mühlpfordt & Wessner, 2009; O'Neill & Martin, 2003). Chat can profitably be integrated with other synchronous media, such as shared whiteboards, and even with asynchronous media like wikis (Stahl, 2009a). The analysis of usage of such environments can reveal group practices that users develop to coordinate their communication and to work together in such integrated chat environments (Markman, 2009; Schönfeldt & Golato, 2003).

While the potential of chat to support group cognition and collaborative learning is still largely a vision, research conducted in the Virtual Math Teams (VMT) Project provides guidance in the design of both technology and pedagogy to pursue this vision. These aspects of the project have been discussed elsewhere, primarily in (Stahl, 2009b). In this chapter, we want to look at some examples of group cognition in synchronous chat. First, we will discuss the methodological issue of the unit of analysis. This is important to clarify because it is second nature for most researchers—even when studying collaborative learning—to focus on the individual learner and the utterances of an individual as the unit of analysis, and thereby to miss the group-cognitive phenomena, which are the focus in the four case studies that follow.

Individual and group learning

Learning—even collaborative learning—has traditionally been considered a change in the knowledge of individual minds. More recently, it has been conceptualized at the opposite extreme in terms of participation in communities of practice (Lave & Wenger, 1991). In general, learning is conceptualized at the individual level and group knowledge building at the community level, despite evidence of the centrality of the small group, particularly in collaborative settings. An intermediate position between these two extremes is to consider how learning takes place in the practices of small groups (Stahl, 2006a). This is particularly appropriate for CSCL contexts, which are designed to support the building of knowledge in small groups and where learning is promoted through the effective interaction of students in online small groups.

Recent work in CSCL and the learning sciences indicates that learning takes place differently in small groups than when students are working on their own (Barron, 2003; Cohen et al., 2002; Schwartz, 1995). That is, if one measures individual learning as a difference between knowledge before and after some intervention, the inclusion of group work as part of the intervention makes a difference. These studies speculate that the difference is due to group processes, such as the practices involved in making ideas or concepts explicit and explaining them to group members. However, these studies were not specifically designed to capture the group processes and to describe how they were involved in group learning. Unfortunately, studies of learning rarely focus on the small-group processes themselves as activities of knowledge building.

We have been conducting a research project since 2002 to explore the group processes involved in synchronous chat activities in the Virtual Math Teams (VMT) Project at Drexel University. This project is based on our theory of group cognition, which we are still elaborating as a basis for understanding core processes underlying collaborative learning theory, design and practice. Investigations in VMT are designed to explore group practices in online collaborative learning of mathematics. The supporting technology is instrumented to capture all the data needed to observe group phenomena rigorously (Stahl, 2009c). We focus our analysis on case studies—some quite brief, others extending across several chat sessions.

Our publications to date have presented focused aspects of this research or described specific practices that seem to be important for understanding collaborative learning. In more theoretical reflections on this, my contribution to the CSCL2 book argued for "rediscovering the CSCL" that tends to be lost in research at the individual-student or isolated-utterance unit of analysis (Stahl, 2002b). At the CSCL 2002 conference, I proposed using interaction analysis to study group perspectives and collaborative knowledge building (Stahl, 2002a). My CSCL 2003 paper differentiated individual interpretation processes from the group meaning-making practices (Stahl, 2003). For CSCL 2005, I asked, "Can collaborative groups think?" (Stahl, 2005) and then at CSCL 2007 looked at the group meaning-making process in some detail (Stahl, 2007).

The VMT research team—along with nine other CSCL labs from around the world—has just published a number of VMT Project case studies of specific group practices (Stahl, 2009b). We are now trying to synthesize our findings and—in this paper—to understand how collaborative learning takes place on the basis of computer-supported group practices. In particular, four recent case studies show mechanisms of group cognition: resolving differences of perspective or approach (Toledo, Zemel & Stahl, 2007), engaging in inquiry or questioning (Zhou, Zemel & Stahl, 2008), creating or maintaining a group problem space (Sarmiento-Klapper, 2009) and coordinating mathematical problem solving across multiple media for communication or reasoning (Çakir, 2009). Here we want to look at the implications of these practices for collaborative learning in our synchronous chat context. This paper summarizes these four illustrative analyses of group practices to show how learning takes place at the small-group level. The question of how this gets individuated—or internalized into the minds or practices of the individual students in the groups—is beyond the scope of this paper and of the methodology of the VMT Project.

It is often assumed that case studies do not lead to generalizable findings of theoretical import. Although the following four sections each focus on specific cases of interaction, they should be understood within the contexts of the larger research effort. The doctoral dissertations from which these studies are excerpted not only each consider multiple similar cases in detail, but also distill in different ways what has been learned more generally from the VMT Project as a multi-year team-research effort. Our sense of group work informally synthesizes rather diverse data from many virtual math team experiences. The VMT data corpus includes well over a thousand student-hours of chat in 370 session logs, covering a broad array of different experimental contexts. Most of these chats involved K-12 students working on math topics in groups of 3 to 6. Some involved college students or researchers—occasionally with as many as a dozen participants typing in the same chat room. Students came from around the US, as well as some from Brazil, Singapore and Scotland. Some seemed to be mathematically gifted, but others were probably average and some were at risk. The technology for early VMT sessions consisted of familiar commercial chat systems; by 2005 a system with chat and a shared whiteboard integrated by graphical referencing was used; and in 2006 this was expanded to include a lobby, a tabbed interface and a wiki repository. The math topics evolved from typical algebra and geometry challenge problems from the Math Forum's Problem-of-the-Week (PoW) service to more open-ended topics like the grid world and patterns of sticks and squares.

For a variety of reasons, some of the chat logs are considered better data than others for analyzing the mechanisms of group cognition. In the spring and summer of 2004, an intensive effort was put into coding ten simple chat sessions (PoW-wows). The VMT Spring Fests in 2005 and 2006 brought student groups together for sequences of four hour-long sessions, providing a glimpse into longer-term development of group dynamics and group learning using text chat integrated with a shared whiteboard. The four case studies summarized here look at excerpts from teams in the VMT Spring Fest 2005 and 2006 data, as well as going back to a 2004 PoW-wow to look at purely textual interaction. In each case, the specific, highly situated analysis presents a concrete instance of phenomena that are visible—in their rich variety and individuality—throughout the VMT data corpus. These case studies shed light on some of the most theoretically fundamental and elusive themes of CSCL, semiotics, information science and learning science. In particular, each of the four studies addresses a major issue that has been influential in the CSCL research literature. Taken as a whole, they significantly advance our understanding of the nature and mechanisms of group cognition, as will hopefully become clear by the end of this paper.

Case study 1: Group-cognitive conflict

The fundamental theories of the learning sciences—going back to the classic texts of both Piaget and Vygotsky—claim that learning is stimulated by an optimal level of differences among conflicting perspectives on a topic. Modern versions of learning theory refer to this claim as "cognitive conflict"—in the socio-cognitive psychological tradition focused on individual cognition (Perret-Clermont & Schubauer-Leoni, 1981)—and as the "inter-animation of perspectives"—in the socio-cultural dialogical tradition focused on collaborative small-group interaction (Wegerif, 2006).

Neo-Piagetian varieties of CSCL, at least, locate the power of collaboration in the attempt to overcome conflicting perspectives, with their attendant psychological tensions. We prefer to deal with the inter-animation of perspectives—the notion that multiple views or approaches can be productive for creative knowledge building in collaborative groups—by looking to see how the alternative perspectives actually interact with each other in group problem-solving efforts. Our analysis illustrates how the eventual resolution of a difference in approach to a problem can drive the group to solve the problem in a way that none of the participants would have individually.

In the previous essay, it was suggested that VMT chats were largely driven forward and sustained by "math-proposal adjacency pairs." These are interactions in which one participant makes a proposal bid to the group for the group's work and this is accepted or rejected by another group member on behalf of the group. The studies of resolution of differences look into a more complicated scenario of this interaction: the resolution of differences between two or more math proposals—initiated by different individuals, operating from within contrasting perspectives on the group topic and entering into conflict with each other. The group may take up their conflict and work through it across a longer sequence of postings, rather than just quickly accepting or rejecting a proposal on its own. Such a group activity can drive the work of the group for a significant period of time. The group response to "cognitive conflict" and the subsequent inter-animation of different perspectives can drive learning at both the individual and group level, as it sustains the chat interaction. The result of the resolution of differences can be an expansion of the joint problem space; group participants build a richer shared understanding of the object of their collaborative undertaking.

While there is widespread agreement on the importance of resolving differences for stimulating learning, there has been little analysis to date of interactional mechanisms by which differences of approach to topics or problems are resolved in small groups. The exploration of such mechanisms requires new qualitative research. It is hard to explore scientifically the resolution of differences in the minds of individuals. However, the resolution of differences within small groups may be observable in traces of their communication and interaction. The VMT Project provides a naturalistic experimental environment that was designed and instrumented to capture the interactions of small groups of students faced with collaborative learning tasks.

Participants in the group problem-solving sessions we have studied engage in a number of activities such as framing the problem or problems, discussing and assessing approaches, executing these approaches and assessing their results as part of performing the activity described as a "problem-solving session." Whether the problem solving is done face-to-face or through computer-mediated communication, as long as there are multiple participants with their respective approaches, procedures and assessment methods, there will need to be some degree of negotiation. Negotiation, defined as "a discussion intended to produce agreement," is a key activity in most group problem solving.

Participants negotiate which approach to use, who is to participate in the unfolding of proffered approaches and in what order competing approaches are to be used. Participants also negotiate how solutions are to be assessed for adequacy and correctness. This interactional process of resolving differences drives the learning activity of the virtual math team by structuring the continuity of the discourse. Participants negotiate when there are competing proposals that appear in their problem-solving interaction. As proposals are advanced, they may be accepted, rejected or ignored. Acceptance is shown in an uptake of the resources offered by the proponent of the proposal. The participants use these resources in similar or compatible ways. Acceptance thus means that the participants build on each other's postings and co-construct their framing of the problem, crafting their solution or assessing the adequacy of their proffered solution. A new posting accepts what was proposed by a previous posting and tries to re-situate it in the new poster's perspective. In the end, the group solves its problem as a result of such back-and-forth motion across differences.

Alternatively, in the face of rejection, participants may adopt other strategies to change the allocation of participation. The spurned proponent may recycle the proposal or post an alternate message, which claims to have some idea that would shed light on the group activity. However, this alternate message would require the other participants to ask the rejected proponent to reveal the idea. If this ploy works, then a counter-proposal may arise and begin another cycle of exchanges. If a proposal is ignored, its proponent may decide to go along with the other proposal, or present a new proposal, or lurk.

These group practices may not appear different from negotiation in a face-to-face setting, since acceptance, rejection or indifference can be communicated through postings as well as through talk. However, in chat acceptance, rejection or indifference may not appear immediately after the proposals to which they would be paired if the interaction were face-to-face. This makes it possible for participants who would otherwise be in an impasse to select parts of a long series of related postings that they can append to their own postings to break an impasse and thereby produce agreement. Thus, in the episode from which Log 1 was taken, we find Mario selectively appropriating the postings of Alice and including them in his own presentation, despite his on-going rejection of her approach. Similarly, we find Alice using the labels instigated by Mario in making her own contrary claims regarding the reliability of labels. They are tasked with proving why a given geometric situation is impossible, and they propose conflicting approaches:

29	Mario	You name where the green line meets the base
30	Alice	B
31	Alice	I have an idea that might help us find whats wrong with the pic.
32	Mario	We could use good ol' Pythag thm to see what BV is
33	Alice	Lets not

Log 1.

Participants recognize agreement when they post tokens of agreement in reaction to other participant's postings. Prior to these displays of agreement, participants show that they are aware that there is some problem, that a solution has to be found, that the solution has to be implemented. The awareness of a problem is expressed in postings that supply additional resources to help frame the problem. For Mario, these additional resources are in the form of labels that eventually frame the problem as a type that can be solved using the Pythagorean theorem. For Alice, labeling is not as consequential. Mario proposes a solution, which is based on the application of the Pythagorean theorem while Alice proposes a different approach to finding a solution. Mario, in proposing the Pythagorean theorem, puts forward an approach that the participants are assumed to be familiar with, while Alice proposes her alternative approach based on details of the given problem description.

We also note that the participants try to negotiate the order in which varying approaches may be applied to the problem at hand. Both Mario and Alice try to get the other participants to apply their approaches first. Both of them work independently and refrain from criticizing each other's approaches until such time as either uses some resource produced by the other to advance their own approach. Thus, Alice uses the labeling "BV" that Mario first used to point out how he cannot produce a correct result with his approach. Mario, in return, uses this claim to proceed to a computation of BV, which then produces a result, which is not directly traceable to the use of the Pythagorean theorem but rather to a set of properties associated with equilateral triangles, octagons and hexagons.

If one conceives of the problem solving as the effort of individuals, then one would predict a strong likelihood that this session would have broken down. Two strong willed students brought incompatible approaches to the given task, and each vigorously resisted the approach of the other. However, through the group-interaction processes of negotiation, the differences were resolved in a productive way that led to a solution of the problem and a continuation of the interaction. The resolution of difference did not take place through a vote among preexisting personal opinions, compromise, bargaining or consensus, but through a subtle and selective building of each participant's proposals upon the up-take of the other participant's proposals. A shared framing of the problem—or a joint problem space—was co-constructed through the inter-animation of alternative perspectives on the problem. Through fine-grained analysis of the chat log, it was possible to characterize various interactional methods that were employed by the group to achieve a productive inter-animation.

The excerpt that was analyzed can be seen to have been driven forward by the interactive moves between participants, motivated by their different perspectives. From a methodological viewpoint, it is important to note that the driving force is not the individuals as agents, but the tension between them. The math solution does not arise directly from the mental representations of the individual students, but from the group effort to respond to the conflicting differences and from the interplay between the participants. Of course, the brains of each student were necessary to interpret the group meanings created in the interaction and to articulate the utterances that were posted in the chat in response to the on-going discourse, but the problem framing, the group problem space, the solution path, the meaning making all took place at the group level in the visible, persistent chat.

What can be said about learning in this case study? If we talk about the group learning—having followed a path to that solution and having arrived at an understanding of the solution of the problem—then we can say that the group learning was driven by the process of interactively resolving the differences of proposed approaches. If, further, we assume that the individual students learned something from the experience, we can say they did so by "individuating" the group lesson, making it their own and integrating it into their personal understanding, where it can serve as a set of resources for future mathematical discourses (including internal discourses of thought). Because the effort to resolve differences in the chat discourse kept both Alice and Mario focused on the proposals of the other, it is likely that they will each internalize something of their opponent's perspective. In this sense, their individual learning will be driven by the confrontation with a perspective that conflicted with their own. Experiences like these could lead to their ability to learn on their own by reading and even by thinking about perspectives that conflict with their own initial ideas. Thus, analysis of this case study seems to provide insight into grand theories of individual and collaborative learning through cognitive conflict and inter-animation of perspectives as driven by the resolution of differences.

Case study 2: Questioning to learn

The study of practices of group questioning investigates another driving force of collaboration. Rather than seeing a question posed in a chat as an outward expression of an individual's mental idea or of an individual's request for information, we look at the methods of formulating and taking up a bid at questioning to see how the meaning and function of the questioning are negotiated interactively. Questioning is seen to be a potentially complex group process, incorporating a wide variety of interactional methods. A question can be part of a math-proposal adjacency pair, putting forward a tentative proposal or reacting to a proposal bid. Questioning within a group can extend across a much longer sequence of adjacency pairs, advancing (or not) the problem-solving trajectory of the group. This analysis of questioning as an interactional achievement of a group—as opposed to a query in an individual mind—signals an innovative interactional approach to information science, with its conceptualizations of knowledge and information seeking that often underlie CSCL theories.

In an online collaborative context like VMT chats, questions are often not simple, well-defined queries for pre-existing information, but should be understood as situated moves within the group dynamic of the problem-solving effort. The object of the questioning is itself an emergent property of the interaction, through which the meaning is successively interpreted, refined and converged upon by the details of how the question is built, read and responded to. Questioning can play an integral role in the social relations among the participants, either positioning individuals as more or less competent or else maintaining peer standings. Question/response interactions are key to pursuing group problem-solving strategies, building a joint problem space and sustaining the team discourse.

We start by asking how it is possible to sustain a productive peer relationship in an online group when the raising of questions often reveals and makes relevant differences among actors in expertise, talent, ability, knowledge or understanding. Pursuing this line of inquiry allows us to look into the mechanisms underlying peer-group interaction. When there are differences in competence, actors need to work out among themselves the social order and the organization of their interaction. We look at how differences are attended to by participants in a collaborative peer group as part of the mechanism by which a group of students collaborate and manage the organization of their participation in ongoing chat interaction around problem solving. In particular, we examine the ways members of a small group (a) introduce differences in situated competencies as interactionally relevant, (b) organize their interaction to attend to these differences and (c) effect repairs where possible or find ways to proceed where repair is ineffective.

There are many ways that differences in competency can be introduced as interactionally relevant. Posing a question is often one way of accomplishing this. For example, an actor can ask a question about what is going on, or indicate there is a problem of understanding, or the actor can show the need for assistance by taking a particular kind of "next step" in a sequentially unfolding set of actions, for instance. When a questioner asks certain kinds of questions, she constitutes and makes relevant differences in expertise, knowledge, etc. as a matter for the recipients to attend to. Thus, not only is the questioner asking a recipient about the matter at hand, she is also instantiating their relationship in terms of the organization of their participation in the interaction (e.g., as questioner and answerer). In examining our data of students' interaction in VMT chats, we have noticed that question-response pairs are frequently invoked for attending to differences in local expertise and competency. For instance, asking a question may imply that the addressee(s) are likely to be able to provide some information that the questioner does not know.

When actors put forward certain questions that do not address explicitly their standing as participants in the interaction, matters of difference in knowledge, understanding, expertise, etc., can be addressed in ways that preserve a peer relationship between questioner and respondent. When actors make the organization of participation explicit in the question-response construction as a matter to be addressed, then the nature of the relationships among interactants becomes a matter of concern that needs to be addressed. Issues of differences in knowledge, understanding or expertise are then made relevant in terms of the way those relationships are worked out. In Log 2 from (Zhou et al., 2008), Nish positions himself as potentially "stupid" sounding; this lessens the possibility that respondents will position him as being less competent and will simply provide the requested explanation. The respondents, 137 and Jason, respond with relevant resources, without putting themselves in a teacher role. However, in line 180 Jason makes explicit the difference in math competency level between Nish and the rest of the group, effectively excluding Nish from full participation in the group work.

```
175    Nish        hope this doesnt sound too stupid, but
wuts a summation

177    137           The sum of all terms from a to b


178    Jason
       http://en.wikipedia.org/wiki/Sigma_notation


180    Jason       don't worry Nish, you'll learn all about
it next year
```

Log 2

In analogy to our analysis of a "failed proposal" in our discussion of math-proposal adjacency pairs in the previous essay, we contrasted a "breakdown" example of a question-response interaction to a successful case in an attempt to specify the characteristics of a "successful question." The analysis suggests the following characteristics, some of which bear resemblance to those for successful proposals:

A clear question structure that elicits a response. Making a report of one's math competency (beginning of line 175) may indicate some problem of understanding, but not present a question of its own. It does not elicit a response from the group. A question on a math topic with a clear structure is more likely to elicit a response without interactional trouble.

Information on what is known by the questioner. A question such as "what's a summation?" may be ambiguous as to what it is really asking for, as there are multiple possible readings of it. Providing information on what the questioner already knows can help rule out some possible readings of the question.

Right timing and interactional context within the sequence of interaction. Posing a question irrelevant to the ongoing discussion takes the risk of interrupting the group and deviating from the topic; careful work is needed to build the context for the question; ignoring this risks failure.

Engagement in the group process. Indication of being engaged in the group process is also helpful in that it contributes to enacting and maintaining the peer relationship. Failing to engage in the group process like Nish does during the response construction can be destructive to the peer relationship.

Question-response interactions are key to pursuing group problem-solving strategies, building a group problem space and sustaining the team discourse. Participants do not just pose questions as information-seeking or help-seeking moves by individuals. Question-response pairs also function at the small-group level as mechanisms for managing peer relationships and organizing participation. They can function to include—or exclude—a group member. They can play an integral role in the social relations among the participants, positioning individuals as more or less competent and maintaining or adjusting peer standings.

Case study 3: Evolving the joint problem space

In order to engage in shared work as a group, there must be a task to work on together—what activity theory refers to as the "object" of the group activity. This must be more than simply a statement of a problem that was given to the group, but needs to be worked out as a "problem space" to which the group can orient itself in an on-going and practical way. We looked at how a group establishes and maintains its "joint problem space" (Sarmiento & Stahl, 2008). Our study grew out of an attempt to understand how groups maintain their continuity of interaction across discontinuities. It extended our understanding of how a joint problem space is maintained by stressing the sequential and temporal aspects of "bridging" methods that are typically employed by virtual math teams to overcome discontinuities that threaten to disrupt their effort. We now see the joint problem space as integrating:

Social aspects (which transform participants into "members" of the interactional group),

Domain content concerns (such as the group's characterization of their problem to be solved) and

Temporal relations (the past, present and future as they are constituted in the unfolding sequentiality of the group interaction).

This joint problem space structures the work and discourse of the group, providing a shared understanding of the references and concerns that are expressed in utterances and behaviors of the individual group members. This analysis replaces the easily misunderstood metaphor of common ground with a richer construct.

Theories of collaborative learning have identified the central role of the joint problem space (JPS) in coordinating work and establishing intersubjective understanding (Teasley & Roschelle, 1993). The concept of problem space had its inception within the information-processing perspective as a characterization of individual problem-solving activity. It was then reformulated and extended within the learning sciences to include the social and domain dimensions. Based on a detailed analysis of sustained online collaborative problem-solving activity by a small group of students over multiple sessions, we propose that the theory of the joint problem space should now be further expanded. In addition to the dimensions of social relations and domain content, which are increasingly recognized in the learning sciences, we argue for the salience of the temporal dimension. Our analysis shows that the joint problem space is co-constructed at the group unit of analysis through the temporal and sequential orientation to inter-subjective meaning making.

The JPS can now be seen as a socio-temporal-semantic field, co-constructed through interactions such as collective remembering and providing the basis for shared understanding of meaning. Processes of group cognition both sustain and are sustained by the JPS. The JPS is seen as an interactional phenomenon at the small-group unit of analysis, rather than as a convergence of mental representations of individuals as is often understood within theories of cognitive change and common ground. That is, the JPS is established and maintained through the sequential relationship of interactions among group participants as they build upon past actions, current situations and future opportunities of their group activity. Individual mental representations are possible spin-offs of the JPS, rather than causes of it.

All of these resources—the knowledge artifacts used and referenced, the sequential organization of cases and the temporal markers of prior activity—are organized in different ways with relation to the participants in a temporal or sequential space. The concept of "deictic field" developed by Hanks (1992) seems especially useful to define the relationship between this new "space" and Barron's domain content and social relational spaces (Barron, 2003). Hanks describes the deictic field as composed first by "the positions of communicative agents relative to the participant frameworks they occupy," for example, who occupies the positions of speaker and addressee as well as other relevant positions. Second, the deictic field integrates "the positions occupied by objects of reference," and finally "the multiple dimensions whereby the former have access to the latter" (p. 193). From this perspective, participants in Log 3 constitute, through interaction, the relevant relative dimensions whereby they are to manage the positioning of agents and relevant objects of reference. They collectively co-construct a field of spatio-temporal indexicality incorporating bridging across sessions to locate activities, events and resources.

144	mathis	letz start working on number 8
145	bob1	we already did that yesterday
146	qw	we did?
147	mathis right and down	but we did it so that there was only
148	bob1	i mean tuesday
149	mathis	i guess we will do it with left and up?
150	qw	It would be almost the same.

Log 3.

In the interaction excerpted here, the three dimensions are intimately intertwined or unified. Participation is managed so that people who were or were not present in the previous session could nevertheless be included in remembering the knowledge constructed then. The knowledge artifacts (paths, formulae, procedures for exploring patterns) of the past are situated in the present work. The temporal discontinuity between sessions is bridged and the sequentiality of the group work is organized within the newly elaborated deictic field that the group incorporated in their joint problem space.

In our analysis of interactions we have observed that the content and relational dimensions are, in fact, relevant to collaborative problem-solving teams. Moreover, in expanding the range of phenomena analyzed to include longitudinal interactions across discontinuities, we have also uncovered time and the sequential unfolding of interaction as a third relevant and important dimension of activity. The interactional field is constituted by the participants to include problem-related objects and communicative agents associated with a prior interaction, and in doing so they position themselves and those resources within specific participation frameworks. The content objects (e.g., knowledge artifacts) and the relations among people (e.g., social positioning) are located within a temporal field, which provides a context for situating past, present and future events, for pointing to the events as temporally structured and for ordering utterances in their sequential relationships. Our central claim is that this temporal/sequential dimension is as essential to understanding collaborative interactions as are the content and relational dimensions.

The theory of group cognition takes as one of its central principles the dialectical relationship between social interaction and the construction of meaning. Meaning is not viewed as pre-existing in the minds of individuals, but as something that is constituted in the discourse within the group (Stahl, 2003). Nor is the group viewed as pre-existing as a set of people, but as a functional unit that constitutes itself in the interaction of its members when they position themselves within their group activity. From this perspective, the social organization of action and the knowledge embedded in such action are emergent properties of moment-by-moment interactions among actors, and between actors and the objects and the activity systems in which they participate collectively. The content space and the relational space, in Barron's terms, are mutually constitutive from this perspective.

Group cognition theory offers a candidate description for how the dynamic process of building knowledge might intertwine the content and relational spaces: "Small groups are the engines of knowledge building. The knowing that groups build up in manifold forms is what becomes internalized by their members as individual learning and externalized in their communities as certifiable knowledge" (Stahl, 2006a, p. 16). Thus, small group interaction can play a pivotal mediating role in the interplay between individual cognition (and the relations among the individuals) and communities of practice (and the knowledge objects that they share). Time as the sequential organization of activity seems to be a resource and an aspect of interaction that plays a significant role in how communities, groups and individuals achieve knowledge through small-group interaction. We have caught a glimpse or two of how temporality is marked and sequentiality is established within the discourse of small groups in VMT.

In our analysis of how small groups "sustain" their group cognition while engaged in brief episodes of online mathematical problem solving, we alluded to two ways in which time might be an important element of individual episodes of problem-solving activity. On the one hand, the collaborative activity involved in solving a problem can be "spread across" hundreds of micro-level interactions. On the other hand, individuals might internalize or individualize the meaning co-constructed through interactions and "sustain" the group cognition by engaging in later individual or group work. In either case, groups are described as sustaining their social and intellectual work by "building longer sequences of math proposals, other adjacency pairs and a variety of interaction methods" (Stahl, 2006b, p. 85).

Our analysis of interactions that bridge gaps across sessions confirms and extends these findings by suggesting that in longitudinal interactions, temporal and sequential resources are central to constituting activity as continuous by constructing and maintaining a group problem space. Interaction is taken here in the full sense that ethnomethodologists give it, as the "ongoing, contingent co-production of a shared social/material world," which, as Suchman argues "cannot be stipulated in advance, but requires an autobiography, a presence and a projected future" (Suchman, 2007). We have just began the work of describing in detail the interactional group practices that allow teams to construct and manage this expanded problem "field" by interweaving content, relational and temporal aspects of interaction.

Case study 4: Coordinating visual, narrative and symbolic reasoning

We now consider how work in the group problem space is conducted when the online environment combines textual postings and graphical drawing media, as in a VMT chat room with shared whiteboard. By looking closely at the practices a student group uses to coordinate chat postings with carefully choreographed inscriptions on the shared whiteboard, we see how deep understanding of math can be effectively promoted through the organization of visual, narrative and symbolic reasoning within group interaction. Although drawings, text and mathematical symbols build knowledge and convey meaning through very different semiotic systems, in VMT sessions they are tightly coordinated and mutually informing. Students new to the environment spontaneously develop and share methods of connecting and coordinating work in these media.

Mathematical insight is often first grounded in visual reasoning with concrete instances, where relationships can be seen and understood concretely. These insights can then be pointed out to others through narratives, which instruct them how to see in the group's shared way. In mathematics, symbolic expressions are effectively employed to articulate, formalize and generalize understandings of relationships, providing means for symbolic manipulations that lead to further conclusions and to different forms of comprehension. The math artifacts that emerge from group work that coordinates visual, narrative and symbolic reasoning are not simple objects, but concepts that can only be understood through the coordination of their multiple realizations in these different types of media. The coordination of group work in the three realms supports deep mathematical understanding (as opposed to rote learning) of individuals by fostering understanding of the multiple realizations of math artifacts. It also enriches the joint problem space of the group's effort by interconnecting the semantic relationships of the three realms within a shared network of meaning.

We recently investigated how a group of three upper-middle-school students put the features of an online environment with dual interaction spaces into use as they collaboratively worked on a math problem they themselves came up with (Çakir, 2009). Our analysis revealed several important insights regarding the affordances of systems with dual interaction spaces. First, we observed that the whiteboard can make visible to everyone the animated evolution of a geometric construction, displaying the visual reasoning process manifested in drawing actions. Second, whiteboard and chat contents differ in terms of mutability of their contents, due to the object-oriented design of the whiteboard, which allows modification and annotation of past contributions. Third, the media differ in terms of the persistence of their contents: whiteboard objects remain in the shared visual field until they are removed, whereas chat content gradually scrolls off as new postings are produced. Although contents of both spaces are persistently available for reference, due to linear progression of the chat window, chat postings are likely to refer to visually (and hence temporally) proximal chat messages and to graphical whiteboard objects. Finally, the whiteboard objects index a horizon of past and future activities as they serve as an interactional resource through the course of related episodes of chat discussion.

Our analysis of this team's joint work also revealed methods for the organization of collaborative work, through which group members co-construct mathematical meaning sedimented in semiotic objects distributed across the dual interaction spaces of the VMT environment. We observed that bringing relevant math artifacts referenced by indexical terms such as "hexagonal array" to other members' attention often requires a coordinated sequence of actions across the two interaction spaces. Participants use explicit and verbal references to guide each other about how a new contribution should be read in relation to prior contents. Indexical terms stated in chat referring to the visible production of shared objects are instrumental in the reification of those terms as meaningful mathematical objects for the participants. Verbal references to co-constructed graphical objects are often used as a resource to index complicated mathematical concepts in the process of co-constructing new concepts. Finally, different representational affordances of the dual interaction spaces allow groups to develop multiple realizations of the math artifacts to which they are oriented. Shared graphical inscriptions and chat postings are used together as semiotic resources in mutually elaborating ways. Methods of coordinating group interaction across the media spaces also interrelate the mathematical significances of the multiple realizations.

Overall, we observed that actions performed in both the chat and whiteboard interaction spaces constitute an evolving historical context for the joint work of the group. What gets done now informs the relevant actions to be performed next, and what was done previously can be reproduced/modified depending on the circumstances of the ongoing activity. As the interaction unfolds sequentially, the sense of previously posted whiteboard objects and chat statements may become evident and/or modified, as in this brief excerpt in Log 4:

12	137	So do you want to first calculate the number of triangles in a hexagonal array?
13	Qwertyuiop	What's the shape of the array? a hexagon?[Reference to line 12]
14	137	Ya [Reference to line 13]
15	Qwertyuiop	ok….
16	Jason	wait-- can someone highlight the hexagonal array on the diagram? i don't really see what you mean...
17	Jason	Hmm.. okay
18	Qwertyuiop	Oops [Reference to Whiteboard]
19	Jason	so it has at least 6 triangles?
20	Jason	in this, for instance [Reference to Whiteboard]

Log 4.

Here the VMT environment's graphical referencing tool is used to coordinate chat postings with previous chat postings as well as with objects on the whiteboard. Through the sequential coordination of chat postings and whiteboard inscriptions, the group successfully solved their self-defined mathematical challenge, to find a formula for the number of small triangles in a hexagonal array of any given side-length. Their interaction was guided by a sequence of proposals and responses carried out textually in the chat medium. However, the sense of the terms and relationships narrated in the chat were largely instantiated, shared and investigated through observation of visible features of graphical inscriptions in the whiteboard medium. The mathematical object that was visually co-constructed in the whiteboard was named and described in words within the chat. Finally, a symbolic expression was developed by the group, grounded in the graphic that evolved in the whiteboard and discussed in the terminology that emerged in the chat. The symbolic mathematical result was then posted to the wiki, a third medium within the VMT environment. The wiki is intended for sharing group findings with other groups as part of a permanent archive of community knowledge building by virtual math teams.

Our case study demonstrates that it is possible to analyze how math problem solving—and presumably other learning achievements—can be carried out by small groups of students. The students can define and refine their own problems to pursue; they can invent their own methods of working; they can use unrestricted vocabulary; they can coordinate work in multiple media, taking advantage of different affordances. Careful attention to the sequentiality of references and responses is necessary to reveal how the group coordinated its work and how that work was driven by the reactions of the group members' interactions with each other. Only by focusing on the sequentiality of the interactions can one see how the visual, narrative and symbolic build on each other as well as how the actions of the individual students respond to each other to co-construct math objects, personal understanding, group agreement and mathematical results that cannot be attributed to any one individual, but which emerge from the interaction as complexly sequenced. This analysis illustrates a promising approach for CSCL research to investigate aspects of group cognition that are beyond the reach of quantitative methods that ignore the full sequentiality of their data.

In our case study, we have seen the establishment of an indexical ground of deictic references co-constructed by the group members as an underlying support for the creation and maintenance of their joint problem space. We have seen that nexus of references created interactionally as group members propose, question, repair, respond, illustrate, make visible, supply symbols, name, etc. In the VMT dual-media environment, the differential persistence, visibility and mutability of the media are consequential for the interaction. Group members develop methods of coordinating chat and drawing activities to combine visual and conceptual reasoning by the group and to co-construct and maintain an evolving shared indexical ground of their discourse.

During the 18 minute excerpt analyzed in this case study, three students construct a diagram of lines, triangles and hexagons, propose a math pattern problem, analyze the structure of their diagram and derive an algebraic formula to solve their problem. They do this by coordinating their whiteboard and chat activities in a synchronous online environment. Their accomplishment is precisely the kind of educational math experience recommended by mathematicians (Livingston, 1999; Lockhart, 2009; Moss & Beatty, 2006). It was not a mental achievement of an individual, but a group accomplishment carried out in computer-supported discourse. By analyzing the sequentiality and indexicality of their interactions we explicated several mechanisms of this group cognition by which the students coordinated the meaning of their discourse and maintained adequate reciprocity of understanding.

The coordination of visual and semiotic realizations of the mathematical objects that the students co-construct provides a grounding of the algebraic formulas the students jointly derive in the line drawings that they inspect visually together. As the students individualize this experience of group cognition, they can develop the deep understanding of mathematical phenomena that comes from seeing the connections among multiple realizations (Sfard, 2008). Our case study does not by any means predict that all students can accomplish similar results under specific conditions, but merely demonstrates that this is possible within a synchronous CSCL setting and that a fine-grained sequential analysis of interaction can study how the group accomplished it.

Group cognition and learning

As a research field, CSCL has been deeply influenced by the theories of Vygotsky (1930/1978). In particular, one can say that CSCL is inspired by his visionary insight that learning takes place originally inter-subjectively (in small groups), and may then be internalized as intra-subjective (individual) learning. To this view, CSCL adds the hope that networked computer technology can bring learners together in new ways to take advantage of the power of collaborative learning. In this paper, we have tried to indicate a way of analyzing group learning that was not available to Vygotsky and that has been too little pursued within CSCL to date. By observing the group practices through which small groups of learners accomplish problem solving and other tasks, we can begin to determine the mechanisms that make knowledge building possible at the small-group level. We can observe group practices with the requisite detail by recording interactions that take place in synchronous chat settings, where the complete context of interaction can be captured, logged and replayed for analysis. Then we can describe the kinds of interactions that take place in group-cognitive conflict, in group inquiry, in maintaining a group problem space or in coordinating group reasoning across multiple media. These group practices set the stage for individual learning by allowing groups to reach achievements that the group's members can take away as skills, resources or methods for their own learning. As Vygotsky noted, the mediations involved in internalization are complex—and we would add that they are hard to observe. However, to understand individual learning as a cultural and developmental process, it seems necessary—and quite possible—first to understand the practices of group cognition that underlie it. We may then find that the traditional conceptualizations of individual learning must be reworked on the model of the small-group practices.

References

Barron, B. (2003). When smart groups fail. *The Journal of the Learning Sciences, 12*(3), 307-359.

Çakir, M. P. (2009). *How online small groups co-construct mathematical artifacts to do collaborative problem solving.* Unpublished Dissertation, Ph.D., College of Information Science and Technology, Drexel University, Philadelphia, PA, USA.

Cohen, E. G., Lotan, R. A., Abram, P. L., Scarloss, B. A., & Schultz, S. E. (2002). Can groups learn? *Teachers College Record, 104*(6), 1045-1068.

Fuks, H., Pimentel, M., & Pereira de Lucena, C. (2006). R-u-typing-2-me? Evolving a chat tool to increase understanding in learning activities. *International Journal of Computer-Supported Collaborative Learning, 1*(1), 117-142. Available at http://dx.doi.org/10.1007/s11412-006-6845-3.

Garcia, A., & Jacobs, J. B. (1998). The interactional organization of computer mediated communication in the college classroom. *Qualitative Sociology, 21*(3), 299-317.

Garcia, A., & Jacobs, J. B. (1999). The eyes of the beholder: Understanding the turn-taking system in quasi-synchronous computer-mediated communication. *Research on Language and Social Interaction, 34*(4), 337-367.

Hakkarainen, K. (2009). A knowledge-practice perspective on technology-mediated learning. *International Journal of Computer-Supported Collaborative Learning, 4*(2), 213-231. Available at http://dx.doi.org/10.1007/s11412-009-9064-x.

Hanks, W. (1992). The indexical ground of deictic reference. In A. Duranti & C. Goodwin (Eds.), *Rethinking context: Language as an interactive phenomenon* (pp. 43-76). Cambridge, UK: Cambridge University Press.

Herring, S. (1999). Interactional coherence in cmc. *Journal of Computer Mediated Communication, 4*(4). Available at http://jcmc.indiana.edu/vol4/issue4/herring.html.

Livingston, E. (1999). Cultures of proving. *Social Studies of Science, 29*(6), 867-888.

Lockhart, P. (2009). *A mathematician's lament: How school cheats us out of our most fascinating and imaginative art forms.* New York, NY: Belevue Literary Press.

Lonchamp, J. (2006). Supporting synchronous collaborative learning: A generic, multi-dimensional model. *International Journal of Computer-Supported Collaborative Learning, 1*(2), 247-276. Available at http://dx.doi.org/10.1007/s11412-006-8996-7.

Lonchamp, J. (2009). A three-level analysis of collaborative learning in dual-interaction spaces. *International Journal of Computer-Supported Collaborative Learning, 4*(3), 289-317. Available at http://dx.doi.org/10.1007/s11412-009-9068-6.

Markman, K. (2009). "So what shall we talk about": Openings and closings in chat-based virtual meetings. *Journal of Business Communication, 46*(150-170). Available at http://job.sagepub.com/cgi/content/abstract/46/1/150.

Moss, J., & Beatty, R. (2006). Knowledge building in mathematics: Supporting collaborative learning in pattern problems. *International Journal of Computer-*

Supported Collaborative Learning, 1(4), 441-465. Available at http://dx.doi.org/10.1007/s11412-006-9003-z.

Mühlpfordt, M., & Wessner, M. (2009). The integration of dual-interaction spaces. In G. Stahl (Ed.), *Studying virtual math teams* (pp. 281-293). New York, NY: Springer. Available at http://dx.doi.org/10.1007/978-1-4419-0228-3_15.

O'Neill, J., & Martin, D. (2003). *Text chat in action.* Paper presented at the ACM Conference on Groupware (GROUP 2003), Sanibel Island, FL.

Perret-Clermont, A.-N., & Schubauer-Leoni, M.-L. (1981). Conflict and cooperation as opportunities for learning. In W. P. Robinson (Ed.), *Communication in development* (pp. 203-234). New York, NY: Academic Press.

Sarmiento, J., & Stahl, G. (2008). *Extending the joint problem space: Time and sequence as essential features of knowledge building.* Paper presented at the International Conference of the Learning Sciences (ICLS 2008), Utrecht, Netherlands. Available at http://GerryStahl.net/pub/icls2008johann.pdf.

Sarmiento-Klapper, J. W. (2009). *Bridging mechanisms in team-based online problem solving: Continuity in building collaborative knowledge.* Unpublished Dissertation, Ph.D., College of Information Science and Technology, Drexel University, Philadelphia, PA, USA.

Scardamalia, M., & Bereiter, C. (1996). Computer support for knowledge-building communities. In T. Koschmann (Ed.), *CSCL: Theory and practice of an emerging paradigm* (pp. 249-268). Hillsdale, NJ: Lawrence Erlbaum Associates.

Schönfeldt, J., & Golato, A. (2003). Repair in chats: A conversation analytic approach. *Research on Language and Social Interaction, 36*(3), 241-284.

Schwartz, D. (1995). The emergence of abstract representations in dyad problem solving. *Journal of the Learning Sciences, 4*(3), 321-354.

Stahl, G. (2002a). Contributions to a theoretical framework for CSCL. In G. Stahl (Ed.), *Computer support for collaborative learning: Foundations for a CSCL community. Proceedings of CSCL 2002* (pp. 62-71). Boulder, CO: Lawrence Erlbaum Associates. Available at http://GerryStahl.net/cscl/papers/ch15.pdf.

Stahl, G. (2002b). Rediscovering CSCL. In T. Koschmann, R. Hall & N. Miyake (Eds.), *CSCL 2: Carrying forward the conversation* (pp. 169-181). Hillsdale, NJ: Lawrence Erlbaum Associates. Available at http://GerryStahl.net/cscl/papers/ch01.pdf.

Stahl, G. (2003). Meaning and interpretation in collaboration. In B. Wasson, S. Ludvigsen & U. Hoppe (Eds.), *Designing for change in networked learning environments: Proceedings of the international conference on computer support for collaborative learning (CSCL '03)* (pp. 523-532). Bergen, Norway: Kluwer Publishers. Available at http://GerryStahl.net/cscl/papers/ch20.pdf.

Stahl, G. (2005). *Group cognition: The collaborative locus of agency in CSCL.* Paper presented at the international conference on Computer Support for Collaborative Learning (CSCL '05), Taipei, Taiwan. Proceedings pp. 632-640: Lawrence Erlbaum Associates. Available at http://GerryStahl.net/pub/cscl2005.pdf & http://GerryStahl.net/pub/cscl2005ppt.pdf.

Stahl, G. (2006a). *Group cognition: Computer support for building collaborative knowledge.* Cambridge, MA: MIT Press. Available at http://GerryStahl.net/mit/.

Stahl, G. (2006b). Sustaining group cognition in a math chat environment. *Research and Practice in Technology Enhanced Learning (RPTEL), 1*(2), 85-113. Available at http://GerryStahl.net/pub/rptel.pdf.

Stahl, G. (2007). *Meaning making in CSCL: Conditions and preconditions for cognitive processes by groups.* Paper presented at the international conference on Computer-Supported Collaborative Learning (CSCL '07), New Brunswick, NJ: ISLS. Available at http://GerryStahl.net/pub/cscl07.pdf.

Stahl, G. (2009a). Designing a mix of synchronous and asynchronous media for VMT. In G. Stahl (Ed.), *Studying virtual math teams* (pp. 295-310). New York, NY: Springer. Available at http://dx.doi.org/10.1007/978-1-4419-0228-3_16.

Stahl, G. (2009b). *Studying virtual math teams.* New York, NY: Springer. Available at http://GerryStahl.net/vmt/book.

Stahl, G. (2009c). Toward a science of group cognition. In G. Stahl (Ed.), *Studying virtual math teams* (pp. 555-579). New York, NY: Springer. Available at http://dx.doi.org/10.1007/978-1-4419-0228-3_28.

Suchman, L. A. (2007). *Human-machine reconfigurations: Plans and situated actions* (2nd ed.). Cambridge, UK: Cambridge University Press.

Teasley, S. D., & Roschelle, J. (1993). Constructing a joint problem space: The computer as a tool for sharing knowledge. In S. P. Lajoie & S. J. Derry (Eds.), *Computers as cognitive tools* (pp. 229-258). Mahwah, NJ: Lawrence Erlbaum Associates, Inc.

Toledo, R. P. S., Zemel, A., & Stahl, G. (2007). *Resolving differences: Twists and turns in a synchronous online collaborative mathematics problem-solving session.* Paper presented at the international conference on Computer-Supported Collaborative Learning (CSCL '07), New Brunswick, NJ. Available at http://GerryStahl.net/vmtwiki/ramon.pdf.

Vygotsky, L. (1930/1978). *Mind in society.* Cambridge, MA: Harvard University Press.

Wegerif, R. (2006). A dialogic understanding of the relationship between CSCL and teaching thinking skills. *International Journal of Computer-Supported Collaborative Learning, 1*(1), 143-157. Available at http://dx.doi.org/10.1007/s11412-006-6840-8.

Zemel, A., & Çakir, M. P. (2009). Reading's work in VMT. In G. Stahl (Ed.), *Studying virtual math teams* (pp. 261-276). New York, NY: Springer. Available at http://dx.doi.org/10.1007/978-1-4419-0228-3_14.

Zhou, N., Zemel, A., & Stahl, G. (2008). *Questioning and responding in online small groups engaged in collaborative math problem solving.* Paper presented at the International Conference of the Learning Sciences (ICLS 2008), Utrecht, Netherlands. Available at http://GerryStahl.net/pub/icls2008nan.pdf.

8.   Temporality of the Joint Problem Space

Johann W. Sarmiento & Gerry Stahl

Our attempts at describing the processes involved in learning and knowledge-building activities depend on our ways of conceptualizing the context in which such activities take place. Here we trace the development of the concept of "problem space" from its inception within the information-processing perspective as a characterization of individual problem-solving activity. We review reformulations and extensions made to the concept within the Learning Sciences, and explore them as attempts to better describe small-group interactions in complex knowledge-building contexts. Using a detailed analysis of sustained, online collaborative problem-solving activity, we propose that a new aspect of the problem space needs to be carefully considered in order to fully account for these kinds of experiences: temporal and sequential orientation to inter-subjective meaning making.

Introduction

The challenge of identifying, describing and assessing the activities that typify the contexts in which learning and knowledge building take place lies at the core of all inquiry in the learning sciences. As Sfard (1998) has argued, even the metaphors that we use to characterize what learning is, work as lenses that focus our attention on particular aspects of learning interactions, while obscuring or ignoring others. Descriptions of features, resources and activities particular to each learning context serve as the building blocks for structuring inquiry about them and offering descriptions of their dynamics. In this paper we use the construct of the "joint problem space" and trace its development within the Learning Sciences as a way to present an expanding view of what is, or needs to be, considered relevant and significant in descriptions of learning and knowledge building activity.

In order to anchor our review of the evolution of the concept of "problem space," we will use data originating from groups participating in the Virtual Math Teams (VMT) project. The VMT project at the Math Forum (http://mathforum.org/vmt/) investigates the innovative use of online collaborative environments to support effective secondary mathematics learning in small groups. Central to the VMT research program are the investigation of the nature and dynamics of group cognition (Stahl, 2006a) as well as the design of effective technological supports for quasi-synchronous small-group interaction. In addition, we investigate the linkages between synchronous interactions (e.g., collaborative chat episodes) and distributed asynchronous interactions at the level of the online community. VMT is currently studying how upper middle school and high school students do mathematics collaboratively in an online environment that integrates electronic chat with a shared whiteboard and a series of support tools for referencing and annotating objects. Particular attention is given to the methods that students deploy to conduct their interactions in such an environment. Taken together, these methods define a culture, a shared set of ways to "make sense together." The methods are subtly responsive to the chat medium, the pedagogical setting, the social atmosphere and the intellectual resources that are available to the participants. These methods help define the nature of the collaborative experience for the small groups.

Joint problem spaces

Joint activity, the kind of activity that takes place when multiple participants engage with each other, offers a unique context for the investigation of human reasoning. Not only are the reasoning processes that characterize joint activity visibly distributed across multiple participants (e.g., Hutchins, 1995; Salomon, 1993), but they are also highly shaped by the way that material and conceptual artifacts are integrated into activity (e.g., Perkins, 1993; Schwartz, 1995) and the way that activity evolves over time (e.g., Brown & Campione, 1994; Lave & Wenger, 1991; Scardamalia & Bereiter, 1991). For instance, in Roschelle (1992) and Teasley & Roschelle (1993), the authors analyze dyads using a physics software simulation to explore concepts such as velocity and acceleration, and propose the notion of a *joint problem space* (JPS) to explain how collaborative activity gets structured in this context. This "knowledge structure" was presented as integrating: *goals, descriptions of the current problem state* and *awareness of available problem-solving actions.* The space was characterized as being "shared" in the sense that both members of the dyad oriented to its construction and maintenance.

At first glance, the concept of a *"joint problem space"* may appear strongly related to the original concept of *"problem space"* advanced within the information-processing perspective on human problem solving which originated in the collaborative work of Allan Newell and Herbert Simon. Newell and Simon (1972) concentrated on building a "process theory" describing the performance of individual "intelligent adults in our own culture," working on short and "moderately difficult problems of a symbolic nature," (p. 3) where "motivation is not a question and emotion is not aroused" (p. 53). To achieve this, they explicitly excluded group activity as well as "long-term integrated activities" involving multiple episodes of action over longer periods (p. 4). Central to their theory is the idea that to solve a task or problem, one must "adapt" to the environment presented by the problem (the *"task environment"*) by constructing an internal representation of the problem's relevant elements (a *"problem space"*). The concept of *problem space* was then introduced as a "neutral and objective way of talking about the responses of the subject, including his internal thinking responses, as he goes about dealing with the stimulus situation" (p.59). This space, mostly viewed as internal or mental but sometimes related to external resources as well (e.g., Kotovsky & Simon, 1990), is commonly presented as a graph with nodes and links. A person is assumed to understand a task correctly when she has successfully constructed a problem space representation containing or "encoding": a set of *states of knowledge* including the *initial state* of the problem, the *goal state* and the necessary intermediate states, as well as *operators* for changing from one state into another, *constraints* determining allowable states and moves, and any other encodings of knowledge such as problem-solving heuristics and the like (pp. 59 & 810). Problem solving proceeds as the subject works from the initial state in her mental space, purposefully creating and exploring possible solution paths, testing and evaluating the results obtained. This process is commonly characterized as "search" on the problem space and search, as an activity, becomes the central phenomena theorized. The level of detail offered about candidate search processes is, undoubtedly, one aspect in which this theory rivals other less specified proposals. For instance, search methods such as *breadth first, depth first, branch and bound, bidirectional, heuristic best first, hill climbing*, etc. have been offered as descriptions of the processes followed by human problem solvers in different contexts (Newell, 1980).

The characterization of the *joint problem space* advanced by Teasley and Roschelle (1993), despite superficial similarities, goes beyond simply being a collective reformulation of the information-processing concept of *problem space*. [This seminal paper straddled the cognitive and interactional perspectives, causing ideological barriers to publication (personal communication Roschelle to Koschmann at CSCL 02 and Teasley to Stahl at

GROUP 07).] From their perspective, social interaction in the context of problem-solving activity occurs *in relation to* a shared conception of the problem which is in itself *constituted through* the collaborative process of coordinating communication, action and representation in a particular context of activity; not restricted to or primarily driven by individual mental states. This perspective as well as the authors' method of analysis are closely related with the ethnomethodological position regarding the nature of shared agreements as *"various social methods for accomplishing the member's recognition that something was said-according-to-a-rule, and not the demonstrable matching of substantive matters."* From this perspective, a common understanding becomes a feature of an interaction (an operation, in Garfinkel's terms) *"rather than a common intersection of overlapping sets"* (Garfinkel, 1967, p.30), as "shared mental models" (Salas & Fiore, 2004) or "common ground" (Clark & Brennan, 1991) sometimes seem to portray. A "shared agreement" or a "mutual conception of the problem" is then the emergent and situated result of the participants' interactions tied to their context of activity. In the words of Roschelle and Teasley, it is *"the coordinated production of talk and action by two participants (that) enabled this construction and maintenance (of the joint problem space) to succeed."*

Beyond the sole identification of relevant resources, an effective account of the problem solving process requires a description of the fundamental activities involved. Roschelle (1992) presents the most compelling description of such activities associated with the joint problem space when he states that the process of the students' incremental achievement of convergent meaning through interaction can be characterized by the four primary features of activity synthesized in Figure 1.

---

a.   The production of a deep-featured situation, in relation to

b.   The interplay of physical metaphors, through the constructive use of

c.   Interactive cycles of conversational turn-taking, constrained by

d.   The application of progressively higher standards of evidence for convergence.

Figure 1. Primary features of the process of achieving convergent conceptual change. From (Roschelle, 1992)

Testing and expanding the proposed construct of the *joint problem space* requires, then, the ability to recognize these features in interaction. In order to do this and to support the next steps in our exploration of the construct of *problem space*, we would like to introduce here one particular problem situation used as part of the Virtual Math Teams (VMT) project mentioned earlier:

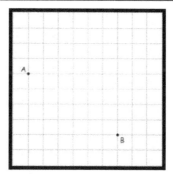

Figure 2. Grid-world task: Pretend you live in a world where you can only travel on the lines of the grid. You can't cut across a block on the diagonal, for instance Your group has gotten together to figure out the math of this place. For example, what is a math question you might ask that involves these two points?

One could argue that the task presented in Figure 2 does not properly specify a problem yet. The "problem" at hand is, in fact, to create a problem. Within the information-processing perspective, the foundational activities which contribute to the creation of a problem are, in fact, poorly understood. As a recent review of psychological research on problem solving stated, "problem-solving research has not revealed a great deal about the processes involved in problem recognition, problem definition, and problem representation (Pretz, Naples, & Sternberg, 2003, p. 9). It is only after a *problem space* has been constructed internally in the mind of a subject, at least partially, that one can start to trace the solution process as a *search process*. However, observing these early phases of problem solving can, indeed, inform us about how problem spaces are constituted in interaction and how some of the features of collaborative activity described by Roschelle contribute to this important phase. For instance, in our study of the ways that small online groups in VMT engaged with this task, we observed a number of activities that could help characterize certain aspects of these early phases of the creation of a problem space. The groups often identified and appropriated specific elements of the task, and purposefully and iteratively structured them into a problematic situation. Resources such as graphical manipulations (e.g., grid annotations), related mathematical concepts (e.g., straight distance), constraints (e.g., you can only travel on the lines of the grid) or analogous problems were used to construct and evolve a set of possible inquiries about this world. We can characterize these constructions as creating a *"deep-featured situation"* in the sense that they embody the sustained exploratory activities of the participants. As an example, many groups promptly oriented to finding the shortest distance between points A and B in the grid world, a familiar problem to school-aged students. Some purposefully attended to the constraints of the grid world while others simply ignored them and proceeded to explore diagonal distances. Building on this initial problem, many groups embarked on the problem of finding the number of shortest paths between any two points on the grid. Figure 3 contains some snapshots of the artifacts the different groups created to help constitute a problem from the original situation.

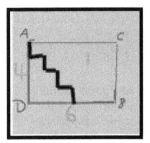 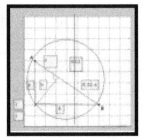 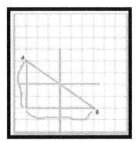

Figure 3. Snapshots of grid-world problem resources created by VMT groups.

In this particular situation, potential problems were constantly defined as sets of artifacts with specific properties (e.g., constraints) sometimes constituted as "discoverables." Multiple trajectories of reasoning were explored, sometimes in concerted fashion, others in parallel. A central aspect of the group's activity seemed to be concerned with "adding structure" to the resources used to think with. From an interactional perspective it certainly does not seem appropriate to characterize such activities as search, although, on the other hand, one could agree that a "space" or network of problem objects and relations was being constructed and that specific features of the resources available were being attended to. Metaphors played a role in some instances but perspectives, or points of view, seemed more interactionally relevant. In this context, the groups did not necessarily orient to the application of "progressively higher standards of evidence for convergence" but, within those teams that seemed more intensively engaged with the grid world as an expansive situation to think with, they seemed to orient strongly to the continuity and sustainability of their inquiry. Overall, these collective problem-solving activities appear to be much more interactive than what the original concept of search in a mental problem space may have suggested (as Kirsh (forthcoming) has eloquently argued for individual problem solving as well). Next, we continue to trace the evolution of the concept of problem space within the Learning Sciences and explore its role in defining the relevant elements that characterize engagement with problem-solving and knowledge-building activity in different contexts.

A dual-space model of collaboration: Content and relational spaces

Barron (2000; 2003) investigated triads of 6th grade students engaged in collaborative mathematical problem solving. Her analysis proposed that it was necessary to differentiate between the *social* and *cognitive* aspects of the interactions observed and investigate the ways in which both are interwoven in the establishment of a joint problem-solving space, especially, when attempting to characterize successful and unsuccessful collaborations. Both cognitive and social aspects are, in a sense, integrated in the features of collaborative activity described by Roschelle (1992) and reproduced in Figure 1. However, Barron's analysis illuminates a new set of specific activities that the participants engaged in when explicitly orienting to this duality, attending to social and cognitive factors in the development and maintenance of a "between-person state of engagement" (p. 349) which resembles the joint conception of the problem proposed by Teasley and Roschelle. Interestingly, patterns of interaction related to a group's inability to attend to common aspects of the problem or to coordinate their reciprocal participation while solving the problem were particularly salient in groups that failed to achieve and maintain "mutual engagement" and, as a result, were unable to capitalize on the ideas and proposals of the group members (p. 311). As a result, Barron proposes a *dual-space model* of collaboration integrating a *content space* pertaining to the problem being solved and a *relational space* pertaining to the ways that participants relate to each other. Naturally, these two spaces are not separate entities but essentially mutually constitutive of each other. Participants simultaneously "attend to and develop" such spaces.

Similar proposals have been made, for instance, in the field of Small Group Research since Robert Bales (1953) first proposed his principle of "equilibrium," which states that a group continuously divides its attention between *instrumental* (task-related) needs and *expressive* (socio-emotional) concerns. More recently, McGrath (1991) suggested in his "Time, Interaction, and Performance" theory that work groups orient towards three "inseparably intertwined" functions: working on the common task together (*production function*), maintaining the communication and interaction among group members (*group well-being* function), and helping the individual member when necessary (*member support function*, p. 151). Poole, also suggested that group decision-making discussions can be characterized by three intertwining "tracks" of activity and interaction: *task progress, relational track*, and *topical focus*. The *task track* concerns the process by which the group accomplishes its goals, such as doing problem analysis, designing solutions, etc. The *relation track* deals with the interpersonal relationships between the group members (e.g., sharing personal information or engaging in social joking). The *topic* track includes a series of issues or concerns the group has over time. Interspersed within these tracks are *breakpoints*, marking changes in the development of strands of work.

The power of these proposals to advance our understanding of group activity lies, however, not in their ability to appropriately name dimensions of interaction or group functions but in their ability to characterize and describe the activities that groups engage in. Consequently, the value of Barron's proposal, in our opinion, lies on her careful way of calling our attention to the interactional methods employed by the students to orient to and constitute the "responsivity" and "connectedness" (p. 353) of their content and relational spaces. In her descriptions, we see participants' degrees of competence in attending and relating to their own "epistemic process" while "tracking and evaluating others' epistemic processes" (p. 310). Similar descriptions have been provided by Engle and Conant as "positioning" (Engle, 2006; Engle & Conant, 2002). In order to expand these concepts, next we extend the type of group phenomena studied from collaborative interactions to longitudinal sequences of joint activity and attempt to inquire about ways in which the concepts of "joint problem space" and "dual problem space" are sufficient to understand them.

Continuity of joint problem spaces in virtual math teams

Undoubtedly, the difficulty of constructing and maintaining a "cognitive" and "social" joint problem space—the intersubjective space of interaction emerging from the active engagement of collectivities in problem solving— represents the central challenge of effective collaborative knowledge building and learning. In fact, several studies have shown that what determines the success of the collaborative learning experience is the interactional manner in which this intersubjective problem space is created and used (Barron, 2003; Dillenbourg *et al.*, 1995; Hausmann, Chi, & Roy, 2004; Koschmann *et al.*, 2005; Wegerif, 2006). Furthermore, the complexity of the challenge of maintaining a joint problem space rises when, as in many naturalistic settings, joint activity is dispersed over time (e.g. multiple episodes of joint activity, long-term projects, etc.) and distributed across multiple collectivities (e.g. multiple teams, task forces, communities, etc.). As a result of these gaps, sustained collaborative learning in small virtual groups and online communities of learners might require that co-participants "bridge" multiple elements of their interactions continuously as they interact over time. Motivated by the need to understand such activities, we set out to investigate the challenges associated with such discontinuities of interaction over time.

Within the Virtual Math Team online community, participating teams might engage in multiple, collaborative sessions over time, they might work on several related tasks over time and learn about the work of other teams. To explore whether VMT teams employ specific methods oriented towards overcoming the discontinuities of time, tasks and participation, during the Spring of 2005 we conducted a pilot case study of five Virtual Math Teams. These virtual teams were each formed with about four non-collocated upper middle-school and high-school students selected by volunteer teachers at different schools across the United States. The teams engaged in synchronous online math interactions for four hour-long sessions over a two-week period. They used the ConcertChat virtual room environment (Wessner *et al.*, 2006), which integrates a chat interface with a shared whiteboard. A new virtual room was provided for each of the sessions, so that participants did not have direct access to the records of their prior interactions. In the first session, the teams were given a brief description of the grid-world presented in Figure 2, where one could only move along the lines of a grid. The students were asked to generate and pursue their own questions about this mathematical world. In subsequent sessions, the teams were given feedback on their work as well as on the work of other teams, and were encouraged to continue their collaboration. Because of the sequential framing of the tasks provided and the continuous relevance of the properties of the grid world, we considered this a propitious setting for the investigation of members' methods related to continuity of knowledge building. We examined each of the 18 sessions recorded, paying special attention to the sequential unfolding of the four problem-solving episodes in which each team participated, to the ways that prior activities were used as resources for later team work, and also to the ways that changes in team membership triggered issues of continuity.

As a result of our analysis, we identified a number of instances where the teams were engaged in several types of "*bridging activity*" aimed at overcoming discontinuities emerging over the multiple episodes of interaction. All teams, although in different levels of intensity, engaged in this type of activity over time. In summary, the instances of bridging identified involved methods related to narrating or reporting past doings as resources for constructing a new task, remembering collectively, and managing the history of the team, among others. Constant comparison through different instances of bridging activity in the entire dataset led to our initial characterization of the structural elements that define these activities and their interactional relevance. Our analysis of the dynamics of bridging activity echoes the construction and maintenance of a "*joint problem space*" (Teasley & Roschelle, 1993) and also agrees with the proposal that such a space integrates *"content"* and *"relational"* dimensions (Barron, 2003). However, throughout our analysis of all instances of bridging activity, we noticed that a third element of interaction reoccurred as a resource and a relevant concern of the participants: The temporal and sequential unfolding of activity (see Figure 4). To illustrate this, let's turn to an actual instance of bridging activity. The conversation reproduced in Figure 5 illustrates how a team oriented to past team activity as resources for framing a current problem-solving task.

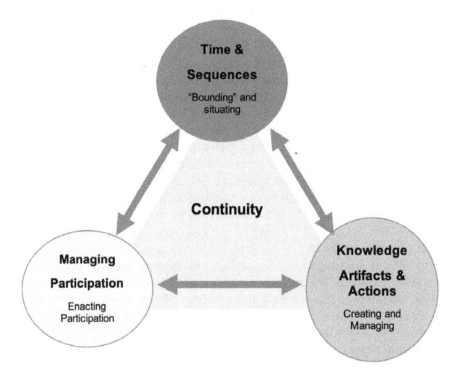

Figure 4. Three dimensions of interaction and their relationship in bridging work

```
144 mathis: letz start working on number 8
145 bob1:   we already did that yesterday
146 qw:     we did?
147 mathis: but we did it so that there was only right
and down
148 bob1:   i mean tuesday
149 mathis: i guess we will do it with left and up?
150 qw:     It would be almost the same.
151 bob1:   it's (|x2-x1|+|y2-y1|-2) choose (|x2-x1|-1)
152 bob1:   try it if you like
153 mathis: nah
154 mathis: if you are so sure...
155 bob1:   i'm not
156 bob1:   actually
157 bob1:   take out the -2 and the -1
158 mathis: then letz check it
```

Figure 5. Chat excerpt of a bridging episode. Spring 2005, Team B, Session two

The first of the three basic interactional dimensions that seem to be at play in bridging activity corresponds to the creation, referencing, manipulation, assessment and re-use of a set of *knowledge artifacts*. This involves constituting the problem-at-hand, identifying which resources are relevant to it, creating tasks, constituting aspects of the problem situation and its resources as known or unknown, among other activities Despite the brevity of the interaction captured in Figure 5, we can recognize some of these artifacts (e.g., problem number 8, "only right and down", "left and up", $(|x2-x1|+|y2-y1|-2)$ choose $(|x2-x1|-1)$, etc.). We can get a glimpse of ways in which they are attended to and manipulated (e.g., "only right and down" is debated as being almost the same as "left and up", the formula provided is offered for assessment, etc.).

Interwoven with the development and use of knowledge artifacts, we also identified the active management of participation as a second relevant dimension at play in this case of bridging activity. From this perspective, teams were actively oriented towards, for instance, who was and was not involved in an activity, who could or should speak about a particular matter and how, which activities (e.g. assessing and responding to assessments) were allocated to participants, etc. In essence, the participants orient to the development in interaction of specific participation frameworks (Goffman, 1981) which "position" team members in relation to each other, the resources at hand and the activities they are engaged in. This positioning activity, for example, situated participants as problem-solving peers, experts, explainers, etc. In addition, the activities they engage in over time position them with different types of access, rights and duties with respect to relevant knowledge artifacts. The excerpt in Figure 5 illustrates this, especially toward the end of this passage, when Bob1 attempts to position Mathis as someone who could do the checking of his solution formula. After Mathis declines and Bob1 states his lack of confidence in the correctness of the formula a new participation framework gets enacted, in which the group together can engage in the work necessary to check and possibly correct the solution provided for this problem.

The first two dimensions of interaction observed matched, very closely, the "content" and "relational" spaces theorized by Barron. However, a recurring third element present in episodes of bridging activity captured our attention both because of its centrality in the interactions analyzed as well as its novelty within the theoretical frameworks considered: the temporal or sequential organization of experience. Temporality and sequentiality are constructs that are often taken for granted and which have only recently recovered their centrality in analyses of joint activity (e.g., Arrow *et al.*, 2004; Lemke, 2001; Reimann, 2007; Sawyer, 2003, Stahl, 2006b). Our analysis suggests, however, that in the types of interactions that we observed, participants orient to time and sequences as central resources for the organization of their collaborative activity. As can be seen in Figure 5, VMT participants visibly oriented to what was done in a different episode of activity or at a different time, to the relationship between what was done before and what is being done now, or to what possible actions might be available at a particular moment as related to what had been achieved so far.

The excerpt reproduced in Figure 6, illustrates a case in which a team is collectively engaged in trying to reconstruct parts of their previous session while initiating their current problem-solving activity. Remembering of past activity unfolds as a collective engagement in which different team members participate dynamically. Some of the current team members were not present in the previous session and yet, they are instrumental in the reconstruction of that past and in shaping its current relevance. This was the fourth session of team E. Towards the beginning of the session (8:22:09 PM) the facilitator (MFMod) suggested in the chat that during the summer the team members could work with their friends on a new problem he posted: the "circle problem."

Later, he added that they could pursue the circle question in "this chat" if they wanted or "any other questions and worlds" that they thought of. Following about a minute of silence, the facilitator posted a message in which he reported how in the previous session the team had "worked on finding a formula for the number of shortest paths between any two points A and B on the grid (...) explored multiple possibilities and figured out that x+y and x^2+y^2 work (where x and y correspond to the # of units you need to travel along x and y axis to get from A to B) but only for some points, not all". Then he suggested that they could continue "exploring more cases" and see if they could find "a general formula," work on the circle problem he had posted earlier, or on any other problem from the "original questions" presented at the beginning of their VMT experience. The team then oriented towards finding a task for themselves, and the following interaction took place:

```
119 8:27:42  drago:     ok

120 8:30:11  gdo: where did u guys last leave off (To
119)

121 8:31:20  MFmod:     I think that the above section I
wrote is where the group last was (To 114)

122 8:31:36  MFmod:     yes?

123 8:31:42  drago:     well

124 8:31:48  gdo: i dont remember that

125 8:31:51  drago:     actually, my internet connection
broke on Tuesday

126 8:31:56  drago:     so I wasn't here

127 8:32:12  MFmod:     so maybe that is not the best
place to pick up

128 8:32:14  estric:    i wasnt able to be here on
tuesday either

129 8:32:50  gdo: how bout u meets

130 8:33:01  meets:     uh...

131 8:33:11  meets:     where'd we meet off....

132 8:33:16  meets:     i remember

133 8:33:22  gdo: i was in ur group

134 8:33:24  meets:     that we were trying to look for a
pattern

135 8:33:27  gdo: but i didn't quite understand it
```

```
136 8:33:34  gdo: can u explain it to us again meets

137 8:33:38  meets:    with the square, the 2by 2
square, and the 3by2 rectangle

138 8:33:42  meets:    sure...

139 8:33:45  meets:    so basically...

140 8:33:45  gdo: o yea

141 8:33:49  gdo: i sort of remember

142 8:33:55  meets:    we want a formula for the
distance between poitns A and B

143 8:34:02  drago:    yes...

144 8:34:05  meets:    ill amke the points

(meets draws two points on the existing grid on the
shared whiteboard)

145 8:34:09  MFmod:    since some folks don't remember
and weren't here why don't you pick up with this idea and
work on it a bit

(meets labels the two points on the grid A and B)

146 8:34:55  meets:    okay

147 8:34:59  meets:    so there are those poitns A and B

148 8:35:08  meets:    (that's a 3by2 rectangle

 149 8:35:28  meets:   we first had a unit square

(meets draws the lines of a 3 by 2 rectangle with points
A and B in its opposing corners)

150 8:35:44  meets:    and we know that there are only 2
possible paths......
```

Figure 6. Chat excerpt of a bridging episode. Spring 2005, Session Four, Team E

This sequence involves a number of interesting interactional features. In particular, a set of temporal and sequential markers (e.g., Tuesday, last, again) and the mixing of different verb tenses are used to index prior events and constitute a present task. In the facilitator's feedback, the declarative assertions constructed with past-tense verbs (e.g., "you worked on finding a formula", "you explored multiple possibilities", "you figured out that x+y and x^2+y^2 work", etc.) were followed by future-oriented suggestions: "you may want to continue exploring more cases and see if you can find a general formula", "you can work on the problem I posted earlier", etc. The uptake by the team of the task assessments and proposals made by the facilitator also involved similar resources. Gdo's request in line 120 for a report of where the group "last" left off seems to use a communicative marker that allows parties in conversation to segment or index specific portions of experiences and relate them in ways that allows them to form sequences of participation and activity. Gdo is orienting the group back to a specific aspect of "last Tuesday," and after Drago and Estric both positioned themselves as not having participated in last Tuesday's session, Meets is then asked directly in lines 129 and 136 to reproduce a past ("again") explanation for the rest ("us").

One of the things that is remarkable about the way this interaction unfolds is the fact that although it might appear as if it was Meets who individually remembered what they were doing last time, the activity of remembering unfolds as a collective engagement in which different team members participate. This is accomplished by marking and using time as a central resource to organize participation and to advance their current problem solving. To organize their present activity, they reproduce a sequence of previously constructed cases (the square, the 2x2 square, and the 3x2 rectangle) and link them to knowledge artifacts and the related knowledge of the group (e.g., stating in line 150 that for the unit square "we know that there are only 2 possible paths"). In fact, later in this interaction there is a point where Meets remembers the fact that they had discovered that there are six different shortest paths between the corners of a 2x2 grid but he reports that he can only "see" four at the moment. Drago, who did not participate in the original work leading to that finding, is able to see the six paths and proceeds to invent a method of labeling each point of the grid with a letter so that he can name each path and help others see it (e.g., "from B to D there is BAD, BCD ..."). After this, Meets was able to see again why it is that there are six paths in that small grid and together with Drago, they proceeded to investigate, in parallel, the cases of a 3x3 and a 4x4 grid using the method just created.

All of these resources—the knowledge artifacts used and referenced, the sequential organization of cases, and the temporal markers of prior activity— are positioned in different ways with relation to the participants in a *temporal or sequential space*. The concept of "deictic field" developed by Hanks (2005) seems especially useful to define the relationship between this new "space" and the existing *content* and *relational* spaces. Hanks describes the deictic field as composed first by *"the positions of communicative agents relative to the participant frameworks they occupy,"* for example, who occupies the positions of speaker and addressee as well as other relevant positions.

Second, the deictic field integrates *"the positions occupied by objects of reference,"* and finally *"the multiple dimensions whereby the former have access to the latter"* (p. 193). From this perspective, participants constitute, through interaction, the relevant relative dimensions whereby they are to manage the positioning of agents and relevant objects of reference. In our analysis, we have confirmed that the *content* and *relational* dimensions are, in fact, relevant to collaborative problem-solving teams.

However, in expanding the range of phenomena analyzed to longitudinal interactions, we have also uncovered time and the sequential unfolding of interaction as a third relevant and important dimension of activity. In the excerpt reproduced in Figure 6, the interactional field is being constituted by the participants to include problem-related objects and communicative agents associated with a prior interaction, and in doing so they position themselves and those resources within specific participation frameworks.

Our central claim is that this third dimension is essential to understanding collaborative interactions of this type. This dimension is essentially interwoven with the content and relational dimensions of the joint problem space. Such interdependency can be seen as characterizing the longitudinal knowledge building of activity systems like the Virtual Math Teams.

Conclusions

The theory of group cognition (Stahl, 2006a) takes as one of its central principles the dialectical relationship between social interaction and the construction of meaning. From this perspective, the organization of action and the knowledge embedded in such action is an emergent property of moment-by-moment interactions among actors, and between actors and the activity system in which they participate collectively. The *content* space and the *relational* space, in Barron's terms, are mutually constitutive from this perspective. *Group Cognition* offers a candidate description for how the dynamic process of building knowledge might intertwine the content and relational spaces: "Small groups are the engines of knowledge building. The knowing that groups build up in manifold forms is what becomes internalized by their members as individual learning and externalized in their communities as certifiable knowledge." (Stahl, 2006a, p. 16). Time and the sequential organization of activity might be a resource and an aspect of interaction that plays a significant role in how groups and individual achieve this.

In our analysis of how groups "sustain" their group cognition while engaged in brief episodes of online mathematical problem solving, we alluded to two ways in which time might be an important element of individual episodes of problem-solving activity (Stahl, 2006b). On the one hand, the collaborative activity involved in solving a problem can be "spread across" hundreds of micro-level interactions. On the other hand, individuals might internalize the meaning co-constructed through interactions and "sustain" the group cognition by engaging in later individual or group work. In either case, groups are described as sustaining their social and intellectual work by "building longer sequences of math proposals, other adjacency pairs and a variety of interaction methods."

The analysis presented here of interactions that bridge gaps across sessions confirms and extends these findings by suggesting that in longitudinal interactions, temporal and sequential resources are central to constituting activity as continuous by constructing and maintaining a joint problem space. Interaction is taken here in the full sense that ethnomethodologists give it, as the "ongoing, contingent co-production of a shared social/material world," and which, as Suchman argues "cannot be stipulated in advance, but requires an autobiography, a presence, and a projected future" (Suchman, 2003). At the moment, our characterization only provides a tentative framework to organize our developing understanding of collaborative learning and knowledge building over time. We have just began the work of describing in more detail the interactional methods that allow teams to construct and manage this expanded problem "field" (e.g., Sarmiento & Stahl, 2007; Stahl, 2006b; Stahl *et al.*, 2006) by interweaving *content*, *relational* and *temporal* aspects of interaction.

References

Arrow, H., Poole, M. S., Henry, K. B., Wheelan, S., & Moreland, R. (2004). Time, change, and development: The temporal perspective on groups *Small Group Research, 35* (1), 73-105.

Bales, R. F. (1953). The equilibrium problem in small groups. In T. Parsons, R. F. Bales & E. A. Shils (Eds.), *Working papers in the theory of action* (pp. 111-161): Free Press.

Barron, B. (2000). Achieving coordination in collaborative problem-solving groups. *Journal of The Learning Sciences, 9* (4), 403-436.

Barron, B. (2003). When smart groups fail. *Journal Of The Learning Sciences, 12* (3), 307-359.

Brown, A., & Campione, J. (1994). Guided discovery in a community of learners. In K. McGilly (Ed.), *Classroom lessons: Integrating cognitive theory and classroom practice* (pp. 229-270). Cambridge, MA: MIT Press.

Dillenbourg, P., Baker, M., Blaye, A., & O'Malley, C. (1995). The evolution of research on collaborative learning. In P. Reimann & H. Spada (Eds.), *Learning in humans and machines: Towards an interdisciplinary learning science* (pp. 189-211). Oxford, UK: Elsevier.

Engle, R. A. (2006). Framing interactions to foster generative learning: A situative explanation of transfer in a community of learners classroom. *Journal of the Learning Sciences, 15* (4), 451-498.

Engle, R. A., & Conant, F. R. (2002). Guiding principles for fostering productive disciplinary engagement: Explaining an emergent argument in a community of learners classroom. *Cognition and Instruction, 20* (4), 399-483.

Garfinkel, H. (1967). *Studies in ethnomethodology.* Englewood Cliffs, NJ: Prentice-Hall.

Goffman, E. (1981). *Forms of talk.* Philadelphia: University of Pennsylvania Press.

Hausmann, R., Chi, M., & Roy, M. (2004). *Learning from collaborative problem solving: An analysis of three hypothesized mechanisms.* Paper presented at the 26nd annual conference of the Cognitive Science society.

Hutchins, E. (1995). *Cognition in the wild.* Cambridge, MA: MIT Press.

Kirsch, D. (forthcoming). Problem solving and situated cognition. In P. Robbins & M. Aydede (Eds.), *Cambridge handbook of situated cognition.* Cambridge: Cambridge University Press.

Koschmann, T., Zemel, A., Conlee-Stevens, M., Young, N., Robbs, J., & Barnhart, A. (2005). How do people learn? In F. H. R. Bromme & H. Spada (Eds.), *Barriers and biases in computer-mediated knowledge communication.* Kluwer .

Kotovsky, K., & Simon, H. A. (1990). Why are some problems really hard: Explorations in the problem space of difficulty. *Cognitive Psychology, 22,* 143-183.

Lave, J., & Wenger, E. (1991). *Situated learning: Legitimate peripheral participation.* Cambridge, UK: Cambridge Univ. Press.

Lemke, J. L. (2001). The long and the short of it: Comments on multiple timescale studies of human activity. *Journal Of The Learning Sciences, 10* (1-2), 17-26.

McGrath, J. E. (1991). Time, interaction, and performance (tip): A theory of groups. *Small Group Research, 22* (2), 147-174.

Newell, A. (1980). Reasoning, problem solving and decision processes: The problem space as a fundamental category. In R. Nickerson (Ed.), *Attention and performance viii.* Hillsdale, NJ: : Erlbaum.

Newell, A., & Simon, H. A. (1972). *Human problem solving.* Englewood Cliffs, NJ: Prentice-Hall.

Perkins, D. N. (1993). Person-plus: A distributed view of thinking and learning. In G. Salomon (Ed.), *Distributed cognitions: Psychological and educational considerations* (pp. 88-110). Cambridge, UK: Cambridge University Press.

Pretz, J. E., Naples, A. J., & Sternberg, R. J. (2003). Recognizing, defining, and representing problems. In J. E. D. a. R. J. Sternberg (Ed.), *The psychology of problem solving* (pp. 3-30). Cambridge, UK: Cambridge University Press.

Reimann, P. (2007). Time is precious: Why process analysis is essential for CSCL, *International Conference on Computer-supported Collaborative Learning 2007.* New Brunswick, NJ.

Roschelle, J. (1992). Learning by collaborating: Convergent conceptual change. *Journal of the Learning Sciences, 2* (3), 235-276.

Salas, E., & Fiore, S. M. (Eds.). (2004). *Team cognition: Understanding the factors that drive process and performance.* Washington, DC: American Psychological Association.

Salomon, G. (1993). *Distributed cognition.* Cambridge, UK: Cambridge University Press.

Sarmiento, J., & Stahl, G. (2007). Group creativity in virtual math teams: Interactional mechanisms for referencing, remembering and bridging, *Creativity & Cognition 2007* (pp. 37-44). Washington, DC: ACM Press.

Sawyer, R. K. (2003). *Group creativity: Music, theater, collaboration.* Mahwah, NJ: Lawrence Erlbaum.

Scardamalia, M., & Bereiter, C. (1991). Higher levels of agency in knowledge building: A challenge for the design of new knowledge media. *Journal of the Learning Sciences, 1,* 37-68.

Schwartz, D. L. (1995). The emergence of abstract representations in dyad problem solving. *Journal Of The Learning Sciences, 4* (3), 321-354.

Sfard, A. (1998). On two metaphors for learning and the dangers of choosing just one. *Educational Researcher, 27* (2), 4-13.

Stahl, G. (2006a). *Group cognition: Computer support for building collaborative knowledge.* Cambridge, MA: MIT Press.

Stahl, G. (2006b). Sustaining group cognition in a math chat environment. *Research and Practice in Technology Enhanced Learning, 1* (2), 85-.

Stahl, G., Zemel, A., Sarmiento, J., Cakir, M., Weimar, S., Wessner, M., et al. (2006). *Shared referencing of mathematical objects in online chat.* Paper presented at the International Conference of the Learning Sciences (ICLS 2006).

Teasley, S. D., & Roschelle, J. (1993). Constructing a joint problem space: The computer as a tool for sharing knowledge. In S. P. Lajoie & S. J. Derry (Eds.), *Computers as cognitive tools* (pp. 229-258). Mahwah, NJ: Lawrence Erlbaum.

Wegerif, R. (2006). A dialogic understanding of the relationship between CSCL and teaching thinking skills. *International Journal of Computer-Supported Collaborative Learning (ijCSCL), 1* (1), 143-157.

Wessner, M., Shumar, W., Stahl, G., Sarmiento, J., Muhlpfordt, M., & Weimar, S. (2006). *Designing an online service for a math community.* Paper presented at the International Conference of the Learning Sciences (ICLS 2006).

9.   Designing Problems to Support Knowledge Building

Gerry Stahl, Juan Dee Wee, Chee-Kit Looi

The Virtual Math Teams (VMT) knowledge-building environment has been used in Singapore and in the United States. It includes support for synchronous, quasi-synchronous and asynchronous online interaction using text chat, whiteboard drawing and wiki summarization. It has been used for groups of students to collaborate on challenge problems in mathematics, on sequences of math curriculum and on whole courses. In this paper, we discuss the design of topics and activities to encourage innovative knowledge building by individuals, small groups and whole classes.

Introduction

The idea of providing computer support for students in school classrooms to build knowledge collaboratively by developing textual knowledge artifacts—much as research communities do with their conference and journal papers—was first proposed by Scardamalia & Bereiter (1994) in connection with their CSILE software. Subsequent analyses of knowledge building in classrooms often focus on the use of CSILE or its successor, Knowledge Forum (Scardamalia & Bereiter, 2006). However, these are asynchronous discussion forums. We have found that discourse among students can be more engaging in synchronous text chat, given the proper context. In particular, the Virtual Math Teams (VMT) environment has been designed to foster collaborative knowledge building by supporting chat in small groups of students. In this paper, we look at how the VMT system has evolved through a design-based research effort to promote knowledge-building discourse among math students.

Many countries have recently made commitments to re-orienting their educational systems more strongly toward the development of creative thinking and deep understanding. Educators and researchers in places like Singapore and Hong Kong—as well as Finland and Canada—have turned to computer-supported approaches using Knowledge Forum and similar software to achieve this transformation. In this paper, we primarily report on trials using VMT in Singapore. Near the end of the paper, we briefly describe some trials with VMT in the USA that suggest ways to move even further toward a pedagogy of creativity, deep learning, collaborative knowledge building and group cognition.

Evolution of the VMT environment

Starting in 2003 from a simple text chat system, the VMT environment has grown to incorporate a shared whiteboard and even a wiki, with many features to support math problem-solving, social networking and communication. The system has been used by students during a number of events organized by researchers at the Math Forum in Philadelphia. Over a thousand student-hours of chat logs have been recorded. During the past year, VMT has started to be used by researchers elsewhere, including in Singapore. The VMT service has been developed to meet the needs of students engaged in collaborative online math problem solving, as well as those of researchers interested in studying such activities.

Figure 1 shows the VMT chat room. The math problem is posted on the shared whiteboard by the teacher or otherwise via the "Workspace" tab. The "Summary" tab functions as an alternative location for students to post their work or summarize the discussion. Content information pertaining to the problem is made available under the "Topic" tab. The "Wiki" tab allows the group to post information that is found to be useful after the discourse. The "Help" tab accesses the VMT user guide.

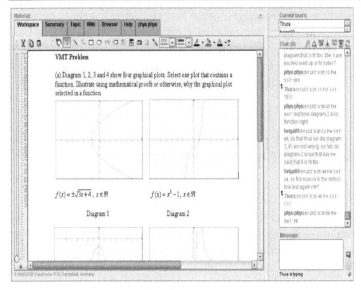

Figure 1: VMT chat room.

Use of VMT in a Singapore junior college

H2 mathematics - VMT curriculum framework

The Singapore Ministry of Education revamped the 'A' level curriculum for 2006 to one (H2 mathematics) that places more emphasis on thinking and communicating (MOE, 2005). The mathematics syllabus had a 10-15% reduction in curriculum content, giving students increased opportunity to reflect and explore problems critically. Stein & Henningsen (1997) argued that it is important for a classroom environment to engage students actively in deep conceptual mathematical activity, to develop their ability in mathematical reasoning. The VMT online environment complements the Ministry's new initiative. It serves as a useful platform for exploration of mathematical ideas, creating opportunities for students to construct and manipulate representations in order to promote their mathematical conceptual understanding (Alagic, 2003). Research studies have shown that collaborative learning is effective in improving academic skills compared to individual study of mathematics (Reglin, 1990; Yetter et al., 2006). The teaching of H2 mathematics supported by the VMT environment allows students to construct mathematical knowledge collaboratively in situations where they are not co-located.

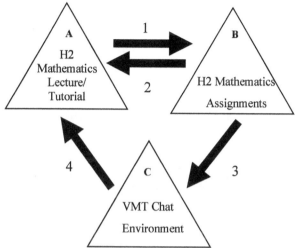

Figure 2: H2 mathematics - VMT curriculum framework.

Figure 2 presents an overview of the H2 Mathematics - VMT Curriculum Framework. Triangle A represents the tutorial/lecture where students learn new mathematics concepts. During tutorials, teachers review mathematical concepts covered in the lectures. Arrow 1 shows students applying the knowledge learned from the lectures/tutorials to solve problems in the assignment. Triangle B represents students applying the learned concepts to solve math problems in assignments. Arrow 2 shows students clarifying doubts with the teacher pertaining to the assignments. Triangle C represents students collaboratively solving math problems using VMT chat. Students form groups to solve mathematical problems similar to those found in the assignment (arrow 3). A focus group session is conducted by the teacher to review the problem-solving process, reinforcing concepts taught earlier (arrow 4) in tutorial sessions. The teacher, through the focus group session is also able to clarify misconceptions or emphasize learning points from the VMT chat in subsequent lectures.

Implementation of VMT trials

A total of 15 teams (45 JC 1 students) from Jurong Junior College participated in the first VMT trials in 2006. Prior to the VMT trials, the students attended training sessions at the college's computer laboratory. The training sessions provided the students with knowledge to navigate around the VMT environment, type mathematical symbols on the shared whiteboard and explore the functionality of VMT. It was the first time that the students had the opportunity to collaborate to solve math problems online. They were told that working in small groups was an experience of team effort to solve the problem and that it would be especially challenging at the beginning. The teacher implemented chat room rules to ensure cooperation and order among team members. The rules included: ensuring that all members were present before commencing the math problem solving; reading up adequately on the topic before logging onto VMT; understanding that quality of participation depends on cooperation among group members; giving fellow team members time to read the question; showing consideration to fellow team members.

Arithmetic and geometric series problems based on traditional problem designs were posted on the shared whiteboard by the teacher. Here is one such problem:

Find an expression for the nth term of the series:

$2 + 22 + 222 + 2222 + \dots.$

and deduce that the sum of the first n terms of the series is:

$$\frac{20}{81}(10^n - 1) - \frac{2n}{9}$$

Students are expected to carefully analyze the series $2 + 22 + 222 + 2222 + \dots.$ and to use their prior experience in problem solving or formulas to derive the nth term of the series. After that, they are to deduce the expression $\frac{20}{81}(10^n - 1) - \frac{2n}{9}$ using the expressions developed in the earlier part. Students accessed VMT from home to solve the problems. Following the VMT sessions, the teacher conducted interviews with participants to review the problem-solving process in VMT.

In 2007, seven new teams (21 JC 1 students) from the same college participated in the second VMT trials using different problem designs. The next section will describe in detail the different types of problem designs implemented in VMT. Prior to the VMT trials, the students attended training sessions at the college's computer laboratory and explored the VMT chat environment through a *Learner-Centered Project Work* assignment. Students in groups consisting of four to five students took turns to act as facilitators to conduct chat meetings, building knowledge from previous chat sessions. The students then worked in groups of three to solve an open-ended math function problem (see figure 3). The students had the opportunity to use the whiteboard tools to construct graphical plots and state their agreed-upon solutions in the summary page (figure 4).

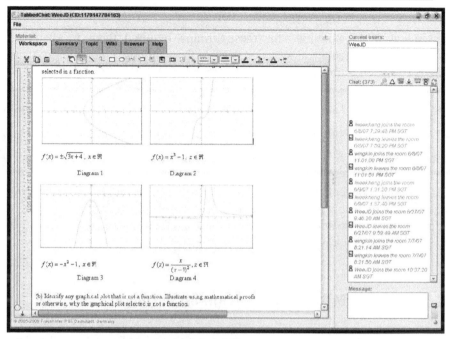

Figure 3: VMT math problem: functions

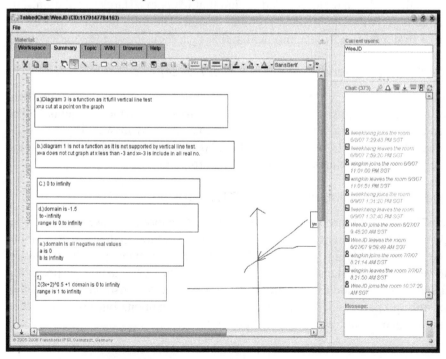

Figure 4: Student solution.

Subsequent VMT activities for these groups required them to focus on discussion of mathematical situations rather than solving a specific problem. Here is one such problem:

The functions f and g are defined $f : x \rightarrow 4x^2 + 3$, $x > 0$ and, $g : x \rightarrow 3 + e^{-2x}$. With the aid of the graph $y = f(x)$, explain why f is a 1-1 function. Find (i) $f^{-1}(x)$ (ii) $f^{-1}g(x)$, giving the domain of each function.

Mathematical concepts were explored and developed as the groups interacted, helping students to obtain a deeper conceptual understanding of the structure of the mathematical situations (problem), rather than focusing on the manipulation of symbols and equations in a routine manner.

VMT problem design in Singapore

Three different designs were used to construct these VMT problems. The first type is the traditional close-ended design that leads to a standard solution. The second type is the open-ended problem design. The third design explores the use of strategies to solve the problem, rather than focusing on the solution itself.

Traditional close-ended problem (TCEP) design

Initial versions of VMT problems used traditional closed-ended problem design. Such designs were adopted from textbooks in which students had to read a given problem, and the solution led to a standard answer. The reasoning process for solving H2 mathematics TCEP designs is minimal compared to the manipulation procedures used to solve the problems.

Traditional open-ended problem (TOEP) design

Subsequent VMT problems were designed to explore the use of traditional open-ended problems to encourage students to reason mathematically about their problem-solving steps. TOEP designs lead to many possible answers. However, such designs are often perceived as not very useful in preparing students for tests and examinations. There is a need to construct problems that not only prepare students academically for examinations but also strengthen their mathematical reasoning in the process.

Polya's problem-solving strategy design

The latest VMT problem was constructed using a hybrid design which combined the merits of both TCEP and TOEP designs. The problem is first constructed using a TCEP design. Solving the problem requires the first two stages of Polya's four stage problem-solving model (Polya, 1952): (1) understanding the problem and (2) devising a plan to solve the problem. Part of the problem-solving process requires students to justify their approaches taken to solve the problem, thus developing their mathematical reasoning. Students collaboratively explore mathematical concepts taught in class and reason about the feasibility of using them to solve hybrid design type problems.

Outcomes of VMT trials in Singapore

Each VMT problem-solving session lasted an average of 2-3 hours. When solving TCEP designs, most groups were able to solve the initial parts of the problem. However, there were often "breaks" in the problem-solving process where one student obtained the answer and shared it with the rest of the group, but did not appropriately show the problem-solving process on the shared whiteboard. Group members acknowledged with a "yes" to indicate understanding, but there was no explicit evidence to demonstrate this understanding.

Students explored different approaches in TOEP designs. There were situations (in the case of the VMT function problems) when curves were wrongly selected from the start, leading to both unproductive and productive discourse. Although the curve selected was wrong and the students did not obtain any of the possible correct solutions, the group applied appropriate mathematical concepts to justify their work, leading to productive knowledge construction.

In the hybrid design, students were able to explore mathematical concepts learned in the class, discussing possible approaches to the solution. There were instances where students queried their group members on the purpose of the suggested approaches, sprouting a series of mathematical conceptual debates on the whiteboard as well as in the chat.

Pivotal moments in the Collaboration Interaction Model

Analysis of the logs of the chats at the junior college resulted in the formulation of a "Collaboration Interaction Model" (CIM), which represented the flow of responses of the students to each other (Wee & Looi, 2007). The graphical representation featured certain "pivotal moments" termed *Pivotal Contribution* in the CIM, which exerted major effects upon the progress of the student groups. The emergence of meaning-making patterns leading to the construction of the *Pivotal Contribution* and patterns of knowledge construction diverging from the *Pivotal Contribution* form the basis for analyzing how shared meaning making is achieved at a group level, rather than at an individual level. Pivotal Contributions are currently viewed from the researcher's perspective. On-going work explores how *Pivotal Contributions* can be understood from the participant's perspective, primarily through focus group sessions conducted by the instructor.

A paper presented at ICCE 2005 in Singapore (and given the "best paper" award there) analyzed how pairs of student chat postings often work to sustain the problem-solving work of a small group of online students (Stahl, 2005). One student makes a bid at a math proposal and then the rest of the group responds, either accepting the proposal and starting to work on it, objecting to it or seeking clarification. Of course, the bid can also be unsuccessful and be ignored by the group. If it is successfully taken up, it can serve like the pivotal moments identified in the CIM and contribute to the online team's group cognition (Stahl, 2006). Data from VMT sessions can also be analyzed in detail to reveal the meaning-making process at work in the group interaction (Stahl, 2007). Through an analysis of the chat interactions in a VMT session—using the CIM approach extended with a close analysis of the verbal content of the proposal bid and uptake—one can observe the meaning-making processes by which teams of students create shared mathematical knowledge.

Analysis of the sessions in Singapore and of recent sessions in the USA using different kinds of tasks suggest ways of further evolving the problem designs to more explicitly promote student explorations to construct and manipulate representations in order to promote their mathematical conceptual understanding.

The VMT Spring Fest

Each year, the VMT project holds a math Festival and invites teams organized by teachers. In 2006, this was organized as an international contest, with prizes to the groups that worked together for four sessions and that were then judged the most collaborative. The first prize was tied by a team in the USA and one in a high school in Singapore. These teams explored the mathematics of sequences. During this contest, a wiki was introduced to allow teams to share their findings with other teams. Interestingly, one of the winning teams was inspired to work on a problem created by another team and shared in the wiki. In the end, they found a mistake in the other team's posting and posted a wiki note with their analysis. This was a first step toward knowledge building in the larger community of the Festival participants, connecting all the teams working in their separate chat rooms.

In Spring 2007, the VMT project tried to integrate the wiki much more closely with the problem solving in the chat rooms. Small groups were encouraged to collaboratively construct summaries of their work each session and to post these summaries to a wiki. All the groups worked on a set of probability problems, whose solutions were organized on the wiki. The idea was that the student groups would contribute to a math knowledge wiki site for students interested in probability. The community of VMT user groups would thereby construct knowledge about school math on the model of Wikipedia— combining knowledge building by the individual students, their teams and an international community.

By having teams create their own questions that interest them about a shared math domain and having them share their analyses with other teams (e.g., through a wiki), we try to combine the advantages of synchronous small group interaction with those of asynchronous community knowledge building.

Supporting extended knowledge building in VMT

Also in Spring 2007, the VMT environment—now expanded to include the chat rooms, a wiki, multiple shared whiteboards, browsers, a portal to the chat rooms and some social networking supports—was used for a graduate online course on human-computer interaction. The course took place over ten weeks, with small workgroups of students meeting online each week to review academic papers and to accomplish weekly design projects. All the group work in chat rooms was summarized by the groups and posted on the wiki for sharing with the instructor and the other groups. The goal of the course was to build knowledge about the design of social networking software. The entire course was run in the VMT environment, with assignments and readings available on the wiki, students forming groups in the portal lobby, student teams reviewing the readings and discussing design tasks in the chat, summarizing on the whiteboard, and posting results on the wiki. The instructor organized the course assignments and the students carried them out over a ten week period, with weekly deliverables, each requiring a couple of online chat collaborations. The class as a whole built up knowledge about the course topic and documented its findings in the wiki, where students in future courses can build upon it further.

The successes of the online course using the VMT environment provides a model of knowledge building over a longer span of time—in this case, ten weeks as opposed to the two weeks of the VMT Festival. Here, the students became quite comfortable in the software environment and in the online collaborative context. The combination of synchronous and asynchronous media—integrated through a number of tools and features—gave the students both flexibility and structure in negotiating the timing and style of their participation. The nature of the assignments and the sharing of their work encouraged creativity, peer feedback and self-reflection.

The context of the use of the VMT chat environment in the USA setting is different from the trials reported from Singapore. The USA participants generally do not know each other from face-to-face activities. In Singapore, the VMT chat environment is used to complement routine lecture/tutorial sessions, allowing interleaving and integration of chat discourse with classroom discourse. In these online sessions, each student already knows the other participants. The teacher has opportunities to bring issues and problems arising from observations of the online group discourse into lecture or tutorial discussions. The teacher can actually reference examples of successful chat discourse and run through the discourse with the students in class, highlighting pivotal moments, constructive suggestions, non-sequitors, and moments when everyone seems to have missed an opportunity to construct further knowledge. This raises interesting research questions, for example, whether modeling and inspecting knowledge building episodes or processes can create better metacognitive awareness in students, leading to better knowledge building.

In each case where VMT has been used, it has become very clear that the most important thing to do is to coordinate the various aspects of the environment and student experience. This includes the design of the problems, the formation and preparation of the groups, the uses of the technology, the seeding of the wiki and of its interconnections in the environment, the instructions to the students, and any feedback given to the students between sessions. It is necessary to structure the entire experience carefully to be a rich but focused knowledge-building experience.

Just as has been found in studies of the use of Knowledge Forum, the "care and feeding" of a knowledge building community is a subtle and elusive business. The larger knowledge building at the classroom level is hard to attain, particularly in school cultures dominated by individualized reward systems.

However, we have found that chat can support a different kind of discourse than discussion forums: it is typically more intense, focused on the resolution of mathematics problems or other designed activities for the small groups. The shared whiteboard provides a flexible area to post drawings and textboxes that serve as knowledge artifacts for the group memory. A wiki can supply a persistent memory store for the community, allowing the outcomes of the chats to be summarized onto web pages that support yet a different kind of discourse. Together, the intermixed digital media support a complex process of knowledge building within different collaborative groupings—individual, team, class and community—and across different temporalities—synchronous, quasi-synchronous and asynchronous.

With the increased complexity of the affordances come increased coordination requirements: the curricular materials and technologies must be carefully designed to work together; the students must learn to navigate the intricacies and to develop appropriate interaction methods.

Usage of the VMT environment in Singapore and the USA has allowed us to identify some of these needs and to begin to explore solutions. Computer support can make new educational settings possible, such as the international VMT Festivals or online courses. It can also put powerful computational and representational tools in the hands of students and allow for increased collaboration. However, in the end, the achievement of progressive educational goals still requires innovative, careful pedagogic planning and sequencing of tasks and problems.

Acknowledgments

We thank the Jurong Junior College, the NIE Learning Sciences Lab, the American NSF, the Math Forum at Drexel University and the VMT team for making this research possible.

References

Alagic, M. (2003). Technology in the mathematics classroom: Conceptual orientation. *Journal of Computers in Mathematics and Science Teaching, 22(4)*, 381-399.

Ministry of Education. (2005). Breadth and flexibility: The new 'A' level curriculum 2006. Singapore: Curriculum Planning and Developmental Division.

Polya, M. (1957). *How to solve it (2nd ed,)*. New York: Doubleday.

Reglin, G. L. (1990). The effects of individualized and cooperative computer assisted instruction on mathematics achievement and mathematics anxiety for prospective teachers. *Journal of Research on Computing in Education, 23,* 404-412.

Scardamalia, M., & Bereiter, C. (1994). Computer support for knowledge-building communities. *The Journal of the Learning Sciences, 3(3)*, 265-283.

Scardamalia, M., & Bereiter, C. (2007). *Knowledge building: Theory, pedagogy, and technology.* In K. Sawyer (Ed.), Cambridge Handbook of the Learning Science. Cambridge, UK: Cambridge University Press.

Stahl, G. (2005). *Sustaining online collaborative problem solving with math proposals.* Paper presented at the International Conference on Computers and Education (ICCE 2005), Singapore.

Stahl, G. (2006). *Group cognition: Computer support for building collaborative knowledge.* Cambridge, MA: MIT Press.

Stahl, G. (2007). *Meaning making in CSCL: Conditions and preconditions for cognitive processes by groups.* Paper presented at the international conference on Computer-Supported Collaborative Learning (CSCL '07), New Brunswick, NJ.

Stein, M. K., & Henningsen, M. (1997). Mathematical tasks and student cognition:. *Journal for Research in Mathematics Education, (28),* 524-549.

Yetter, G., Gutkin, T.B., Saunders, A., Galloway, A. M., Sobansky, R. R. & Song, S. Y. (2006). Unstructured collaboration versus individual practice for complex problem solving: A cautionary tale. *The Journal of Experimental Education, 74(2)*, 137-159.

Wee, J.D, & Looi, C.-K. (2007). *Model for analysing collaborative knowledge construction in a quasi-synchronous chat environment.* Paper presented at the International Conference on Computers-Supported Collaborative Learning (CSCL '07). Chat Analysis Workshop, New Brunswick, NJ.

10. Enhancing Mathematical Communication for Virtual Math Teams

Gerry Stahl, Murat Perit Çakir, Stephen Weimar, Baba Kofi Weusijana & Jimmy Xiantong Ou

The Math Forum is an online resource center for pre-algebra, algebra, geometry and pre-calculus. Its Virtual Math Teams (VMT) service provides an integrated web-based environment for small teams of people to discuss math and to work collaboratively on math problems or explore interesting mathematical micro-worlds together. The VMT Project studies the online math discourse that takes place during sessions of virtual math teams working on open-ended problem-solving tasks. In particular, it investigates methods of group cognition that are employed by teams in this setting. The VMT environment currently integrates social networking, synchronous text chat, a shared whiteboard for drawing, web browsers and an asynchronous wiki for exchanging findings within the larger community. A simple version of MathML is supported in the whiteboard, chat and wiki for displaying mathematical expressions. The VMT Project is currently integrating the dynamic mathematics application, GeoGebra, into its collaboration environment. This will create a multi-user version of GeoGebra, which can be used in concert with the chat, web browsers, curricular topics and wiki repository.

Introduction

The Virtual Math Teams (VMT) Project has conducted research since 2003 on how to support small teams of students around the world to collaborate in online discussions of stimulating mathematical topics. The project has developed an extensive web-based environment and logged about a thousand sessions of usage. Analysis of usage has resulted in over a hundred academic publications (see http://GerryStahl.net/vmt/pubs.html)—the most important of which are collected in *Group Cognition* (Stahl, 2006) and *Studying Virtual Math Teams*

(Stahl, 2009)—and six doctoral dissertations (Çakir, 2009; Litz, 2007; Mühlpfordt, 2008; Sarmiento-Klapper, 2009; Wee, 2009; Zhou, 2010) (see summaries in Çakır, Zemel & Stahl, 2009; Sarmiento & Stahl, 2008).

The VMT environment—available at the Math Forum—currently includes a social-networking portal (http://vmt.mathforum.org/VMTLobby/), a Java application that integrates synchronous text chat with a shared whiteboard, social awareness indicators, and an asynchronous community wiki. We are currently porting the dynamic math GeoGebra system (http://www.geogebra.org) into the VMT environment. The integration of the open-source GeoGebra code will enable it to function in a multi-user, synchronous online environment. Integration into the VMT environment will support simultaneous text chat discussion of dynamic math diagrams, graphical referencing between chat and diagrams, scrollable history of chat and diagrams, and pasting of diagrams into the associated wiki.

The integration of GeoGebra into the VMT environment will provide significant mathematical content and functionality to enhance mathematical exploration and communication by virtual math teams. The integration includes the ability to support importing and exporting of GeoGebra dynamic worksheets; this will allow teachers and students to take advantage of available curricular materials. It will also provide a multi-user version of GeoGebra for the community of teachers and students currently using single-user versions of GeoGebra. The Math Forum plans to release the new system for worldwide usage, providing a convenient online venue for students to engage in synchronous collaborative learning within a rich environment for mathematical inquiry and knowledge-building interaction.

The Math Forum: An online service and resource center for school math

The Math Forum manages a website (http://mathforum.org) with over a million pages of resources related to mathematics for middle-school and high-school students, primarily on algebra and geometry, mostly user generated (as a forerunner of the Web 2.0 philosophy). This site is well established; a leading online resource for improving math learning, teaching and communication since 1992, the Math Forum is now visited by several million different visitors a month. A community has grown up around this site, including teachers, mathematicians, researchers, students and parents—using the power of the Web to learn math and improve math education. The site offers a wealth of problems and puzzles, online mentoring, research, team problem solving, collaborations and professional development. Studies of site usage show that students have fun and learn a lot; that educators share ideas and acquire new skills; and that participants become increasingly engaged over time (Renninger & Shumar, 2002).

The Math Forum offers a number of online services, including the following. Most of these services were developed with research funding and volunteer support; some of the established services now charge a nominal fee to defray part of their operating costs:

- *The Problem of the Week (PoW)*. This popular service posts a different problem every other week during the school year in a number of categories, such as math fundamentals, pre-algebra, algebra or geometry. Challenging non-standard math problems can be answered online or offline. Students can submit their solution strategies and receive feedback from mentors on how to improve their presentations. The best solution descriptions are posted on the Math Forum site.

- *Ask Dr. Math*. Students and others receive mathematics advice from professionals and expert volunteers.

- *Math Tools*. Visitors to the site explore the world of interactive tools for understanding math concepts and communicate with teachers using them in their classrooms, discussing and rating the tools.

- *Teacher2Teacher*. Classroom teachers and educators from around the world work together to address the challenges of teaching and learning math.

- *Other*. Math Forum staff also provide online mentoring and teacher professional development, lead face-to-face workshops and work with teachers in their math classrooms, under contracts with school districts.

- *Virtual Math Teams (VMT)*. The VMT service builds on the highly successful Problem-of-the-Week service. Students who once worked by themselves on PoW problems can now work on more open-ended problems with a group of peers. This can be organized in a variety of ways and can bring many advantages, as discussed in the following sections.

The VMT Project: A new form of math education

The Virtual Math Teams Project explores the potential of the Internet to link learners with sources of knowledge around the world, including other learners, information on the Web and stimulating digital or computational resources. It offers opportunities for engrossing mathematical discussions that are rarely found in most schools (Boaler, 2008; Lockhart, 2009). The traditional classroom that relies on one teacher, one textbook and one set of exercises to engage and train a room full of individual students over a long period of time can now be supplemented through small-group experiences of VMT chats, incorporating a variety of adaptable and personalizable interactions (Scher, 2002).

While a service like PoW or VMT may initially be used as a minor diversion within a classical school experience, it has the potential to become more. It can open new vistas for some students, providing a different view of what mathematics is about. By bringing learners together, it can challenge participants to understand other people's perspectives and to explain and defend their own ideas, stimulating important comprehension, collaboration and reflection skills (Sfard, 2008; Stahl, 2008).

As the VMT library grows in the future, it can guide groups of students into exciting realms of math that are outside traditional high school curriculum, but are accessible to people with basic skills (see Figures 1 and 2). Such areas include: patterns, combinatorics, symbolic logic, probability, statistics, finite math, number theory, infinity, group theory, matrices, non-Euclidean geometries. Many math puzzles and games also build mathematical thinking and stimulate interest in exploring mathematical worlds (Livingston, 1999).

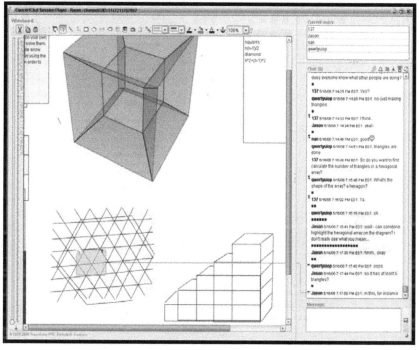

Figure 1. Image of actual student online collaborative work on patterns, showing the importance of shared visualizations tied to the math discourse. Here, a student points from his chat message to a smallest hexagon pattern composed of 6 triangles.

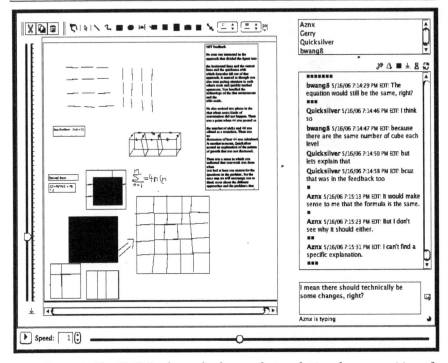

Figure 2. The VMT Replayer displays a chat exploring the composition of different 3-D pyramids. (Note the VCR interface of the Replayer at the bottom of Figure 2).

Ultimately, whole curricula within mathematics could be structured in terms of sequences of VMT topics with associated learning resources (Boaler, 2008; Cobb, Yackel & McClain, 2000; Lockhart, 2009; Moss & Beatty, 2006). Students could form teams to explore these sequences, just as they now explore levels within video-game environments. A Problem-Based Learning (PBL) approach could cover both the breadth and depth of mathematical fields, just as PBL curricula currently provide students at numerous medical schools with their academic training in face-to-face collaborative teams (Barrows, 1994; Koschmann, Glenn & Conlee, 1997). In varying degrees, students could pursue their own interests, learning styles, social modes and timing. Assessments of student progress could be built in to the computational environment, supplementing and supporting teacher or mentor judgments. The collaborative, small-group VMT approach would be very different from previous automated tutoring systems that isolated individual learners, because VMT is built around the bringing together of groups of students to interact with one another. Students can work with peers in other schools, even from other countries and cultures.

Promoting knowledge building through math discourse

For most non-mathematicians, arithmetic provides their paradigm of math. Learning math, they assume, involves memorizing facts like multiplication tables and procedures like long division. But for mathematicians, math is a matter of defining new concepts and arguing about relations among them. Math is a centuries-long discourse, with a shared vocabulary, ways of symbolically representing ideas and procedures for defending claims. It is a discourse and a set of shared practices. Learning to talk about math objects, to appreciate arguments about them and to adopt the practices of mathematical reasoning constitute an education in math.

To mathematicians since Euclid, math represents the paradigm of creative intellectual activity. Its methods set the standard throughout Western civilization for rigorous thought, problem solving, and argumentation. We teach geometry to instill in students a sense of deductive reasoning. Yet, too many people end up saying that they "hate math" and that "math is boring" or that they are "not good at math" (Boaler, 2008; Lockhart, 2009). They have somehow missed the true experience of math cognition—and this may limit their lifelong interest in science, engineering and technology.

According to a recent "cognitive history" of the origin of deduction in Greek mathematics (Netz, 1999), the primordial math experience in 5th and 4th Century BC was based on the confluence of labeled geometric diagrams (shared visualizations) and a language of written mathematics (asynchronous collaborative discourse), which supported the rapid evolution of math cognition in a small community of math discourse around the Mediterranean that profoundly extended mathematics and Western thinking. The vision behind VMT is to foster communities of math discourse in online communities around the world. We want to leverage the potential of networked computers and dynamic math applications to catalyze groups of people exploring math and experiencing the intellectual excitement that Euclid's colleagues felt—leveraging emerging 21st Century media of shared math visualization and collaborative math discourse.

Classical training in school math—through drill in facts and procedures—is like learning Latin by memorizing vocabulary lists and conjugation tables: one can pass a test in the subject, but would have a hard time actually conversing with anyone in the language. To understand and appreciate the culture of mathematics, one has to live it and converse with others in it. Math learners have to understand and respond appropriately to mathematical statements by others and be able to critically review and constructively contribute to their proposals. The VMT Project creates worlds and communities in which math can be lived and spoken.

The learning sciences have transformed our vision of education in the future (Sawyer, 2006; Stahl, Koschmann & Suthers, 2006). New theories of mathematical cognition (Bransford, Brown & Cocking, 1999; Brown & Campione, 1994; Greeno & Goldman, 1998; Hall & Stevens, 1995; Lakatos, 1976; Lemke, 1993; Livingston, 1999) and math education, in particular, stress collaborative knowledge building (Bereiter, 2002; Scardamalia & Bereiter, 1996; Schwarz, 1997), problem-based learning, dialogicality (Wegerif, 2007), argumentation (Andriessen, Baker & Suthers, 2003), accountable talk (Michaels, O'Connor & Resnick, 2008), group cognition (Stahl, 2006), and engagement in math discourse.

These approaches place the focus on problem solving, problem posing, exploration of alternative strategies, inter-animation of perspectives, verbal articulation, argumentation, deductive reasoning, and heuristics as features of significant math discourse (Powell, Francisco & Maher, 2003). By articulating thinking and learning in text, they make cognition public and visible. This calls for a reorientation to facilitate dialogical student practices as well as requiring content and resources to guide and support the student discourses. Teachers and students must learn to adopt, appreciate and take advantage of the visible nature of collaborative learning. The emphasis on text-based collaborative learning can be well supported by computers with appropriate computer-supported collaborative learning (CSCL) software.

Students learn math best if they are actively involved in discussing math. Explaining their thinking to each other, making their ideas visible, expressing math concepts, teaching peers and contributing proposals are important ways for students to develop deep understanding and real expertise. There are few opportunities for such student-initiated activities in most teacher-led classrooms. The VMT chat room provides a place for students to build knowledge about math issues together through intensive, engaging discussions. Their entire discourse and graphical representations are persistent and visible for them to reflect on and share.

Research in designing an online chat community

The VMT Project is an effort to explore some of the opportunities and issues posed above. In order to understand the experience of people and groups collaborating online in the VMT service, the researchers in the project look in detail at the interactions as captured in computer logs. In particular, the project is studying groups of three to six middle- or high-school students discussing mathematics in chat rooms.

The VMT Project was designed to foster, capture and analyze instances of "group cognition" (Stahl, 2006). The project is set up so that every aspect of the communication can be automatically captured when student groups are active in the online community, so that the researchers have access to everything that enters into the communication and is shared by the participants. All interaction takes place online, so that it is unnecessary to videotape and transcribe. Each message is logged with the name of the user submitting it and the time of its submission. Similarly, each item placed in the shared whiteboard is tagged with the name of its creator and its creation or modification time. The chat is persistent and the history of the whiteboard can also be scrolled by participants, and later by researchers.

Although many things happen "behind the scenes" during chat sessions—such as the production of the messages, including possible repairs and retractions of message text before a message is sent, or things that the participants do but do not mention in the chat—the researcher sees everything that the participants *share* and all see. While the behavior of a participant may be influenced on an individual basis—such as by interactions with people outside of the chat or by the effects of various social and cultural influences—the researchers can generally infer and understand these influences to the same extent as the other participants (who often do not know each other outside of the chats). These "external" factors (including the participants' age, gender, ethnicity, culture) only play a role in the group interaction to the extent that they are somehow brought into the discourse or "made relevant" in the chat. In cases where they play a role in the group, then, they are also available to the researchers.

In particular, the sequentiality of the chat messages and of the actions in the whiteboard is maintained so that researchers can analyze the phenomena that take place at the group level of interaction among participants. The other way in which the group interaction may be influenced from outside of activities recorded in the chat room is through general background knowledge shared by the participants, such as classroom culture, pop culture or linguistic practices. If the participants meet on the Internet and do not all come from the same school and do not share any history from outside of the VMT chats, then researchers are likely to share with the participants most of the background understanding that the participants themselves share.

This is not to say that the researchers have the same experience as the participants, but their resources for understanding the chat are quite similar to the resources that the participants had for understanding and creating the chat, despite the dramatic differences between the participant and researcher perspectives. Participants experience the chat in real time as it unfolds on their screen. They are oriented toward formulating their messages to introduce into the chat with effective timing. Researchers are engaged in analyzing and recreating what happened, rather than participating directly in it. They are oriented toward understanding why the messages were introduced when and how they were.

The VMT Project wants to understand how groups construct their shared experience of collaborating online. While answers to many questions in human-computer interaction have been formulated largely in terms of individual psychology, questions of collaborative experience require consideration of the group as the unit of analysis. Naturally, groups include individuals as contributors and interpreters of content, but the group interactions have structures and elements of their own that call for different analytic approaches. In particular, the solving of math problems in the chat environment gets accomplished collaboratively, interactionally. That is, the cognitive work is done by the group.

We call this accomplishment *group cognition*—a form of distributed cognition that may involve advanced levels of cognition like mathematical problem solving and that is visible in the group discourse, where it takes place. It is possible to conduct informative analyses of chats at the group unit of analysis, without asking about the individuals—e.g., their motivations, internal reflections, unexpressed feelings, intelligence, skills, etc.—beyond their participation in the group interaction. Of course, there are also intriguing questions about the interplay between group cognition and individual cognition, but we generally do not consider those in the project.

The VMT Project is studying how small groups of students do mathematics collaboratively in online chat environments. We are particularly interested in the *methods* that the chat members must develop to conduct their interactions in an environment that presents new affordances for interaction. "Member methods" (Garfinkel, 1967) are interactional patterns that participants in a community adopt to structure and give meaning to their activities. A paradigmatic example of member methods is the set of conventions used by speakers in face-to-face conversation to take turns talking (Sacks, Schegloff & Jefferson, 1974). The use of such methods is generally taken-for-granted by the community and provides the social order, meaning and accountability of their activities. Taken together, these member methods define a group culture, a shared set of ways for people interacting to make sense together of their common world. The methods adopted by VMT participants are subtly responsive to the chat medium, the pedagogical setting, the social atmosphere and the intellectual resources that are available to them. These methods help define the nature of the collaborative experience for the small groups that develop and adopt them. Through the use of these methods, the groups construct their collaborative experience. The chat takes on a flow of interrelated ideas for the group, analogous to an individual's stream of consciousness. The referential structure of this flow provides a basis for the group's experience of intersubjectivity and of a shared world.

As designers of educational chat environments, we are particularly interested in how small groups of students construct their interactions in chat media that have different technical features. How do the students learn about the meanings that designers embedded in the environment and how do they negotiate the methods that they adopt to turn technological possibilities into practical means for mediating their interactions? Ultimately, how can we design with students the technologies, pedagogies and communities that will result in desirable collaborative experiences for them? Our response to the question of how cognitive tools mediate collaborative communities is to point to the methods that interactive small groups within the community spontaneously co-construct to carry out their activities using the tools.

The VMT Project pioneered the study of online collaborative math discourse— both its nature and modes of computer support for it. The studies in (Stahl, 2009) present some of the most important of the publications related to the project. They include a number of dissertation-level case studies of interactions in the VMT environment by middle-school, high-school and junior-college students, which analyze: how math problem solving can be effectively conducted collaboratively among students who have never met face-to-face; how the structure of text chat interaction differs from spoken conversation; how the media of graphical diagrams, textual narratives, and symbolic representations can be intimately interwoven to build deep math understanding; how deictic referencing is important to establishing shared understanding; how students co-construct a joint problem space; how collaborative meaning making and knowledge building are accomplished in detail; how online math discourse can be supported by a software environment that integrates synchronous and asynchronous media with specialized math tools; and how a methodology based on interaction analysis can be used for a science of group cognition (Stahl, 2010a; 2010b).

VMT: A multi-user platform for synchronous and asynchronous math discourse

In our design-based research at the VMT Project, we started by conducting chats in a variety of commercially available environments, including AOL Instant Messenger, Babylon, WebCT and Blackboard. Based on these early investigations, we concluded that we needed to include a shared whiteboard for drawing geometric figures and for persistently displaying notes. We also found a need to minimize "chat confusion" by supporting explicit referencing of response threads. We decided to adopt and adapt ConcertChat, a research chat environment with special referencing tools (Mühlpfordt & Wessner, 2005). By collaborating with the software developers at Fraunhofer IPSI in Germany, our educational researchers have been able to successively try out versions of the environment with groups of students and to gradually modify the environment in response to what we find by analyzing the chat logs.

The ConcertChat environment—which is now available in Open Source—integrates text chat with a shared whiteboard. A unique feature of ConcertChat is its support for graphical referencing. It allows for three forms of referencing from the text chat:

- A chat message can point to one or more earlier textual postings with a bold connecting line. When that message appears in the chat as the last posting or as a selected posting, a bold line appears connecting the text to the selected chat posting above.

- While someone types a new chat message, they can select and point to a rectangular area in the whiteboard. When that message appears in the chat as the last posting or as a selected posting, a bold line appears connecting the text to the area of the whiteboard.

- While someone types a new chat message, they can select and point to a graphical object in the whiteboard. When that message appears in the chat as the last posting or as a selected posting, a bold line appears connecting the text to the area of the whiteboard.

This referencing is just one form of integration of media in the VMT environment. The overall technological integration of the VMT Lobby (or portal), chat room/shared whiteboard, and wiki should be understood theoretically as a pedagogical integration of learning at the individual, small-group and community levels. The VMT Lobby provides a portal for the *individual user* to browse the people and topics of the community and to select a room for group work. The chat rooms are basically meeting and work places for the *small groups* as they engage in synchronous collaborative learning. The wiki, on the other hand, primarily provides an asynchronous *community space* in which the work of all groups is coordinated, commented upon and perhaps summarized.

Figure 3. The VMT Lobby, with social networking features on the left and a list of chat rooms on the right, organized by math subject and problem topics.

The *VMT Lobby* provides a social networking portal for students to log into the system (see Figure 3). It includes tools for defining and viewing personal profiles. In general, students in a VMT group have no knowledge about each other except for what is revealed in the chat interaction; with the functionality available in the VMT Lobby, they can define their own profiles and view profiles of each other, as well as send messages to individuals or groups in their communities. Communities are defined for various VMT constituencies, such as participants in a given Spring Fest or in a given course. There is also support for defining buddies, listing favorite chat rooms, etc. In addition, there is an interface for searching and browsing available chat rooms, usually listed for a given community. This provides access to chat rooms on different topics. Students may be told by their teachers to find certain rooms, may be invited by buddies, may search for rooms on interesting topics or may create new rooms and invite peers to join them.

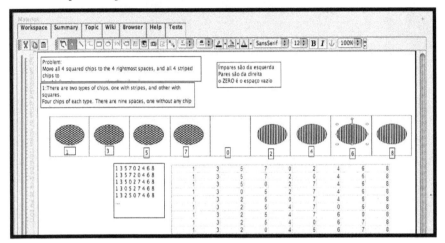

Figure 4. A team including students in Newark and in Brazil collaborated on the chips combinatorics problem. They dragged circles representing game chips according to specific rules. They could then scroll the history of the "Workspace" shared whiteboard to animate the sequence of moves taken. Note that the students have added a new tab named "Teste" in addition to the tabs defined for this curriculum topic.

A typical *VMT chat room* consists of the text chat interface on the right and a shared whiteboard on the left. The history of the whiteboard state can be scrolled through, much like that of the chat, but unlike the chat it usually retains inscriptions in the visible board as long as they are relevant. VMT chat rooms have a tabbed interface, with multiple workspaces—and users can add additional spaces as needed (see Figure 4). One kind of workspace is the shared *Workspace*, supporting graphics and text boxes. Another is a similar shared whiteboard, intended for preparing a *Summary* of the group's work for posting to a special wiki page associated with this chat room. A third tab may display the *Topic* for the room, stored on a wiki page by an instructor. A *Wiki* tab displays a page of the VMT wiki; a special page is created for each room, linked to other pages on the Topic, math Subject or Community. A *Browser* tab provides a simple multi-user web browser that can support the graphical referencing tool from the chat and a history scrollbar. The final tab displays wiki pages containing the VMT *Help* manual and associated information.

The *VMT wiki* acts as a digital library repository for summaries of work posted by teams. If there is a course that involves multiple chats by several teams, a wiki home page can be constructed for the course. The home page would then point to pages describing the course and each assignment. Group assignments are all posted to linked wiki pages. The course wiki includes index pages that bring together the student assignments in various combinations and allow the instructor to post feedback that is visible to all. The student groups can also rate and provide feedback to each other's previous reports.

The VMT wiki can be used flexibly to structure mini-repositories. For instance, a wiki page for the VMT Spring Fest 2007, which involved probability problems, provided a knowledge-building space, analogous to Wikipedia (see Figure 5). That is, anyone in the community could add information to this catalog of knowledge about K-12 probability as well as browsing the space. The space was seeded with a number of different probability problems and several strategies for solving such problems. During the Fest, student groups were to each initially select a problem and try to solve it with one of the strategies. Then they would post a summary of their solution path on the wiki page linked to from the home page for that problem and that strategy. Subsequent work would involve trying the same strategy on other problems or other strategies on the same problem, followed by comparing the results posted by other groups. The idea was that this kind of knowledge-building repository could persist and evolve through use in the future.

The VMT environment has come a long way from the simple AOL Instant Messaging system to the current lobby/chat/tabbed-spaces/wiki multiple-interaction space. In part, this increased complexity parallels the shift from simple math exercises to open-ended explorations of math worlds, from one-shot meetings to multiple-session Fests, from problem-solving tasks to knowledge-building efforts. Along with the considerable gain in functionality come substantial increases in complexity and the potential for confusion. This has been countered by trying to extend and supplement the integration approaches of ConcertChat. The graphical referencing and the history scrollbars have been extended to the multiple tabs. New social awareness notices have been added to track which tab each group member is viewing or referencing.

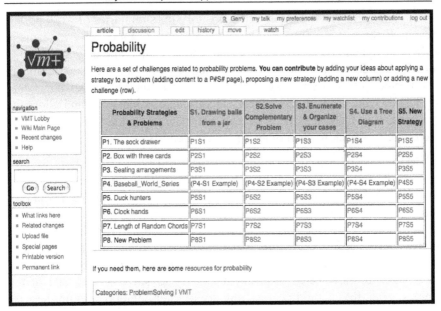

Figure 5. A VMT wiki page associated with chat rooms exploring proability topics.

The VMT collaboration environment has been tuned to the needs of high-school math students. There are specifically math-oriented functions—like a partial implementation of MathML for displaying equations (see http://vmt.mathforum.org/VMTLobby/VMTHelp/mathequations.html) and the whiteboard's stock of Euclidean shapes. In addition, there are tools for integrating the multiple work spaces—like the graphical referencing from chat, the creation of wiki pages corresponding to each chat room and the automatic posting of summary text to the proper wiki page.

Integration across modules has been important. Logins and passwords have been unified across the Lobby, chat rooms and wiki, so that logging into one automatically logs into the others. People registered in one module show up in the profiles and messaging system, by their selected community. When a new chat room is created, it is categorized by a community (e.g., a school), subject (e.g., combinatorics), a topic (e.g., Week 3's assignment) and a group (e.g., Team D). A new wiki page is generated for posting the summary from this room. The MediaWiki functionality of categories automatically associates this new page with aggregation pages for the community, subject, topic and group.

GeoGebra: Dynamic math support for group cognition

Our next major enhancement to the VMT environment is to port the single-user GeoGebra application into VMT as a multi-user component of the tabbed chat room. This will allow groups of users to co-develop and co-explore a GeoGebra geometric construction. They will be able to chat about the drawing and reference parts of it from their chat postings. There will be a history slider, so users can scroll back and forth, watching the changes take place in the drawing for convenient review and reflection.

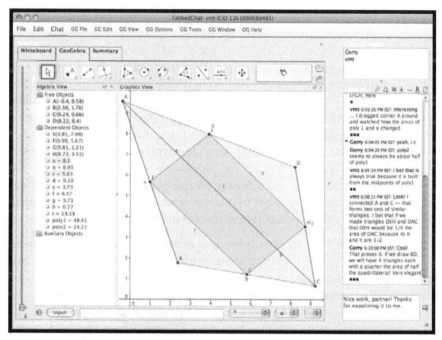

Figure 6. A GeoGebra construction created and discussed collaboratively in a prototype of the VMT 2.0 learning environment. (Not real interaction data.)

The project is porting GeoGebra—a comprehensive and well established application for dynamic math exploration—to the VMT learning environment described above. It will make the application fully multi-user. It will integrate the application in a tab of the environment (see Figure 6). GeoGebra is a particularly appropriate dynamic math application for this project because its source code is freely available as open source, there is a development community to support on-going development, the lead developer and the founder are consulting with us, the application supports a wide range of math from Euclidean construction to calculus and 3-D, GeoGebra has won international prizes, and it has been translated into about 50 languages.

Like all other dynamic math applications, GeoGebra now exists only as a single-user application. While users can send their static constructions to each other, display screen images, or awkwardly include a view of the GeoGebra application within other environments (Blackboard, Moodle, Elluminate, etc.), only one person can dynamically manipulate the construction. Our port will convert GeoGebra to a client-server architecture, allowing multiple distributed users to manipulate constructions simultaneously and to all observe everyone's actions in real time. Every action in the GeoGebra tab will be immediately broadcast by the server to all collaborating clients.

In addition, incorporation of GeoGebra in the VMT environment framework allows users to engage in text chat while manipulating the construction. Importantly, users can graphically point from a chat posting to an area of the construction that they want to index—an important support for math discourse that is unique to VMT (or its now-defunct basis, ConcertChat). They can also scroll back and forth through the history of the GeoGebra construction, animating its evolution—a powerful way to explore many mathematical relationships (see Figure 4 above). In addition, a complete record of the collaborative construction is available to the participants, their teachers and project researchers, allowing them to analyze and reflect upon the complete interaction, including the construction actions synchronized with the chat.

The VMT version of GeoGebra will be compatible with the standard version. Thus, constructions can be imported and exported seamlessly between the two versions. This will facilitate use of legacy GeoGebra curriculum within the collaborative VMT environment. Images of GeoGebra co-constructions can be created and pasted by users into the VMT wiki or into Word documents. Logs of the corresponding chats can also be saved as spreadsheet files and pasted into documents.

The integration of GeoGebra will significantly enhance the mathematical domain-orientation of the VMT system. On the other hand, for the GeoGebra community, it will make available for the first time truly multi-user dynamic geometry support within a rich collaborative environment. With the flexible system of tabbed components, a curriculum designer, instructor or even a student can define topics for rooms with just GeoGebra and chat or with a more complicated mix of additional browsers and support components.

For researchers of math learning, the enhanced environment provides a flexible laboratory for hosting virtual math teams engaged in GeoGebra-based tasks. The entire interactions of these teams will be logged in detail. Not only can the logs be generated in a variety of convenient formats, but also the team interactions can actually be replayed from the logs like digital videos for careful study. With these tools, researchers can explore the group cognition of small teams accomplishing creative problem solving involving geometric constructions that are shared, visible and dynamic.

Making GeoGebra multi-user has involved many technical, underlying changes to the software and has necessitated a number of trade-offs and design decisions. In terms of the software architecture, we treated the GeoGebra application as a client and embedded it in a Concert-Chat tab. Every action performed in the tab is immediately broadcast across the Internet to the VMT server. The server logs the action in its database and then broadcasts the action to the client of every user who is logged into the same room, including the originating client. In this way, each action performed by someone in a given VMT room is displayed identically for everyone who is working together. Minimizing Internet traffic is a major concern, especially with potentially large GeoGebra interdependent objects, and we had to make changes to Concert-Chat and GeoGebra implementations to keep traffic volume under control.

A major issue with multi-user systems is what to do when two users try to do conflicting things at the same time. We have recently implemented a locking mechanism, so that when two clients are creating objects at the same time or are manipulating the same object simultaneously, the changes are not broadcast until the end of the operations. This causes some delay in sharing what people are doing; however, we believe it is necessary to avoid serious confusion. Imagine if several clients were moving point A in opposite directions at the same time. If the system broadcast changes every tenth of a second, point A would be jumping back and forth wildly, making it hard for either user to move it sensibly. Where would point A end? We have decided to have point A end where the last user to release it leaves it. If two clients were simultaneously creating an initial triangle ABC, then without locking we would get multiple points with the same names. Our locking mechanism avoids these problems by noting the conflict and assigning different names to the points, but at some cost to mutual awareness.

In the near future, we plan to try to implement two mechanisms to counteract the negative consequences of delayed mutual awareness: (1) labeling actions and (2) simulating dragging. (1) We would like to display awareness notices in the drawing area stating who is creating, editing or moving a graphical object. This would indicate when multiple users are simultaneously at work, and perhaps some of the users would then wait to see what the others have done. (2) If point A were dragged to a new position, ending up, say, 5 units to the right, rather than having point A suddenly jump to the new position in everyone's client, we would simulate the dragging motion by interpolating 10 steps at tenth-of-a-second intervals. Then point A would appear to move to its new position through a smooth and straight motion. This would not be true to the original dragging motion, but would give some feel for a dragging manipulation, which we believe to be important to the GeoGebra manipulation experience.

Of course, other trade-offs are possible, depending upon the technical architecture. We are trying certain approaches and testing them out. We hope to soon have students trying our system. Gradually, we will learn of additional problems and evolve some solutions. The experience will never be the same as having a group of geometers standing around a physical whiteboard—although in some ways it will be better because there will be a permanent record of all interactions, which can be replayed for reflection and analysis. We hope that the integration of GeoGebra with text chat will help to overcome problems that arise from imperfect mutual awareness by allowing people to discuss in text what they are doing in constructions.

Mathematics is often thought of as a solitary experience. However, our findings in the Virtual Math Teams Project show that it can be an exciting, engaging, motivating and rewarding experience when conducted collaboratively. To promote this effectively online, one must provide a carefully crafted set of tools. We believe that GeoGebra can play an important role as a central tool in the VMT environment and we look forward to working with the GeoGebra development and user community to tune our environment to meet the needs of math education globally.

The following two essays discuss related aspects of the VMT project. The first outlines our view of mathematics learning and proposes a set of complementary methodologies for analyzing how small online student groups could engage in mathematical discourse in the VMT system with GeoGebra. The other describes our research on incorporating conversational agents in this system. The best source for the theoretical background of VMT is (Stahl, 2006); a recent compilation of case studies of students interacting in VMT is (Stahl, 2009).

We hope the enhanced VMT environment will provide an attractive and effective platform for collaborative mathematical discourse and will appeal to students, teachers and researchers.

Acknowledgements

This research has been funded in part by grants from the National Science Foundation (NSF): "Dynamic Support for Virtual Math Teams" award DRL-0835383, "Exploring Adaptive Support for Virtual Math Teams" award DRL0723580, "Engaged Learning in Online Communities" award SBE-0518477, "IERI: Catalyzing & Nurturing Online Workgroups to Power Virtual Learning Communities" award IERI 0325447, "Collaboration Services for the Math Forum Digital Library" award DUE 0333493 and by a grant from the Office of Naval Research (ONR), "Theories and Models of Group Cognition." We would like to thank Markus Hohenwarter and Michael Borcherds for their support and assistance in porting GeoGebra to VMT.

References

Andriessen, J., Baker, M., & Suthers, D. (Eds.). (2003). *Arguing to learn: Confronting cognitions in computer-supported collaborative learning environments.* Dordrecht, Netherlands: Kluwer Academic Publishers. Computer-supported collaborative learning book series, vol 1

Barrows, H. (1994). *Practice-based learning: Problem-based learning applied to medical education.* Springfield, IL: SIU School of Medicine.

Bereiter, C. (2002). *Education and mind in the knowledge age.* Hillsdale, NJ: Lawrence Erlbaum Associates.

Boaler, J. (2008). *What's math got to do with it? Helping children learn to love their most hated subject: And why it is important for America.* New York, NY: Viking.

Bransford, J., Brown, A., & Cocking, R. (Eds.). (1999). *How people learn: Brain, mind, experience, and school.* Washington, DC: National Research Council Web: http://books.nap.edu/html/howpeople1/

Brown, A., & Campione, J. (1994). Guided discovery in a community of learners. In K. McGilly (Ed.), *Classroom lessons: Integrating cognitive theory and classroom practice* (pp. 229-270). Cambridge, MA: MIT Press

Çakir, M. P. (2009). *How online small groups co-construct mathematical artifacts to do collaborative problem solving.* Unpublished Dissertation, Ph.D., College of Information Science and Technology, Drexel University, Philadelphia, PA, USA

Çakir, M. P., Zemel, A., & Stahl, G. (2009). The joint organization of interaction within a multimodal CSCL medium. *International Journal of Computer-Supported Collaborative Learning, 4*(2), 115-149. Web: http://GerryStahl.net/pub/ijCSCL_4_2_1.pdf Doi: http://dx.doi.org/10.1007/s11412-009-9061-0

Cobb, P., Yackel, E., & McClain, K. (2000). *Symbolizing and communicating in mathematics classrooms: Perspectives on discourse, tools, and instructional design.* Mahwah, NJ: Lawrence Erlbaum Associates.

Garfinkel, H. (1967). *Studies in ethnomethodology.* Englewood Cliffs, NJ: Prentice-Hall.

Greeno, J. G., & Goldman, S. V. (1998). *Thinking practices in mathematics and science leraning.* Mahwah, NJ: Lawrence Erlbaum Associates.

Hall, R., & Stevens, R. (1995). Making space: A comparison of mathematical work in school and professional design practices. In S. L. Star (Ed.), *The cultures of computing.* Oxford, UK: Blackwell Publishers

Koschmann, T., Glenn, P., & Conlee, M. (1997). Analyzing the emergence of a learning issue in a problem-based learning meeting. *Medical Education Online, 2*(1). Web: http://www.utmb.edu/meo/res00003.pdf

Lakatos, I. (1976). *Proofs and refutations: The logic of mathematical discovery.* Cambridge, UK: Cambridge University Press.

Lemke, J. L. (1993). *Talking science: Language, learning and values.* Norwood, NJ: Ablex.

Litz, I. R. (2007). *Student adoption of a computer-supported collaborative learning (CSCL) mathematical problem solving environment: The case of the math forum's virtual math teams (VMT) chat service.* Unpublished Dissertation, Ph. D., School of Computer and Information Sciences, Nova Southeastern University, Florida

Livingston, E. (1999). Cultures of proving. *Social Studies of Science, 29*(6), 867-888

Lockhart, P. (2009). *A mathematician's lament: How school cheats us out of our most fascinating and imaginative art forms.* New York, NY: Belevue Literary Press.

Michaels, S., O'Connor, C., & Resnick, L. B. (2008). Deliberative discourse idealized and realized: Accountable talk in the classroom and in civic life. *Studies in the Philosophy of Education, 27*(4), 283-297

Moss, J., & Beatty, R. (2006). Knowledge building in mathematics: Supporting collaborative learning in pattern problems. *International Journal of Computer-Supported Collaborative Learning, 1*(4), 441-465 Doi: http://dx.doi.org/10.1007/s11412-006-9003-z

Mühlpfordt, M. (2008). *Integration dualer interaktionsräume: Die verknuepfung von textbasierter synchroner kommunikation mit diskreten konstruktionswerkzeugen. (the integration of dual-interaction spaces: The connection of text-based synchronous communication with graphical construction tools [in German]).* Unpublished Dissertation, Ph. D., Fakultaet fuer Mathematik und Informatik, Fern Universitaet, Hagen, Germany

Mühlpfordt, M., & Wessner, M. (2005). Explicit referencing in chat supports collaborative learning. In T. Koschmann, D. D. Suthers & T.-W. Chan (Eds.), *Computer-supported collaborative learning 2005: The next ten years! (proceedings of CSCL 2005)* (pp. 460-469). Taipei, Taiwan: Mahwah, NJ: Lawrence Erlbaum Associates

Netz, R. (1999). *The shaping of deduction in Greek mathematics: A study in cognitive history.* Cambridge, UK: Cambridge University Press.

Powell, A. B., Francisco, J. M., & Maher, C. A. (2003). An analytical model for studying the development of mathematical ideas and reasoning using videotape data. *Journal of Mathematical Behavior, 22*(4), 405-435

Renninger, K. A., & Shumar, W. (2002). *Building virtual communities.* Cambridge, UK: Cambridge University Press.

Sacks, H., Schegloff, E. A., & Jefferson, G. (1974). A simplest systematics for the organization of turn-taking for conversation. *Language, 50*(4), 696-735. Web: www.jstor.org

Sarmiento, J., & Stahl, G. (2008). *Extending the joint problem space: Time and sequence as essential features of knowledge building.* Paper presented at the International Conference of the Learning Sciences (ICLS 2008), Utrecht, Netherlands. Web: http://GerryStahl.net/pub/icls2008johann.pdf

Sarmiento-Klapper, J. W. (2009). *Bridging mechanisms in team-based online problem solving: Continuity in building collaborative knowledge.* Unpublished Dissertation, Ph.D., College of Information Science and Technology, Drexel University, Philadelphia, PA, USA

Sawyer, R. K. (Ed.). (2006). *Cambridge handbook of the learning sciences.* Cambridge, UK: Cambridge University Press

Scardamalia, M., & Bereiter, C. (1996). Computer support for knowledge-building communities. In T. Koschmann (Ed.), *CSCL: Theory and practice of an emerging paradigm* (pp. 249-268). Hillsdale, NJ: Lawrence Erlbaum Associates

Scher, D. (2002). *Students' conceptions of geometry in a dynamic geometry software environment.* Unpublished Dissertation, Ph. D. , School of Education, New York University, New York, NY

Schwarz, B. B. (1997). Understanding symbols with intermediate abstractions: An analysis of the collaborative construction of mathematical meaning. In L. B. Resnick, R. Saljo, C. Pontecorvo & B. Burge (Eds.), *Discourse, tools, and reasoning: Essays on situated cognition* (pp. 312-335). Berlin, Germany: Springer

Sfard, A. (2008). *Thinking as communicating: Human development, the growth of discourses and mathematizing.* Cambridge, UK: Cambridge University Press.

Stahl, G. (2006). *Group cognition: Computer support for building collaborative knowledge.* Cambridge, MA: MIT Press. 510 + viii pages. Web: http://GerryStahl.net/mit/

Stahl, G. (2008). Book review: Exploring thinking as communicating in CSCL. *International Journal of Computer-Supported Collaborative Learning, 3*(3), 361-368. Web: http://GerryStahl.net/pub/Sfardreview.pdf Doi: http://dx.doi.org/10.1007/s11412-008-9046-4

Stahl, G. (2009). *Studying virtual math teams.* New York, NY: Springer. 626 +xxi pages. Web: http://GerryStahl.net/vmt/book Doi: http://dx.doi.org/10.1007/978-1-4419-0228-3

Stahl, G. (2010a). Group cognition as a foundation for the new science of learning. In M. S. Khine & I. M. Saleh (Eds.), *New science of learning: Computers, cognition and collaboration in education.* New York, NY: Springer. Web: http://GerryStahl.net/pub/scienceoflearning.pdf

Stahl, G. (2010b). How I view learning and thinking in CSCL groups. *Research and Practice in Technology Enhanced Learning (RPTEL).* Web: http://GerryStahl.net/pub/rptel2010.pdf

Stahl, G., Koschmann, T., & Suthers, D. (2006). Computer-supported collaborative learning: An historical perspective. In R. K. Sawyer (Ed.), *Cambridge handbook of the learning sciences* (pp. 409-426). Cambridge, UK: Cambridge University Press. Web: http://GerryStahl.net/cscl/CSCL_English.pdf in English, http://GerryStahl.net/cscl/CSCL_Chinese_simplified.pdf in simplified Chinese, http://GerryStahl.net/cscl/CSCL_Chinese_traditional.pdf in traditional Chinese, http://GerryStahl.net/cscl/CSCL_Spanish.pdf in Spanish, http://GerryStahl.net/cscl/CSCL_Portuguese.pdf in Portuguese, http://GerryStahl.net/cscl/CSCL_German.pdf in German, http://GerryStahl.net/cscl/CSCL_Romanian.pdf in Romanian, http://GerryStahl.net/cscl/CSCL_Japanese.pdf in Japanese

Wee, J. D. (2009). *Reinventing mathematics problem design and analysis of chat interactions in quasi-synchronous chat environments.* Unpublished Dissertation, Ph. D., National Institute of Education, Nanyang Techological University, Singapore

Wegerif, R. (2007). *Dialogic, education and technology: Expanding the space of learning.* New York, NY: Kluwer-Springer.

Zhou, N. (2010). *Investigating information practices of collaborative online small groups engaged in problem solving.* Unpublished Dissertation, Ph.D., College of Information Science and Technology, Drexel University, Philadelphia, PA, USA

Authors

Gerry Stahl, College of Information Science & Technology, Drexel University, Philadelphia, USA, email: Gerry@GerryStahl.net

Murat Perit , College of Information Science & Technology, Drexel University, Philadelphia, USA, email: mpc48@drexel.edu

Stephen Weimar, The Math Forum, Drexel University, Philadelphia, USA, email: steve@MathForum.org

Baba Kofi Weusijana, The Math Forum, Drexel University, Philadelphia, USA, email: baba@MathForum.org

Jimmy Xiantong Ou, The Math Forum, Drexel University, Philadelphia, USA, email: xiantong.ou@gmail.com

11. Analyzing the Discourse of GeoGebra Collaborations

Gerry Stahl, Carolyn Penstein Rosé, Sean Goggins

This is a position paper presenting a perspective on fundamental assumptions about doing, teaching and learning mathematics in the presence of computer and communicative technologies. Doing, teaching and learning mathematics are activities that centrally involve discourse. Computer and communication technologies can facilitate collaborative interactions around mathematical topics. This can make the processes of doing, teaching and learning mathematics visible to researchers in the traces of small-group interaction. Analysis of the discourse can reveal processes of mathematical group cognition. We argue for a view of mathematics as discourse and for a specific set of complementary approaches to analyzing collaborative math discourse.

Collaborative mathematics

The argument against discourse-based approaches to math education—like inquiry learning and collaborative learning—is generally that students must first learn the basic facts before they can speculate on their own. The major worry expressed about learning through peer discourse is that the group of students will come up with the wrong answer or an incorrect theory. The proposed solution is that education must "go back to the basics" and focus on delivering the basic facts of each field to all the students first, and then, if there is time left over, allow students to discuss their own ideas based on the foundation of knowledge of these facts. Mathematics is taken as the clearest example of this argument. Make sure that students have memorized their number facts first, then drill them on applying algorithmic manipulations such as long division. If there is any place for discovery learning, it must come later. Of course, there is never extra time because once the facts of one area of math have been practiced, it is time to move on to the next in a never-ending sequence of math areas (Boaler, 2008; Lockhart, 2009). Similarly, with science, the approach is to have students memorize the basic terminology and facts of one scientific field after another. The assumption is always that there is a fixed body of factual knowledge that forms the uncontested basics of each field of math and science.

However, neither math nor science works that way in reality. Each actual field of math and science has evolved and grown through controversy and over-turning of one position after another. Math and science are the products of inquiry, dialog and controversy at the level of the creation of individual results and at the level of the formulation of theories for whole areas.

For instance, the expansion of the concept of number in the history of math proceeded through the repeated criticism of the limits of each historical concept: from the integers to rationals, to irrationals, to imaginary and complex, to transfinite, to infintesimal, to hyperreal, …. (Lakoff & Núñez, 2000). If one follows a particular theorem, such as Lakatos' (1976) study of refutations of proofs of Euler's theorem, one sees that historical progress in professional mathematics proceeds not by collecting more and more facts, but by reconceptualizations and constructive criticism. Individual proofs of professional mathematics also proceed through complex paths of inquiry, speculation and critique—although this path of discovery is obscured in the linear logic of published presentations.

An interesting example of innovative mathematical proof arose this past year when Timothy Gowers, a renowned professional mathematician, invited others to participate in a virtual math team effort to find a new proof for a theorem which had only been proven until then in a very indirect and obscure way (Polymath, 2010):

> The work was carried out by several researchers, who wrote their thoughts, as they had them, in the form of blog comments at http://gowers.wordpress.com. Anybody who wanted to could participate, and at all stages of the process the comments were fully open to anybody who was interested. This open process was in complete contrast to the usual way that results are proved in private and presented in a finished form. The blog comments are still available, so although this paper is a polished account of the DHJ argument, it is possible to read a record of the entire thought process that led to the proof. (p. 4)

As Gowers (Gowers & Nielsen, 2010) observed from a look at the trace of the collaborative effort, even at the highest levels of math problem solving, consideration of false starts is integral to the process:

The working record of the Polymath Project is a remarkable resource for students of mathematics and for historians and philosophers of science. For the first time one can see on full display a complete account of how a serious mathematical result was discovered. It shows vividly how ideas grow, change, improve and are discarded.... Even the best mathematicians can make basic mistakes and pursue many failed ideas. (p. 880)

Analyzing discourse

In the VMT Project, we study the traces of online collaborative interactions of small groups of students discussing math topics in order to observe the methods of students engaged in math problem-solving discourse (Stahl, 2006; 2009b). We use various approaches to analyzing the discourse. In order to work effectively together, students must make their thinking visible to their collaborators. They can do this in many ways, dependent upon the affordances of the online environment. The VMT environment, for instance, supports chat texting, shared whiteboard drawing, GeoGebra constructions, graphical referencing, wiki postings and math symbols. Because the VMT system captures a complete trace of the group interactions, the thinking that the students make visible to each other is also visible to researchers.

One approach that we take to the analysis of student interactions is to conduct *data sessions* in which a group of researchers collaboratively view the log of what took place in a VMT chat room and slowly step through the interaction (see Section 4 below). This way, we get interpretations of what took place, as seen from the various personal perspectives of researchers with different methodological training. Building on such relatively informal observations, individual researchers can then look more systematically at the trace data and develop analyses of the student-student interactions using concepts and techniques of conversation analysis (Schegloff, 2007), as adapted to online math discourse.

Also, we can look at the relations among the students through *social-network* analysis (see Section 5 below). This way we can quantitatively measure the different roles (e.g., leaders and responders) in the discourse of different groups during various sessions. We can see what the lines of communication were and we can correlate social roles with other characteristics, including measures of math learning.

A third approach is to *code* individual lines of chat for different kinds of interactional moves that may be of interest (see Section 6 below). Then, statistical analysis can reveal patterns in the discourse. In addition, we can correlate individual student learning with characteristics of the chats. For instance, we might compare math test results of individual students before and after the VMT sessions to see who learned the most and then see which groups contained students who learned more or less than students in other groups. Knowing how well students in different groups learned, we can compare the statistical characteristics of the discourse in the different groups.

Conversation analysis and discourse analysis

In *Group Cognition* (Stahl, 2006), we argued that we do not yet have a science of small groups. Current approaches in education, psychology and related fields focus either on the individual or the community, but not on the intermediate small group as the unit of analysis. For instance, most discussions of small groups either reduce group phenomena to individual behaviors or to cultural factors. The VMT Project has been trying to define in a preliminary way a science of groups appropriate to understanding computer-supported collaborative learning (Stahl, 2010a). We are interested in the specifically group-level phenomena. Focused on the group unit of analysis, our approach adopts the analytic approach of Conversation Analysis (CA) and adapts it from informal social conversation of mainly dyads to online, task-oriented interaction of small groups; in the VMT case, the groups are usually four or five high school students discussing mathematical relationships, using text chat and a shared whiteboard.

In the past year, we have been trying to apply CA techniques in a systematic way to the coding of VMT chat logs (Stahl, 2009a; 2010b). In doing so, we have begun to suspect that these CA techniques are at too fine-grained a level to capture the most important group-cognitive processes in small-group problem solving. While it is true that the adjacency-pair structure on which CA analysis focuses provides much of the interactional fabric of small-group cognitive work, (a) it is at too detailed a level to describe the important methods of mathematical group cognition, (b) it is often deviated from in the complexity of text chat by multiple participants and (c) it fails to capture the larger problem-solving processes that are fundamental to mathematical tasks. At the other extreme, Discourse Analysis (DA) (Gee, 1992) is too high-level, oriented toward the socio-cultural issues, such as power relationships and gender.

Just as we have previously maintained that a small-group-level science of group cognition is needed to fill the theoretical lacuna between individual-level psychology and community-level social science, we now propose that an analytic method is needed that fills the gap between CA and DA. We call this new method Group-Cognition Analysis (GCA). It builds on the adjacency-pair structure fore-grounded by CA, but looks at the longer sequences that are so important to mathematical problem solving and explanation. Unfortunately, GCA is extremely time consuming and involves tedious, detailed, multi-dimensional analysis of the words, references and utterances that go into longer sequences; therefore, we are interested in computer-supported statistical analysis and automated coding to assist and complement this analysis process.

Analyzing interaction structure

To complement the ethnomethodologically informed interaction analysis, we will analyze VMT chat logs using content analysis (Krippendorff, 2004) and social-network analysis (Wasserman & Faust, 1992). The content analysis will be executed using the following two rubrics. The unit of analysis for this work will be a complete unit of group conversation.

The first rubric will evaluate the development of group identity within the small groups, using Tajfel's (1978) description of group communication as inter-group, inter-personal, intra-group and inter-individual. Inter-group communication is communication across groups, and only rarely occurs in VMT data. Inter-personal communication takes place between two individuals. Intra-group communication is within the group, where all members participate in the dialogue. An utterance addressing an individual member in the presence of the whole group is coded as inter-individual communication.

The second rubric will evaluate trace data for knowledge co-construction using a rubric developed by Gunawardena et al (1997). Two raters will score the conversations on these rubrics and measure inter-rater reliability using Krippendorf's alpha (2004). This type of analysis has been performed by Goggins (2009) on asynchronous communication records. The contrast with the results from synchronous chat data will provide a helpful comparison of synchronous and asynchronous knowledge co-construction in small groups.

Social-network analysis will be performed on group interactions in order to determine if there are patterns of networked interaction that correspond with the development of group identity or the co-construction of knowledge. The resulting networks will be bi-partite (users and objects) and regular. Since the networks in online chats are closed and small, we will focus our analysis on small network evolution over time and on elaborating semantically meaningful measures of tie strength.

Tracking longitudinal evolution will involve developing a time-series set of network views, possibly addressing the state of the network as a feature that contributes to other forms of analysis. We will also explore the advantages of deriving measures of tie strength from the results of machine-learning algorithms, response-time lag and length of sustained interaction between pairs of group members.

Automated language analysis

In recent years, the computer-supported collaborative learning community has shown great interest in automatic analysis of data from collaborative-learning settings, building on and extending state-of-the-art work in text mining from the language-technologies community. Automatic analysis approaches as we know them today are only capable of identifying patterns that occur in a stable and recognizable way. Although those patterns can be arbitrarily complex, there are limitations to contexts in which an approach of this nature is appropriate. These approaches are most naturally usable within research traditions that value abstraction and quantification. The most natural application of such technology is within traditions that employ coding-and-counting approaches to analysis of verbal data. Thus, we do not see this at all as a replacement for the two frameworks discussed above, but as a synergistic approach. By nature, empirical-modeling approaches involving statistics and machine learning are mainly useful for capturing what is typical. In contrast, within many qualitative-research traditions, it is the unusual occurrences and practices that are worthy of study. Thus, it is unlikely that such technology would be directly usable for producing the kind of findings that are valued within those traditions. However, what it may be able to assist with is finding the unusual occurrences within a mass of data, which might then be worthy of study in a more qualitative way.

Machine-learning algorithms can learn mappings between a set of input features and a set of output categories, allowing us to automatically generate coded categories for input utterances. Language-analysis software does this by using statistical techniques to find characteristics of hand-coded "training examples" that exemplify each of the output categories. The goal of the algorithm is to learn rules by generalizing from these examples in such a way that the rules can be applied effectively to new examples. In order for this to work well, the set of input features provided must be sufficiently expressive, and the training examples must be representative.

Once candidate input features have been identified, analysts typically hand code a large number of training examples. The previously developed TagHelper tool set (Rosé et al., 2008) and more recent SIDE tool set (Mayfield & Rosé, to appear) both have the capability of allowing users to define how texts will be represented and processed by making selections in their GUI interfaces. In addition to basic text-processing tools such as part-of-speech taggers and stemmers—which are used to construct a representation of the text that machine-learning algorithms can work with—a variety of algorithms from toolkits such as Weka (Witten & Frank, 2005) are included in order to provide many alternative machine-learning algorithms to map between the input features and the output categories. Based on their understanding of the classification problem, machine-learning practitioners typically pick an algorithm that they expect will perform well. Often this is an iterative process of applying an algorithm, seeing where the trained classifier makes mistakes, and then adding additional input features, removing extraneous input features or experimenting with algorithms. SIDE, in particular, includes an interface for supporting this process of error analysis, which aids in the process of moving forward from a sub-optimal result. Our automatic analysis technology is extensively discussed in our recent article investigating the use of text-classification technology for automatic collaborative-learning process analysis (Rosé et al., 2008).

Conclusion

In this position paper, we have argued that traditional assumptions about doing, teaching and learning mathematics focused on the acquisition of basic math facts by individuals misses the central role of discourse in doing, teaching and learning mathematics. This does not mean that we believe that groups of students should just be left to talk about math without any guidance, as though this would lead them to reproduce centuries of mathematical advances. Rather, we believe that it is important for researchers to study closely the nature of mathematical discourse within small groups discussing strategically designed math topics and supported by powerful computer tools, like GeoGebra. In particular, we have identified a research opportunity for pursuing such a research agenda by studying the traces of online collaborative learning of math to observe the individual and group cognition that is made visible there. We have proposed a set of complementary approaches to the analysis of student online math discourse with the potential to describe group-cognitive moves that contribute to math learning.

Our argument here has focused on certain methodologies that we believe can be fruitfully applied to the detailed and rigorous analysis of online collaborative learning of mathematics. This should not be taken as a rejection of the validity of other approaches, not referenced in our position paper, but as a proposal for a specific approach that we are investigating. We believe that the complex of issues surrounding the analysis of computer-supported collaborative mathematics learning calls for a multiplicity of methodologies.

References

Boaler, J. (2008). What's math got to do with it? Helping children learn to love their most hated subject: And why it is important for America. New York, NY: Viking.

Cobb, P. (1995). Mathematical learning and small-group interaction: Four case studies. In P. Cobb & H. Bauersfeld (Eds.), The emergence of mathematical meaning. (pp. 25-130). Mahwah, NJ: Lawrence Erlbaum Associates.

Gee, J. P. (1992). The social mind: Language, ideology, and social practice. New York, NY: Bergin & Garvey.

Goggins, S. (2009). Knowledge management, social identity and social network structure in completely online groups. Unpublished Dissertation, Ph.D., Information Science & Technology, University of Missouri.

Gowers, T., & Nielsen, M. (2010). Massively collaborative mathematics. Nature. 461(15), 879-881.

Gunawardena, C. N., Lowe, C. A., & Anderson, T. (1997). Analysis of a global online debate and the development of an interaction analysis model for examining social construction of knowledge in computer conferencing. Journal of Educational Computing Research. 17, 397-343.

Krippendorff, K. (2004). Reliability in content analysis: Some common misconceptions and recommendations. Human Communication Research. 30, 411-433.

Lakatos, I. (1976). Proofs and refutations: The logic of mathematical discovery. Cambridge, UK: Cambridge University Press.

Lakoff, G., & Núñez, R. (2000). Where mathematics comes from: How the embodied mind brings mathematics into being. New York City, NY: Basic Books.

Livingston, E. (1999). Cultures of proving. Social Studies of Science. 29(6), 867-888.

Lockhart, P. (2009). A mathematician's lament: How school cheats us out of our most fascinating and imaginative art forms. New York, NY: Belevue Literary Press.

Mayfield, E., & Rosé, C. P. (to appear). An interactive tool for supporting error analysis for text mining: Demo. Paper presented at the Human Language

Technologies: The 11th Annual Conference of the North American Chapter of the Association for Computational Linguistics.

Netz, R. (1999). The shaping of deduction in Greek mathematics: A study in cognitive history. Cambridge, UK: Cambridge University Press.

Papert, S. (1980). Mindstorms: Children, computers and powerful ideas. New York, NY: Basic Books.

Polymath, D. H. J. (2010). A new proof of the density hales-jewett theorem. arXiv. Web: http://arxiv.org/abs/0910.3926v2

Powell, A. B., Francisco, J. M., & Maher, C. A. (2003). An analytical model for studying the development of mathematical ideas and reasoning using videotape data. Journal of Mathematical Behavior. 22(4), 405-435.

Rosé, C., Wang, Y.-C., Cui, Y., Arguello, J., Stegmann, K., Weinberger, A., et al. (2008). Analyzing collaborative learning processes automatically: Exploiting the advances of computational linguistics in computer-supported collaborative learning. International Journal of Computer-Supported Collaborative Learning. 3(3), 237-271. Doi: http://dx.doi.org/10.1007/s11412-007-9034-0

Sawyer, R. K. (Ed.). (2006). Cambridge handbook of the learning sciences. Cambridge, UK: Cambridge University Press.

Schegloff, E. A. (2007). Sequence organization in interaction: A primer in conversation analysis. Cambridge, UK: Cambridge University Press.

Sfard, A. (2008). Thinking as communicating: Human development, the growth of discourses and mathematizing. Cambridge, UK: Cambridge University Press.

Stahl, G. (2006). Group cognition: Computer support for building collaborative knowledge. Cambridge, MA: MIT Press. 510 + viii pages. Web: http://GerryStahl.net/mit/

Stahl, G. (2009a). Keynote: How I view learning and thinking in CSCL groups. Paper presented at the International Conference on Computers and Education (ICCE 2009). Hong Kong, China. Web: http://GerryStahl.net/pub/iccekeynote2009.pdf

Stahl, G. (2009b). Studying virtual math teams. New York, NY: Springer. 626 +xxi pages. Web: http://GerryStahl.net/vmt/book Doi: http://dx.doi.org/10.1007/978-1-4419-0228-3

Stahl, G. (2010a). Group cognition as a foundation for the new science of learning. In M. S. Khine & I. M. Saleh (Eds.), New science of learning: Computers, cognition and collaboration in education. New York, NY: Springer. Web: http://GerryStahl.net/pub/scienceoflearning.pdf

Stahl, G. (2010b). The structure of collaborative problem solving in a virtual math team. Paper presented at the Conference for Groupware (GROUP 2010). Sanibel Island, FL. Web: http://GerryStahl.net/pub/group2010.pdf

Stahl, G., Koschmann, T., & Suthers, D. (2006). Computer-supported collaborative learning: An historical perspective. In R. K. Sawyer (Ed.), Cambridge handbook of the learning sciences. (pp. 409-426). Cambridge, UK: Cambridge University Press. Web: http://GerryStahl.net/cscl/CSCL_English.pdf in English, http://GerryStahl.net/cscl/CSCL_Chinese_simplified.pdf in simplified Chinese, http://GerryStahl.net/cscl/CSCL_Chinese_traditional.pdf in traditional Chinese, http://GerryStahl.net/cscl/CSCL_Spanish.pdf in Spanish, http://GerryStahl.net/cscl/CSCL_Portuguese.pdf in Portuguese,

http://GerryStahl.net/cscl/CSCL_German.pdf in German,
http://GerryStahl.net/cscl/CSCL_Romanian.pdf in Romanian,
http://GerryStahl.net/cscl/CSCL_Japanese.pdf in Japanese

Stahl, G., Ou, J. X., Cakir, M. P., Weimar, S., & Goggins, S. (2010). Multi-user support for virtual geogebra teams. Paper presented at the First North American GeoGebra Conference. Ithaca, NY. Web:
http://GerryStahl.net/pub/geogebrana2010c.pdf

Stahl, G., Rosé, C. P., O'Hara, K., & Powell, A. B. (2010). Supporting group math cognition in virtual math teams with software conversational agents. Paper presented at the First North American GeoGebra Conference. Ithaca, NY. Web:
http://GerryStahl.net/pub/geogebrana2010a.pdf

Tajfel, H. (Ed.). (1978). Differentiation between social groups: Studies in the social psychology of intergroup relations. Oxford, UK: Academic Press.

Wasserman, S., & Faust, K. (1992). Social network analysis: Methods and applications. Cambridge, UK: Cambridge University Press.

Witten, I. H., & Frank, E. (2005). Data mining: Practical machine learning tools and techniques (2nd ed.). San Francisco, CA: Morgan Kaufmann.

12. Supporting Group Math with Software Conversational Agents

Gerry Stahl, Carolyn Penstein Rosé, Kate O'Hara, Arthur Powell

This is a research paper on a new tool to support dynamic mathematics in education. The research explores the use of software agents to engage in synchronous interaction with a small group of students working online in the Virtual Math Teams environment. The purpose of the agents is to facilitate discourse by the students that promotes their collaborative learning. In particular, the conversational agents try to encourage academically productive talk, in which students work together in ways that are accountable to each other and to their task. The agents are currently being tested in student groups working on problems in combinatorics. This research will soon be extended to student groups using a multi-user version of GeoGebra.

The vision of software agents used to support collaborative online work with dynamic math

The vision of the Virtual Math Teams (VMT) Project (Stahl, 2009b) is to open up an online opportunity for students to get together in small groups to discuss mathematics. The educational theory behind this is that learning mathematics centrally involves developing skills in mathematical discourse (Sfard, 2008). While the Internet allows students from around the world to enter into conversation with each other, turning that abstract possibility into a practical experience with educational benefits requires more than generic online communication media (Stahl, 2006). The VMT environment supplies some of the kinds of tools needed for sharing and discussing mathematical constructions and relationships. It also allows educators to develop well-designed and motivating math topics for exploration and discussion. The VMT environment is currently being extended to incorporate a multi-user version of GeoGebra—see the previous two chapters.

In order to enhance the focus of students on math topics and to guide them in productive directions, forms of scaffolding or scripting their discussion are probably important (Kobbe et al., 2007). Of course, well-conceived topic statements can go a long way toward setting a discussion off in a promising direction from the start (Powell et al., 2009). Also, following up on the small-group work with various kinds of feedback afterwards can help to overcome problematic student understandings. For instance, a teacher can annotate or formally assess the work after an online session, student groups can comment on each other's findings or class discussion following the online group work can check the thinking of individual groups and bring multiple approaches into contact with each other.

In addition to scaffolding before and after the small-group work, it is possible to guide the collaborative process synchronously. It may not be practical to expect a teacher who is supervising several groups to interact effectively with all of them simultaneously. The groups may even be meeting at times when a teacher is not available. In fact, groups of students may decide to discuss math topics with no teacher involved. Our research looks at the possibility of using software conversational agents to guide the student discourse synchronously in some productive way. Software agents have proven to be effective in guiding the mathematical work of individual students. In addition, progress in computer analysis of natural (human) language makes it feasible to design software that can parse typed utterances and respond to them based on their characteristics. This provides the motivation for our investigations of the use of "conversational agents" in the VMT environment (Cui et al., 2009).

Conversational agents

We have integrated the agent technology developed by Carolyn Rose's research group (Cui et al., 2009) into the VMT environment developed by Gerry Stahl's research group (Stahl, 2009a). The conversational agents appear in the VMT interface just like human chat participants (see Figure 1).

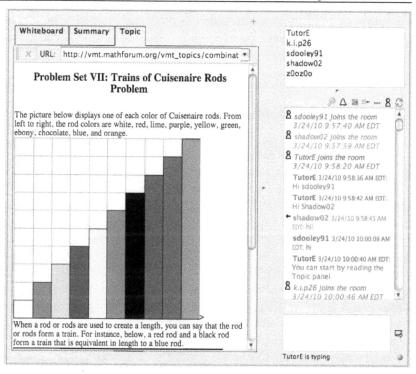

Figure 1. The VMT collaborative-math-learning environment. Note along the right-hand side of the interface that a software agent named TutorE is listed as a current user, as the poster of several chat utterances and as the current chat typist.

There have already been several successful studies of student groups benefitting from the support of automatically triggered conversational agents that enrich the interaction between students (Kumar & Rosé, 2010); many of these studies have employed a version of the Virtual Math Teams environment augmented with this form of dynamic collaborative-learning support (Cui et al., 2009; Kumar & Rosé, 2009). For example, early evaluations measured the extent to which students learned more in conditions when automatic support was offered in the environment in comparison to conditions where it was not (Kumar, Gweon et al., 2007; Kumar, Rosé et al., 2007; Wang et al., 2007). These early studies showed that addition of a support agent into the environment increased pre to post-test learning gains by about one standard deviation, which is a full letter grade. Subsequent studies compared alternative versions of this form of automatic support. These evaluations showed additional increases in effectiveness as we have refined the design of the support. For example, Chaudhuri et al. (2009) showed that students learned more when the support agents allowed the students to put off discussion with the support agents until they were ready to give it their full attention. Ai et al. (to appear) showed that students learned more when the support agents engaged in social behavior in addition to only offering cognitive support.

Academically productive talk

It is quite easy to program agents to greet students as they enter a VMT chat room and to prompt students to say something when everyone is quiet for an extended period or to prompt a specific student to contribute when that student has been particularly quiet. Another agent strategy might be to suggest mathematical content that is relevant to a current stage of problem solving. This might build on the intelligent tutoring technologies developed for guiding individual math learning. Intelligent tutors maintain a model of one or more standard solutions to a problem and also develop a model of the student understanding or problem-solving strategy, which is then compared step by step with the correct solution. Such an approach may be more problematic where there is a group of students with different understandings and where the goal of the math topic is more to explore than to derive the correct answer. So we are also experimenting with an alternative approach of generic guidance for math discourse and collaboration.

An approach called "academically productive talk" seems promising for scaffolding collaborative math discourse. Academically productive talk strategies have developed in response to observed difficulties that teachers have in maintaining mathematical rigor and reasoning in their class discussions (Michaels, O'Connor & Resnick, 2008). Academically productive talk has three dimensions: accountability to the community, accountability to math knowledge and accountability to accepted standards of reasoning. The concept of academically productive talk thus highlights the need to combine appropriate classroom discourse, mathematical rigor and student reasoning to achieve powerful mathematics instruction and learning.

The academically productive talk form of classroom interaction is one in which a facilitator (or an agent) poses a question that calls for a relatively elaborated response (in mathematics, both a solution and a reason for the solution) and then presses the group as a whole to develop explanations for the solution. The process includes extended exchanges between teacher and student and among students, and includes a variety of talk moves, such as asking other students to explain what the first respondent has said, challenging students—sometimes via posing of counter examples, or "re-voicing" a student's contribution ("So let me see if I've got your idea right. Are you saying…?"), which makes the student's idea, reformulated by the teacher, available to the entire group.

Experiments with combinatorics

We are currently conducting a series of experiments using a curriculum of problems in combinatorics (Powell, Lai & O'Hara, 2009) specifically designed for the VMT Project by Arthur Powell's research group. This involves eight problems:

1.   The Towers Problem Set

2.   The Pascal's Triangle Problem Set

3.   The Pizza Problem Set

4.   The Pizza with Halves Problem Set

5.   The World Series Problem Set

6.   The Taxicab Problem Set

7.   The Cuisenaire Rods Problem Set

8.   Final Compare-and-Contrast Problem Set

The problems are closely related to each other and to Pascal's triangle (Powell & Lai, 2009), which is introduced in the second problem. A high school class on finite math taught by Kate O'Hara is working on these problems in small groups. They work on each problem for about two sessions, gradually gaining insight into the structure of typical combinatorics problems.

In these experiments, conversational agents play different roles, as discussed above. In the first place, we have tried a broad range of degrees of intervention. We often use a "wizard-of-oz" approach, in which a human researcher plays the role of the software agent, without the student participants knowing. This makes it easier to try many different approaches, without being too concerned about the practicality of programming them.

In some sessions, the agents play a rather directive role, similar to that of a teacher-centered discourse. Here, the agent recommends steps for students to take, asks questions and provides content-related feedback. The students become quite focused on interacting with the agents—even more than with each other. They ask the agents to tell them if they have the correct answer and sometimes even ask the agent to give them the answer.

In other sessions, the agent greets the students at the beginning and then informs them that they are accountable for their own discourse and math work, but that the agent is available to answer questions. In such cases, the agent plays the role of an interactive help system without being intrusive. Students can easily access the agent by addressing it in the chat, just as they would address a peer or teacher.

Probably the most interesting role for the agents is as promoters of academically productive talk. Here, they monitor the discourse and occasionally intervene to encourage mutual understanding among the students in a group. Thus, they promote accountability to the collaborative community, to math knowledge and to accepted standards of reasoning in their class.

Experiments with GeoGebra

When the students finish their sessions on combinatorics, we will move on to dynamic geometry topics involving the use of GeoGebra. Our VMT 2.0 environment, currently in alpha testing in several experimental classrooms, includes a multi-user version of GeoGebra. In Figure 2, a quadrilateral has been constructed and the midpoints of its edges have been connected. The chat participants are discussing the ratio of the area of the interior quadrilateral to that of the original one.

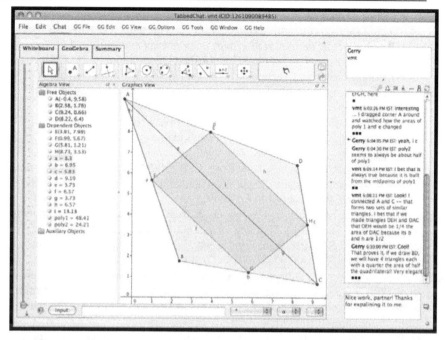

Figure 2. A GeoGebra construction created and discussed collaboratively in the VMT 2.0 learning environment.

Of course, the work in Figure 2 is just a scenario, not actual student data. When we conduct experiments with student groups we will be interested in how they integrate work in GeoGebra with the chat discourse. As an additional layer, we will have the interactions in the chat between students and conversational agents. An added challenge for development of our software agents will be the question of whether the agents need to analyze the work in the GeoGebra tab or whether they can just focus on the chat discourse.

We hope that our experience with these studies will help us to determine the most effective roles for conversational agents in facilitating virtual GeoGebra teams.

References

Ai, H., Kumar, R., Nguyen, D., Nagasunder, A., & Rosé, C. P. (to appear). *Exploring the effectiveness of social capabilities and goal alignment in computer-supported collaborative learning.* Paper presented at the Intelligent Tutoring Systems.

Boaler, J. (2008). *What's math got to do with it? Helping children learn to love their most hated subject: And why it is important for America.* New York, NY: Viking.

Çakir, M. P. (2009). *How online small groups co-construct mathematical artifacts to do collaborative problem solving.* Unpublished Dissertation, Ph.D., College of Information Science and Technology, Drexel University. Philadelphia, PA, USA.

Çakır, M. P., Zemel, A., & Stahl, G. (2009). The joint organization of interaction within a multimodal CSCL medium. *International Journal of Computer-Supported Collaborative Learning. 4*(2), 115-149. Web: http://GerryStahl.net/pub/ijCSCL_4_2_1.pdf Doi: http://dx.doi.org/10.1007/s11412-009-9061-0

Chaudhuri, S., Kumar, R., Howley, I., & Rosé, C. P. (2009). *Engaging collaborative learners with helping agents.* Paper presented at the Conference on Artificial Intelligence in Education (AI in Ed 2009).

Cui, Y., Kumar, R., Chaudhuri, S., Gweon, G., & Rosé, C. P. (2009). Helping agents in VMT. In G. Stahl (Ed.), *Studying virtual math teams.* (ch. 19, pp. 335-354). New York, NY: Springer. Web: http://GerryStahl.net/vmt/book/19.pdf Doi: http://dx.doi.org/10.1007/978-1-4419-0228-3_19

Kobbe, L., Weinberger, A., Dillenbourg, P., Harrer, A., Hämäläinen, R., Häkkinen, P., et al. (2007). Specifying computer-supported collaboration scripts. *International Journal of Computer-Supported Collaborative Learning. 2*(2), 211-224. Doi: http://dx.doi.org/10.1007/s11412-007-9014-4

Kumar, R., Gweon, G., Joshi, M., Cui, Y., & Rosé, C. P. (2007). *Supporting students working together on math with social dialogue.* Paper presented at the *SLaTE Workshop on Speech and Language Technology in Education.*

Kumar, R., & Rosé, C. P. (2009). *Building conversational agents with basilica.* Paper presented at the North American Chapter of the Association for Computational Linguistics.

Kumar, R., & Rosé, C. P. (2010). *Engaging learning groups using social interaction strategies.* Paper presented at the North American Chapter of the Association for Computational Linguistics.

Kumar, R., Rosé, C. P., Wang, Y. C., Joshi, M., & Robinson, A. (2007). *Tutorial dialogue as adaptive collaborative learning support.* Paper presented at the *Conference on Artificial Intelligence in Education (AIED 2007).*

Litz, I. R. (2007). *Student adoption of a computer-supported collaborative learning (CSCL) mathematical problem solving environment: The case of the math forum's virtual math teams (VMT) chat service.* Unpublished Dissertation, Ph.D., School of Computer and Information Sciences, Nova Southeastern University. Florida.

Lockhart, P. (2009). *A mathematician's lament: How school cheats us out of our most fascinating and imaginative art forms.* New York, NY: Belevue Literary Press.

Michaels, S., O'Connor, C., & Resnick, L. B. (2008). Deliberative discourse idealized and realized: Accountable talk in the classroom and in civic life. *Studies in the Philosophy of Education. 27*(4), 283-297.

Mühlpfordt, M. (2008). *Integration dualer interaktionsräume: Die verknuepfung von textbasierter synchroner kommunikation mit diskreten konstruktionswerkzeugen. (the integration of dual-interaction spaces: The connection of text-based synchronous communication with graphical construction tools [in German]).* Unpublished Dissertation, Ph.D., Fakultaet fuer Mathematik und Informatik, Fern Universitaet. Hagen, Germany.

Powell, A. B., Borge, I. C., Floriti, G. I., Kondratieva, M., Koublanova, E., & Sukthankar, N. (2009). Challenging tasks and mathematics learning. In E. J. Barbeau & P. J. Taylor (Eds.), *Challenging mathematics in and beyond the classroom: The 16th icmi study.* New York, NY: Springer.

Powell, A. B., & Lai, F. F. (2009). Inscriptions, mathematical ideas and reasoning in VMT. In G. Stahl (Ed.), *Studying virtual math teams.* (ch. 13, pp. 237-259). New York, NY: Springer. Web: http://GerryStahl.net/vmt/book/13.pdf Doi: http://dx.doi.org/10.1007/978-1-4419-0228-3_13

Powell, A. B., Lai, F. F., & O'Hara, K. (2009). *Supplemental curriculum unit for online, collaborative problem solving in VMT.* Web: http://GerryStahl.net/vmt/combinatorics.pdf

Renninger, K. A., & Shumar, W. (2002). *Building virtual communities.* Cambridge, UK: Cambridge University Press.

Sarmiento, J., & Stahl, G. (2008). *Extending the joint problem space: Time and sequence as essential features of knowledge building.* Paper presented at the International Conference of the Learning Sciences (ICLS 2008). Utrecht, Netherlands. Web: http://GerryStahl.net/pub/icls2008johann.pdf

Sarmiento-Klapper, J. W. (2009). *Bridging mechanisms in team-based online problem solving: Continuity in building collaborative knowledge.* Unpublished Dissertation, Ph.D., College of Information Science and Technology, Drexel University. Philadelphia, PA, USA.

Scher, D. (2002). *Students' conceptions of geometry in a dynamic geometry software environment.* Unpublished Dissertation, Ph.D., School of Education, New York University. New York, NY.

Sfard, A. (2008). *Thinking as communicating: Human development, the growth of discourses and mathematizing.* Cambridge, UK: Cambridge University Press.

Stahl, G. (2006). *Group cognition: Computer support for building collaborative knowledge.* Cambridge, MA: MIT Press. 510 + viii pages. Web: http://GerryStahl.net/mit/

Stahl, G. (2009a). Designing a mix of synchronous and asynchronous media for VMT. In G. Stahl (Ed.), *Studying virtual math teams.* (ch. 16, pp. 295-310). New York, NY: Springer. Web: http://GerryStahl.net/vmt/book/16.pdf Doi: http://dx.doi.org/10.1007/978-1-4419-0228-3_16

Stahl, G. (2009b). *Studying virtual math teams.* New York, NY: Springer. 626 +xxi pages. Web: http://GerryStahl.net/vmt/book Doi: http://dx.doi.org/10.1007/978-1-4419-0228-3

Stahl, G., Ou, J. X., Cakir, M. P., Weimar, S., & Goggins, S. (2010). *Multi-user support for virtual geogebra teams.* Paper presented at the First North American GeoGebra Conference. Ithaca, NY. Web: http://GerryStahl.net/pub/geogebrana2010c.pdf

Stahl, G., Rosé, C. P., & Goggins, S. (2010). *Analyzing the discourse of geogebra collaborations.* Paper presented at the First North American GeoGebra Conference. Ithaca, NY. Web: http://GerryStahl.net/pub/geogebrana2010b.pdf

Wang, H. C., Rosé, C. P., Cui, Y., Chang, C. Y., Huang, C. C., & Li, T. Y. (2007). *Thinking hard together: The long and short of collaborative idea generation for scientific inquiry.* Paper presented at the *Conference on Computer-Supported Collaborative Learning (CSCL 2007).* New Brunswick, NJ.

Wee, J. D. (2010). *Reinventing mathematics problem design and analysis of chat interactions in quasi-synchronous chat environments.* Unpublished Dissertation, Ph.D., National Institute of Education, Nanyang Techological University. Singapore.

Zhou, N. (2009). *Investigating information practices of collaborative online small groups engaged in problem solving.* Unpublished Dissertation, Ph.D., College of Information Science and Technology, Drexel University. Philadelphia, PA, USA.